The Clinton Wars

THE
Clinton
Wars

The Constitution, Congress, and War Powers

Ryan C. Hendrickson

Vanderbilt University Press
Nashville

© 2002 Vanderbilt University Press
All rights reserved
First Edition 2002

This book is printed on acid-free paper.
Manufactured in the United States of America

Library of Congress Cataloging-in-Publication Data

Hendrickson, Ryan C., 1969-
  The Clinton wars : the constitution, Congress, and
war powers / Ryan C. Hendrickson.— 1st ed.
    p. cm.
Includes bibliographical references and index.
ISBN 0-8265-1413-8 (cloth : alk. paper)
ISBN 0-8265-1414-6 (pbk. : alk. paper)
    1. War and emergency powers—United States—
History. 2. Clinton, Bill, 1946- 3. United States—Military
policy. I. Title.
KF5060 .H46 2002
973.929—dc21

                                        2002003863

Contents

Acknowledgments

This book has been a journey that began in graduate school at the University of Nebraska–Lincoln in 1993 and culminated with the end of the Clinton administration. While this book was being researched and written, many people provided comments or critiques or were simply supportive of my efforts. Many former colleagues and professors from my graduate school years deserve my thanks, including Lloyd Ambrosius, Joe Blankenau (now at Wayne State College), Phil Dyer, John Hibbing, Pete Maslowski, Jonathan Strand (now at the University of Nevada–Las Vegas), and Elizabeth Theiss-Morse. Among those at the University of Nebraska, most importantly, I thank Dave Forsythe, who critiqued much of the book, challenged me in ways that I will always appreciate, and provided helpful advice at all stages of the book.

In my first teaching position at Lambuth University in Jackson, Tennessee, many former colleagues were also supportive of my research interests. I thank especially Ellis Arnold, Randy Austin (now at Newan University), Gene Davenport, Dalton Eddleman, Don Huneycutt, Lyda Kowalski, and Wilburn Lane.

In my current position at Eastern Illinois University, Andy McNitt kindly commented on portions of the manuscript, and Rich Wandling was especially supportive of my writing endeavors. In addition, EIU's Council on Faculty Research provided me a summer writing grant that helped me complete the book. Several chapters of this book were presented at meetings of the International Studies Association and the International Studies Association–Midwest, and I also want to thank those who commented on my research at those meetings, especially Peter Schraeder of Loyola University. I also very much appreciate the advice provided by the anonymous reviewers of this manuscript, who prodded me to produce what I hope will be a more useful contribution to the study of American foreign policy. In acknowledging all those who assisted me, I note that the final responsibility for the content and interpretations rests with me alone.

Portions of this book have been published elsewhere in slightly different form. Chapter 4 is based in part on my article "War Powers, Bosnia, and the 104th Congress," reprinted with permission from *Political Science Quarterly* 113, no. 2 (Summer 1998): 241–58. A version of Chapter 5 appeared previously as "American War Powers and Terrorists: The Case of Usama Bin Laden" in *Studies in Conflict and Terrorism* 23, no. 3 (2000): 161–74, published by Taylor and Francis. Portions of Chapter 4 and Chapter 7 also appeared as "Clinton's Legal Dominion: War Powers in the Second Term" in *National Security Studies Quarterly* 5, no. 1 (1999): 29–64.

Many other family members and friends deserve my thanks, including Jerry and Mary Hendrickson, G. McCluskey, and Marguerite Clohisy. Finally, and most importantly, thank goodness for my wife, Tece. The book would not have been possible without her encouragement, patience, and love.

Introduction

The question of who has authority to deploy American troops and use military force abroad is one of the most profound and important constitutional issues raised since the republic's founding. In the aftermath of the terrorist strikes on the United States on September 11, 2001, this issue surfaced again on the American political agenda. American foreign policy entered a new era in the days that followed, in which President George W. Bush and the United States Congress essentially declared war against terrorists and all those who support terrorism around the world. On September 14, upon President Bush's request, the U.S. Senate and House of Representatives granted the president authority to use "all necessary and appropriate force" and to take military action "in order to prevent any further acts of international terrorism."[1] This is not the first time that the commander in chief has been given wide military powers to confront national security threats. In 1964, Congress passed the Gulf of Tonkin Resolution, which gave President Lyndon B. Johnson the authority to use "all necessary measures" to combat the North Vietnamese communists during the cold war. President Johnson's and later President Richard M. Nixon's military actions in Vietnam eventually led to tense relations between the Oval Office and Congress and to a bitterly divided American public. In response to both presidents' perceived military powers during the Vietnam War, in 1973 Congress passed the War Powers Resolution (WPR), which sought to restrict the president's power to engage in prolonged military excursions abroad. With the United States now engaged in a new war against terrorism, with a similarly empowered commander in chief, the relevance of war powers policy and the importance of understanding the history of the issue are as great as they have ever been.

Historically, the question of war powers has produced much tension between America's executive and legislative branches. In the aftermath of the Mexican War and President James Polk's orchestration of the events leading to America's entry into the conflict, Congressman Abraham Lincoln (R-Ill.) wrote the following in a letter to a colleague:

> The provision of the Constitution giving the war-making power to Congress was dictated, as I understand it, by the following reasons: Kings had always been involving and impoverishing their people in wars, pretending generally, if not always, that the good of the people was the object. This our convention understood to be the most oppressive of all kingly oppressions, and they resolved to so frame the Constitution so that no one man should hold the power of bringing oppression upon us.[2]

With a striking degree of similarity, over 150 years later, Senator Larry Craig (R-Idaho) stated only hours before the United States' participation in the North Atlantic Treaty Organization's (NATO's) bombing campaign in Kosovo:

> I have to think this administration's policy is inconsistent with constitutional government and the rule of law. Let us not forget the Constitution of the United States gives the sole power to declare war to the Congress, article I, section 8—not to the President, but to the Congress. Nothing in the laws or the Constitution of the United States suggests that a determination by the United Nations Security Council or the North Atlantic Treaty Organization is a substitute.[3]

Likewise, Congressman Charles Canady (R-Fla.) added:

> I also want to state my great concern about the commencement of this war without the authorization of the Congress. The President does not have the constitutional authority unilaterally to decide that the United States will wage war on a sovereign Nation which has not attacked or threatened the United States. Absent truly exigent circumstances, the armed forces of the United States should be sent into conflict only when duly authorized by this Congress.[4]

Thus, the power to use force continues to generate confusion, frustration, and lament from some members of Congress.

Past studies of American war powers generally fall into one of three categories. In the first, scholars have examined judicial interpretations of war powers. Most analysts argue that the federal courts have avoided the development of substantive and meaningful guidelines on war powers.[5] In the second group, others provide broad historical examinations of war powers, emphasizing the manner in which Congress and the president battled over the authority to use force abroad over the last two centuries. During the nineteenth century, presidents generally sought congressional authorization or approval prior to using force. Yet Congress since World War II has often been depicted by this group of historians as an acquiescent body that has allowed the president to assert nearly unilateral powers as commander in chief.[6] The third category focuses on single uses of force in American foreign policy. Much of this literature addresses the War Powers Resolution (WPR), which was passed in 1973 over President Nixon's veto.[7] The vast majority of scholarship on the WPR maintains that it has failed miserably in generating greater consultation and shared decision-making powers between the president and Congress.[8] As in the second group, most analysts in the third group concur that Congress avoids invoking its war powers and prefers to let the president assume the full political risks associated with using force. At the same time, they say, presidents during the cold war made unilateral claims as commander in chief, which in large part were accepted by members of Congress.[9]

In the aftermath of the Clinton presidency, this book provides a comparative analysis of the Clinton administration's uses of force and major troop deployments abroad, as well as a broad examination of war powers and the congressional-executive interplay during the Clinton era.

At the beginning of the Clinton presidency it could be expected that the president and Congress would be on a more equal footing with regard to war powers. President Clinton entered the White House with limited foreign policy experience as governor of Arkansas. Congressional Republicans and other partisan critics were also quick to note that the president had dodged the draft during the Vietnam War, and consequently they doubted his ability to lead in foreign policy. Bill Clinton also became the first individual to enter the White House after the cold war, in a new era of strategic ambiguity. No longer did the United States have the "evil empire" of the Soviet Union to contend with and define its central foreign policy objectives. Rather, the parameters of national security were much more ambiguous. What now constituted the United States' national security interests? Who was the new military threat to the United States? Had global environmental issues and other transnational threats catapulted themselves onto the security agenda? All of these questions remained unanswered. In times such as these, one could reasonably expect that Congress would have a greater ability to shape the American foreign policy agenda and have a more influential position vis-à-vis the president in defining America's national security interests.[10] Prima facie, the international strategic climate provided Congress the opportunity to serve as a stronger check on the commander in chief and break the pattern of deferential behavior it had followed so frequently during the cold war.

Another important element of the Clinton presidency was the election of a new Republican majority to the House and Senate in 1994. Many of the newly elected Republicans took their seats with great ideological zeal for their conservative causes. One of these interests was a commitment to "strengthen" U.S. foreign policy and to limit the president's ability to deploy American forces in United Nations peacekeeping operations.[11] With so many highly motivated partisans entering Congress, and with their campaign promises on record in their "Contract with America," one might expect that the Republican majority would take its constitutional war powers more seriously, particularly after the United States' political debacle in Somalia in 1993. Many of the new Republicans and their leadership promised constituents across the United States that they would not let the Clinton administration involve American troops in further United Nations operations unless specifically approved by Congress. Upon taking their seats, House members passed the National Security Revitalization Act, which sought to limit the president's ability to use force through the United Nations, and new Senate Majority Leader Bob Dole's (R-Kans.) "Peace Powers" bill similarly called for restraints on the commander in chief. Congressional assertiveness on war powers seemed like a reasonable expectation when the GOP gained majority status.

During the Clinton presidency, NATO, for the first time since its creation in 1949, authorized and eventually used military force in Bosnia and later in Kosovo. Since NATO had never before used force, it was unclear how Congress would interpret its role vis-à-vis NATO, especially in light of the new foreign policy vigor expressed by the Republican majority in 1995.

Finally, the politics of impeachment in 1998 and 1999 and President Clinton's personal admission that he had "misled" the public added another new and potentially important dynamic to the war powers interplay. Clinton's ability to lead and control Washington's agenda was certainly damaged during these precarious times. Again, the Republican majority in Congress had another opportunity to assert itself in foreign policy making, with the potential to wield considerable influence over the commander in chief in his weakened state. Yet despite the political pressures associated with impeachment, Clinton struck the alleged terrorist outposts of Usama Bin Laden[12] in Sudan and Afghanistan only three days after admitting he had "misled" the nation about his relationship with a White House intern. Clinton also ordered the bombing of Iraq on the eve of the House impeachment proceedings and used American troops in NATO strikes on Kosovo in 1999 one month after his acquittal by the Senate on the impeachment charges.

Although the political climate at various times during the Clinton era suggested the potential for a more assertive Congress, the pattern of congressional deference established in the cold war remained the norm. However, the reasons for this deference vary in each instance. This book's central argument is that Congress's deference to the president during this period is not merely an institutional norm but a pattern determined by the political conditions at the time of the use of force, by the choices made by key individual members of Congress, and often by partisan political considerations. Understanding this deference and the congressional-executive interplay demands a case-by-case analysis of the major uses of America's armed forces during the Clinton presidency.

Notable exceptions to the pattern of congressional deference occurred during President Clinton's impeachment crisis, which injected a new element to the war powers interplay. Although Clinton still exercised considerable leadership as commander in chief, the events surrounding the impeachment encouraged more substantive dialogue between the president and Congress, especially prior to the strikes against Usama Bin Laden. Clinton also took additional steps to consult with Congress prior to the use of force in Kosovo, in part because of strategic and diplomatic concerns, but also because of Congress's highly partisan demeanor at the time. However, this level of consultation was the exception and probably will not have a long-term impact on the presidency or Congress. Rather, in keeping with this book's theme, it was the domestic political conditions *at the time* that were fundamental in shaping the broader war powers interplay.

ORGANIZATION OF THE BOOK

In order to set a foundation for this study, the book begins with a historical analysis of war powers. Chapter 1 includes a discussion of the views about war powers held by delegates to the Constitutional Convention and follows with an appraisal of the history of the United States' agreements to participate in the United Nations and NATO, which have become key aspects of presidential claims to wide authority as commander in chief. It continues with a discussion of the debates surrounding the formation of the War Powers Resolution, as well as its weaknesses in practice. (The resolution is included as an appendix.) This chapter establishes the legal, constitutional, and historical context of war powers that Bill Clinton inherited upon entering the White House.

The book follows with six case studies of the most prominent military deployments and uses of force during the Clinton years.[13] These cases include chapters on the United States' deployments to Somalia, Haiti, and Bosnia; the strikes on Usama Bin Laden in 1998; NATO's actions in Kosovo; and the numerous military strikes on Iraq. Each chapter includes a short background on the conflict and U.S. foreign policy in the respective country or region prior to the use of force. This historical background is followed by an examination of the presidential-congressional interplay in each case.[14] When relevant, analogies are drawn with past uses of force in recent American foreign policy in order to illustrate important differences witnessed during the Clinton years. Chapter 5, which examines Clinton's strikes against Usama Bin Laden, includes a more extensive comparison with President Ronald Reagan's strikes on Libyan leader Muammar Qaddafi in 1986, because of the important similarities and differences in these cases. Each chapter concludes with an assessment of Congress's and the president's compliance with the Constitution and the War Powers Resolution. Where appropriate, each chapter addresses the impact and relevance of international organizations on the constitutional and political authority to use American forces abroad. As president, Bill Clinton turned to international organizations—the United Nations and NATO—for authority to use force. As will be demonstrated, these multilateral endorsements were used to insulate the president from congressional assertions of power and to protect the president's own perceived constitutional powers.

In sum, this study seeks a more comprehensive explanation for Congress's deference on war powers and an appraisal of constitutional war powers during the Clinton presidency. Since the end of World War II, and now in the post–cold war era, the balance of power has increasingly tilted toward the commander in chief. Unfortunately, this imbalance is increasingly the norm and appears to have become even more deeply grounded in American political practice after eight years of the Clinton presidency. The decision to use force in the United States' constitutional democracy was intended to be made within a democratic context. While congressional deference with regard to war powers was the norm during Clinton's tenure as president, analyses of additional domestic (and sometimes international) political factors surrounding each major use of force or deployment by Clinton provide new explanations for Congress's acquiescence to the president and for Clinton's infrequent efforts to consult with Congress. With the end of the Clinton era and a new "war" on terrorism, there is a renewed necessity to understand the United States' policy-making process on the use of force abroad and the constitutional requirements surrounding war powers.

1   War Powers
in American History

Since the republic's founding, American presidents have engaged in over three hundred different uses of force abroad. During the same time, Congress passed only five declarations of war. To the casual observer, it may seem that as commander in chief, the president is entitled to unilateral military powers and acts in a perfectly constitutional manner when deploying troops without congressional approval. From this logic, it follows that Congress is supposed to be a secondary player in American foreign policy and should remain at a distance when it comes to the decision to use of force abroad. Some politicians and scholars alike contend that the president should be the empowered branch of government when it comes to using the military abroad. Based on political practice, especially since World War II, it is understandable how one could come to this conclusion, although such a view neglects the founding fathers' views on checks and balances, as well as key treaties negotiated by the United States Congress that protected and reaffirmed Congress's constitutional war powers.

Advocates of Presidential War Powers

One of the strongest proponents of presidential war powers was Senator Barry Goldwater (R-Ariz.). Goldwater argued that when the founding fathers discussed war powers at the Constitutional Convention and decided to assign Congress the power to "declare" rather than "make" war, they intended that the president should be in charge of military decisions. Congress should only speak to support the president. In his view, Congress may decide to declare war or not, but the president has an independent leadership role in his constitutional war powers.[1] Former senator and secretary of defense nominee John Tower (R-Tex.) likewise argued that the president should not be encumbered by Congress in foreign policy making. While Tower's critique of Congress was broader in scope than Goldwater's, Tower still maintained that the president should be allowed to respond quickly in the nation's interest if a military need exists. Tower believed that more often than not Congress gets in the president's way, to the detriment of U.S. foreign policy.[2]

Advocates of a strong commander in chief might also point to Federalist Paper No. 74 to support this position, in which Alexander Hamilton wrote: "Of all the concerns of government, the direction of war most peculiarly demands those qualities which distinguish the exercise of power by a single hand. The direction of war implies the direction of a common strength; and the power of directing and employing the common strength forms a usual and essential part of the definition of the executive authority." Hamilton's vision of the presidency clearly emphasized an empowered commander in chief.

Other students of war powers argue similarly that Congress should not be involved in use-of-force decisions. Robert Bork maintains that it is mistake to place "law" over national interests in American foreign policy. Rather, he argues that morality should be the president's guide and Congress should stay out of use-of-force decisions and use only public opinion as its guide to either critique or applaud the president.[3] Others maintain that because Congress consists of so many different members, lacks expertise in foreign policy, and often thinks in parochial terms, any military decision "short of war" should be left with the president alone.[4] Given the heightened perception that Congress has become increasingly partisan over the last decade and spends much of its time running for reelection rather than immersing itself in the study of public policy, this argument at first glance may seem very attractive to students of American foreign policy, as well as the wider public.

Perhaps the strongest piece of evidence cited by those who advocate a strong, empowered president is Supreme Court Justice George Sutherland's written opinion in *U.S. v. Curtiss-Wright Export Corporation et al.* (1936). In this decision, which involved the export of military arms to Bolivia and Paraguay, Sutherland argued that the president is not limited by the Constitution in foreign policy making and has sovereign powers in foreign affairs. Sutherland wrote that the president is the "sole organ of the federal government in the field of international relations," and has "plenary and exclusive" power as president.[5] Sutherland's position clearly implied that Congress was meant to play a secondary role in American foreign policy making and called for a powerful commander in chief. The Supreme Court essentially reaffirmed this decision during the Vietnam War, when the Court refused to rule on two major war powers questions brought before it. The Court denied certiorari in *Mora v. McNamara*, in which the petitioners asked the Court to rule on whether American military activities in Vietnam were illegal, and thus in violation of the constitution's war powers clause.[6] In 1970, the Court again refused in *Commonwealth of Massachusetts v. Laird* to determine if the president was in violation of the war powers clause because Congress had not declared war in Indochina.[7] In its refusal to act, the Court affirmed the status quo: presidential leadership in military and foreign affairs. The petitioners would not be allowed to change the president's foreign policy ambitions simply because Congress had not declared war. By implication, the president was allowed to engage American troops in combat without specific war declarations from Congress and, to some degree, had military powers independent of Congress.

Political practice or custom may also lead to the conclusion that Congress is not to be involved in use-of-force decisions. Since World War II, the United States has fought wars in Korea and Vietnam and has used force in the Dominican Republic, Grenada, Libya, Panama, and Iraq, as well as other foreign countries. In none of these cases did Congress specifically declare war. In the Korean War, the Truman administration noted: "That the President's power to send the Armed Forces outside the country is not dependent on Congressional authority has been repeatedly emphasized by numerous writers."[8] Truman's explanation was accepted and even vigorously defended by some members of Congress. With such a precedent in place and repeatedly reaffirmed by presidential leadership in military affairs during the cold war, it seems that a norm of presidential leadership is now an accepted part of the American foreign policy process. These sentiments were echoed by Secretary of Defense Richard Cheney prior to the United States' use of force in the Persian Gulf War: "I do not believe the president requires any additional authority from Congress. . . . Of the more than two hundred occasions in American history when presidents have committed U.S. military force, on only five of those occasions was there a prior declaration of war."[9] Similar arguments for presidential power were pronounced by former President George Bush. Even when Bush deployed over 400,000 forces in the Persian Gulf War in 1990, he only went to Congress to "request" its approval, maintaining that he was not required by the Constitution or the War Powers Resolution to gain congressional authorization. After Congress voted to support Operation Desert Storm, Bush noted: "As I made clear to congressional leaders at the outset, my request for congressional support did not, and my signing this resolution does not, constitute any change in the long-standing positions of the executive branch on either the President's constitutional authority to use the Armed Forces to defend vital U.S. interests or the constitutionality of the War Powers Resolution."[10] Bush expressed his feelings on executive authority most bluntly in his 1992 presidential election campaign, when he stated that he did not need the approval from "some old goat" in Congress to oust Saddam Hussein from Kuwait.[11] As is demonstrated in the chapters to follow, the belief that members of Congress should not get in the president's way when national security matters arise remains quite popular today.

Others also argue that if presidents gain United Nations Security Council approval, they are not obligated to seek congressional authorization. Senator William Knowland (R-Calif.) argued that Truman's deployment of troops in Korea was clearly part of a United Nations "police action" and thus could not be defined as "war."[12] Other senators of both parties made similar arguments about Truman's claim for broad presidential powers under the aegis of the United Nations.[13] More recently, this position has been articulated by Thomas M. Franck and Faiza Patel, who argue that members of Congress understood that the United Nations' military actions were akin to "police actions" and therefore would not require congressional approval. They also note that the UN Security Council was to be an empowered institution that could act quickly to achieve its mandate. In their view, the United Nations moved the world from an "old order" to a "new order," built upon international cooperation and the new policing power of the United Nations.[14] Thus these authors hold that when the president seeks to use force in a United Nations military operation, congressional authorization is not required.

An additional argument occasionally advanced in favor of a strong commander in chief deals with the modern global security environment.

Even though the founders may have favored an assertive Congress in 1789, today's world of nuclear threats, terrorists, and a presumed necessity for occasional quick military strikes, Congress's "checking" powers are no longer feasible or advisable: national security interests cannot allow for a slow, deliberative, and open discussion of American military interests and strategic objectives. With devastating weapons that could strike the United States quickly, American national security interests demand a president who is independent from partisan, myopic, and self-interested members of Congress.

Thus a number of ostensibly legitimate arguments suggest that the president should be the sole decision maker when it comes to the use of force abroad. Constitutional arguments, appeals to Supreme Court decisions, political practice over time, and the need for an assertive commander in chief in the modern security environment may lead the public, Congress, and certainly the chief executive to favor a strong commander in chief.

Despite political practice since World War II, evidence from the Constitutional Convention and other events in American history suggest that Congress was intended to be fully engaged in war powers decisions. While current political practice, some scholarship, and a number of Supreme Court decisions argue for a president who is nearly imperial in foreign policy making, these arguments run counter to the founders' intentions, the legislative history of the UN Participation Act of 1945, the Senate's approval of the North Atlantic Treaty in 1949, and the passage of the War Powers Resolution in 1973. While Congress has allowed near presidential sovereignty in military affairs, it has simultaneously avoided unambiguous constitutional and other legal responsibilities regarding its war powers.

The Constitution

During the Constitutional Convention, the issue of war powers did not receive a great deal of attention. Yet, from the few short passages that were recorded on the subject in James Madison's *Notes of Debates in the Federal Convention of 1787*, much can be learned. It is first worth noting the founders' respect for the most basic constitutional principle: the belief in checks and balances. The founding fathers feared a monarchial chief executive. It was in this vein that in the Constitution's first draft,

Congress and not the president was given the power to "make" war. After weeks had gone by, on Friday, August 17, 1789, the founders returned to reconsider the war power. The discussion of war powers began with Pierce Bulter's calling for the "vesting of the power in the President." He believed that the chief executive would never make war unless it was supported by the public. Butler's remarks apparently produced vigorous opposition.

James Madison and Elbridge Gerry moved to insert the word *declare* in place of "make" and noted that the president would only have the power to "repel sudden attacks." Roger Sherman followed by noting that war should be difficult to enter into. Elbridge Gerry also responded to Bulter's proposal by noting that "he never expected to hear in a republic a motion to empower the Executive alone to declare war." George Mason followed by noting that he was against the executive having the war power, but was also against the Senate having the power. He also supported the motion to insert "declare" rather than "make."[15]

After these discussions, Madison and Gerry's motion was voted on. Of the ten state delegations who fielded a vote, seven voted for the motion, two against, and Massachusetts abstained.[16] The historical record of Madison's notes strongly suggests that the president was to be limited as commander in chief. War was not intended to be easily entered into but rather would entail a checking mechanism on the chief executive. From the *Notes*, one can conclude that the president was allowed to use force without congressional approval only in the event of an attack upon the United States.

Besides the power to declare war, the founders also gave Congress the power to "provide for the common defense; . . . To grant letters of Marque and Reprisals; . . . To raise and support Armies; . . . To provide and maintain a Navy;" and "To provide for calling forth the Militia to execute the Laws of the Union, suppress Insurrections and repel Invasions."[17] Thus, in many respects Congress was the empowered body with regard to military matters. It is quite clear that the modern presidential assertion of unilateral power as commander in chief does not square with the founding fathers' intent.[18] The founders saw Congress as the body that would make the final decision about entering into war.

Advocates of presidential war powers may retort by arguing that in situations short of war, the president has certain military prerogatives; that is, Congress has a legitimate and well-specified duty when it comes to "war" but otherwise should follow the president as he protects American interests abroad. This argument, however, assumes a semantical distinction in the word *war* that the founders never implied. As established, Congress was given a host of military powers. Only "sudden attacks" upon the United States provided the president justification to use force without Congressional consent. The presidency was never intended to be an independent institution with autonomous military authority.[19]

The evidence of Madison's *Notes* is supported by the historical record of the ratifying conventions. Once the Constitutional Convention was concluded in Philadelphia, approval from eleven of thirteen state conventions was needed for the document's formal adoption. In these conventions, war powers again was not a central issue. Yet when the issue arose, the historical account is well chronicled. David Gray Adler notes that at the New York Convention, Robert R. Livingston stated that the newly created Congress had the same war powers as the Congress under the Articles of Confederation, which granted all war powers to the Congress.[20] At the Pennsylvania Convention, James Wilson also maintained that the president would not have the power to take the nation into war. He stated:

> This [new] system will not hurry us into war; it is calculated to guard against it. It will not be in the power of a single man, or a single body of men, to involve us in such distress; for the important power to declare war is vested in the legislature at large: this declaration must be made with the concurrence of the House of Representatives: from this circumstance we may draw a certain conclusion that nothing but our national interest can draw us into a war.[21]

Other founders, including James Irdell of North Carolina and Charles Pinckney of South Carolina expressed essentially identical arguments in their respective states. Throughout all ratification hearings, there was virtually no debate over the meaning of the war power.[22] Objectors may note Hamilton's Federalist Paper No. 74. Yet when asked specifically about the war power in the ratifying debates, all founders concurred that Congress was endowed with the power to initiate war, not the president.

Supreme Court decisions in the first years of the republic further clarify the founding fathers' intentions with regard to war power. Two decisions especially stand out. In *Talbot v. Seeman* (1801), Chief Justice John Marshall noted that Congress has the "whole powers" of war, and that "Congress may authorize general hostilities."[23] Moreover, in *United States v. Smith* (1806), founding father and Supreme Court Justice William Patterson stated that the president could never lawfully initiate a war but only had the power to respond to attacks upon the United States. Only Congress had the power to initiate hostilities abroad with another nation currently not at war with the United States.[24] Such an interpretation closely follows what James Madison recorded from the Constitutional Convention.

In sum, it is inaccurate to conclude that the Constitution gave the president unilateral powers as commander in chief. The vast majority of the recorded evidence points to a Congress that was to be the final arbiter in determining when force was used. The president was to listen to congressional wishes on the use of force and had only limited military powers to respond to sudden attacks upon the United States. The arguments provided by Goldwater, Bork, and modern presidents on the wide powers of the commander in chief run counter to the evidence available from the historical record of the Constitution's creation, the ratification debates, and the early decisions of the Supreme Court. These principles were reaffirmed when the United States joined the United Nations in 1945.

The United Nations

The central role of the United Nations in President Clinton's foreign policy has led to further obfuscation of war powers responsibilities. Prior to using force or deploying troops abroad in a peacekeeping operation, Clinton gained the United Nations Security Council's approval for military operations in Somalia, Haiti, and Bosnia. However, the legislative history of the United States' entry into the United Nations demonstrates that Congress reserved the right to authorize American participation in any UN military deployment.

Prior to the end of World War II, the House of Representatives and the Senate recognized the need for an international institution that would be more effective than the League of Nations in promoting world peace.[25] In 1943, both chambers of Congress supported resolutions calling for an "international organization" that would foster world peace. Yet these resolutions included important qualifiers to future membership; American troops would only participate in military actions of such an organization in accordance with the United States' "constitutional process."[26] This qualifier clearly implied that Congress would be involved in use-of-force decisions if the United States did join such an organization.

When the Truman administration sought Congress's approval for joining the United Nations, members of Congress were concerned about a loss of their own war powers. Under Chapter 7 of the United Nations Charter, the UN Security Council is allowed to authorize the use of force by its member states in order to "contribute to the maintenance of international peace and security." Article 25 of the UN Charter also stipulates that all member states "agree to accept and carry out the decisions of the Security Council." Once the Security Council made a decision, it would then negotiate a special agreement with its own Military Staff Committee, which would be in charge of carrying out the mission. Prima facie, it appears that the Security Council gained a new grant of military authority, stripping Congress of its constitutional war powers.

In response to the fears expressed by members of Congress, however, President Truman sent a telegram to Congress avowing, "When any such agreement or agreements are negotiated, it will be my purpose to ask the Congress by appropriate legislation to approve them."[27] Article 43 (3) of the United Nations Charter also reads that any agreement between the United Nations Military Staff Committee and its members "shall be subject to ratification by signatory states in accordance with the respective *constitutional processes*."[28] This language reflects the view of Congress's war powers expressed by President Franklin Roosevelt prior to American participation in the United Nations. Four members of Congress were also active participants in the writing of the UN Charter in San Francisco in 1945, resulting in the protection of member states' "constitutional processes" when the UN authorized enforcement actions.[29]

Congress further solidified this understanding of its role in UN military operations when it passed the United Nations Participation Act of 1945. Section 6 of the act states that any agreement between the United States and the UN Security Council "shall be subject to the approval of the Congress by appropriate Act or joint resolution."[30] Moreover, other assurances were clearly articulated by representatives of the Truman administration, which assured that Congress would have the right to prevent U.S. military participation in UN operations.[31]

In sum, when the United States joined the United Nations, Congress gained assurances from the Truman administration and applied statutory language that guaranteed its role of authorizing American participation in any United Nations military operation. Congress ensured that the president had no independent authority to authorize American participation in Security Council operations. In short, Congress did not forfeit its own war powers to the president in 1945.

In practice, however, Article 43 agreements have never been negotiated. With the exception of the United States' participation in the Persian Gulf War, Congress has also allowed American participation in UN military operations without granting specific authorization. For example, in 1950 when the Truman administration gained the United Nations Security Council's approval to defend South Korea from North Korean aggression, Congress allowed Truman to act without specific legislative approval. Because the United States was warring with communists in a war supported by most Americans, few members of Congress found it in their political self-interests to raise constitutional process concerns, Article 43, or the UN Participation Act. Article 43 and the UN Participation Act have largely disappeared from political debate surrounding American participation in UN operations. Although Congress protected its war powers upon joining the United Nations, it has traditionally neglected those powers since that time.

NATO Membership: 1949

Similar to the history of the UN Participation Act, the record of the North Atlantic Treaty, which created NATO, likewise demonstrates that congressional war powers were important to U.S. senators as they began their deliberations over American membership in NATO in 1949. With the heightened fears and belief that the Soviet Union represented a threat to Western Europe in the years immediately following World War II, the United States and its western allies supported the creation of a new military alliance that would deter Soviet military aggression in Western Europe.[32] Yet in creating such an alliance with a real deterrent power, the Senate was also concerned about the abdication of its own war powers. One of the most controversial aspects of the North Atlantic Treaty was Article 5, which reads:

> The Parties agree that an armed attack against one or more of them in Europe or North America shall be considered an attack against them all and consequently they agree that, if such an armed attack occurs, each of them, in exercise of the right of individual or collective self-defence recognised by Article 51 of the Charter of the United Nations, will assist the Party or Parties so attacked by taking forthwith, individually and in concert with the other Parties, such action as it deems necessary, including the use of armed force, to restore and maintain the security of the North Atlantic area.[33]

This article is crucial for providing the necessary deterrent but also appears to commit its members to an automatic defense of their allies. While most senators had no qualms about making a strong stand against communist aggression, many expressed strong reservations concerning Article 5's impact on congressional war powers, fearing that it would render Congress powerless in the decision to wage war.

Anticipating these concerns, in his written statement before the Senate Foreign Relations Committee in 1949 Secretary of State Dean Acheson stated about Article 5: "This naturally does not mean that the United States would automatically be at war if one of the other signatory states were victim of an armed attack. Under our Constitution, the Congress alone has the power to declare war. The obligation of this Government under article V would be to take promptly the action it deemed necessary to restore and maintain the security of the North Atlantic area. That decision would, of course, be taken in accordance with our constitutional procedures."[34] In response to questions from Senate Foreign Relations Chair Tom Connally (D-Tex.) and Senator Arthur H. Vandenberg (R-Mich.), Acheson reiterated the point that there would never be an automatic declaration of war as a result of the North Atlantic Treaty or any military strikes against a NATO ally.[35]

In another important exchange, Senator Forrest C. Donnell (R-Mo.) asked Acheson for further elucidation of the definition of "constitutional procedures." Acheson replied: "The words you have just read, so far as the declaration of war is concerned, obviously mean that Congress is the body in charge of constitutional procedure. . . . Article 5,

Senator, does not enlarge, nor does it decrease, nor does it change in any way, the relative constitutional position of the President and the Congress."[36]

Further evidence that the Truman administration sought no expansion of the president's powers as commander in chief is provided in the response of former Undersecretary of State Robert A. Lovett, who was closely involved in creating the NATO charter, to scrutiny from Senator Donnell by expanding on Acheson's theme and interpretation of Article 5:

> Mr. Lovett: I think the power of the President is clearly fixed by the Constitution and I see nothing in this treaty which in any way runs counter to it.
> Senator Donnell: And what is that power of the President which you see so clearly placed and fixed by the Constitution?
> Mr. Lovett: The power of the President, and the limitations on that power, would require a declaration of war to be made by the Congress.[37]

It is also worth noting that prior to the Senate's agreement to approve the North Atlantic Treaty, in 1948, Senator Vandenberg introduced a Senate resolution supporting a new military alliance with Western Europe, which gained the Senate's wide approval. Vandenberg's resolution declared the Senate's support of "association of the United States by *constitutional process*, with such regional and other collective arrangements as are based on continuous and effective self-help and mutual aid, and as affect its national security."[38] Again, the word choice of "constitutional process" is not random, implying that Congress was the institution that declared war. Vandenberg's personal letters demonstrate this point unambiguously.[39] Thus, as established by this earlier discourse that later resurfaced in the 1949 Senate hearings, the phrase "constitutional process" implied that Congress would be a meaningful player in the decision to use force in NATO.

In sum, much evidence suggests that the Senate and the Truman administration fully understood that NATO's charter did not alter or diminish Congress's war powers. In the aftermath of the hearings, one proposal was offered that explicitly required a declaration of war before the president could use force in support of NATO actions. This provision was rejected handily by the Senate. However, this does not necessarily imply that the Senate gave away its war powers or retreated from its earlier expressed concerns. Rather, it is more likely that the Senate sought to make Article 5 a credible deterrent to the Soviet Union and trusted in Acheson's assurances that Congress's war powers had not been modified.[40]

From a constitutional perspective, nothing in the Constitution allows the Senate to eliminate powers that also belong to the House. As Congress's other chamber, the House too was granted war powers as part of the Congress's ability to declare war. The fact that the Senate signed a treaty allowing American participation in NATO does not imply that the House forfeited its war powers. Thus the evidence is quite strong that American membership in NATO did not infringe upon Congress's war powers. The Senate's dialogue with Acheson demonstrates this point especially well: all actions under NATO required respect for the United States' "constitutional procedures."

Unlike the United Nations, NATO did not engage in military operations until 1994, forty-five years after its creation. Congress and the president never in practice faced constitutional war powers questions with regard to NATO authorizations to use force during the cold war. The Clinton administration broke new political ground with NATO's first use of force in 1994, but the historical record from 1949 is clear.

The War Powers Resolution of 1973

Although the history of the UN Participation Act and the Senate's deliberations about joining NATO provide much insight into congressional perceptions of its own war powers, it was American participation in the Vietnam War that forced Congress to reevaluate the perceived imbalance of powers between the White House and Congress. In 1973, Congress overrode President Nixon's veto and passed the War Powers Resolution (WPR), which sought to reassert Congress's war powers. Although the WPR has received much scholarly analysis and criticism, it continues to be very relevant to the war powers interplay as a source of tension and profound disagreement between members of Congress and the president.

In 1964, Congress approved the Tonkin Gulf Resolution after two American naval ships were allegedly attacked by North Vietnamese forces.[41] The resolution authorized President Johnson "to take all necessary measures to repel any armed attack against the forces of the

United States and to prevent further aggression."[42] In effect, Congress's resolution provided Johnson the blank check he sought to begin a full-scale military operation in Vietnam. Throughout the fighting in Southeast Asia, this resolution was the principal means by which Johnson and later President Richard Nixon argued that Congress had given them the power to use force.[43] However, as the United States slipped further and further into the conflict, and as a perceived "imperial presidency" unfolded, Congress began to reevaluate its ability to control the commander in chief. Many members of the House and Senate argued that Presidents Johnson and Nixon had exploited their power as commander in chief, illegally relegating Congress to a secondary role in American foreign policy.[44]

One of the first members of Congress to express such concerns was Senator J. William Fulbright (D-Ark.), chairman of the Senate Foreign Relations Committee. Fulbright had become disturbed about the perceived war powers imbalance in 1965, when President Johnson deployed thirty thousand American troops to the Dominican Republic without congressional consultation.[45] In response to this deployment, coupled with the United States' growing military presence in Vietnam, Fulbright introduced a "Sense of the Senate" resolution that noted that "a national commitment" to another nation would only come with the joint support of the Congress and the president. Fulbright noted: "There is no need at this time to rehearse all the evidence in support of this view, held by most members of this body, that the authority of Congress in many respects has been dwindling throughout the years since our entry into the Second World War. . . . In no area is the constitutional imbalance more striking and more alarming than in the field of foreign policy."[46] His resolution, which passed unanimously, did not have the force of law, but it did send an important signal to the president about the perceived constitutional imbalance.[47]

Fulbright's efforts were followed by a proposal from Senator Jacob Javits (D-N.Y.), on June 15, 1970, when he introduced the first version of what became the War Powers Resolution. In its initial form, the resolution allowed the president to use force without a declaration of war to defend the United States against an attack, to defend American troops upon attack, to protect the lives and property of U.S. nationals abroad, and to comply with a "national commitment" made jointly by the president and Congress. In any of these situations, the president was given thirty days to gain a declaration of war from the Congress. Otherwise, the troops would have to be brought back to the United States.[48] In the House similar resolutions were offered, with the notable exception that many representatives wanted to give the president more leeway by granting a 120-day period to gain congressional approval after a military deployment. Eventually, after considerable debate, the Senate and House compromised and passed an amended version of Javits' bill, the War Powers Resolution (WPR).[49]

In the WPR's introduction, its authors noted that the resolution's intention was "to fulfill the intent of the framers of the Constitution of the United States and insure that the collective judgement of both the Congress and the President will apply to the introduction of United States Armed Forces into hostilities."[50] More specifically, the WPR created a number of restrictions on the president's ability to use force abroad. The president was only allowed to use force under three circumstances: a declaration of war by Congress, statutory approval from Congress, or a national emergency in which the United States' "territories or possessions" were attacked.[51] Otherwise, any occasions when U.S. armed forces are introduced into hostilities or "into a situation where imminent involvement in hostilities is clearly indicated by the circumstances," fall under the purview of the WPR. This included occasions when U.S. armed forces are introduced into the "territory, airspace or waters of a foreign nation, while equipped for combat."[52] Thus, the WPR was intended to have wide application, including situations short of war. It was meant to place a check against not only the deployment of ground troops but also the use of force by aircraft and ships at sea. This interpretation is supported by Congressman Paul Findley's (R-Ill.) remarks in the *Congressional Record* on the day Congress overrode Nixon's veto:

> The language was carefully drafted so it could not conceivably be interpreted by a President as congressional authorization for the introduction of Armed Forces into hostilities abroad. Of course, Presidents have made such introductions in the past, and Presidents in the future may do the same. But no future President can cite this language as the authority for such action.
>
> In the absence of a declaration of war or other specific authority by Congress, only one use of Armed Forces in conflict abroad is recognized.

That lone exception is a national emergency created by an attack on our Armed Forces or upon our own territory.[53]

Presumably, the WPR also applies to peacekeeping deployments if U.S. troops are "equipped for combat" upon their deployment. It also seems reasonable to conclude that the WPR applies when U.S. troops are deployed under UN Security Council Chapter 7 authorization, in that they would be "equipped for combat" and authorized to use force if necessary.

Another of the WPR's central components is the "consultation" requirement found in Section 3. This requires that "the President in every possible instance should consult with Congress" before and after troops are introduced into hostilities. The resolution also requires that the president report to Congress any use of force within forty-eight hours of undertaking a miliary action. Furthermore, the resolution stipulates that after notifying Congress, the president has sixty days (with the possibility of a thirty-day extension) to gain congressional approval. If approval is not given, the president must recall the troops and cease the use of force.[54]

In response to the WPR, President Nixon argued that it was an unconstitutional infringement on the commander in chief's powers, which has been echoed by every president since 1973.[55] However, in speaking about the resolution, many members of the House and Senate rose to support the restoration of Congress's war power: Clement Zablocki (D-Wis.) called the resolution "a legitimate effort to restore [Congress's] rightful and responsible role under the Constitution." Spark Matsunaga (D-Hawaii) said, "It merely enunciates a procedure by which we in the Congress may assert that sole power vested in the Congress, the power to declare war." Hugh Carey (D-N.Y.) declared, "We are simply restating and making more explicit what is our constitutional function with regard to peace-keeping, and with regard to the powers to make war." And Michael Harrington (D-Mass.) noted that it "would help restore the lawful authority of Congress in the process of committing our Nation to war."[56] Senator Javits, while disappointed with the House compromise, nonetheless later noted that its primary intent was to restore the war powers balance and reassert Congress's constitutional powers.[57] Thus the scope of the WPR was intended to be quite broad, with Congressman Carey's interpretation even including "peace-keeping." The resolution was intended to involve Congress in all use-of-force decisions except national emergencies created by an attack upon the United States.

Not all members of Congress supported the WPR. Some argued that the resolution in fact enlarged the president's powers and allowed the chief executive to wage war for ninety days without Congressional approval. Others felt that the resolution was an unnecessary effort to assert powers that Congress already had.[58] Yet despite these misgivings, the overwhelming feeling at the time was that Congress had reestablished itself as a player in military decisions and was seeking to right the wrong of allowing the commander in chief to act with apparently unlimited power during the Vietnam War.

As noted in the introduction, most scholarship on the WPR maintains that it has failed. Its failure can be attributed partially to Congress's unwillingness to exercise it and to all subsequent presidents' unwillingness to abide by it. Other literature has noted its poorly articulated statutory language. Robert Katzman's analysis of the WPR is particularly useful in highlighting these weaknesses. He notes that in practice, "consultation" has often amounted to little more than "notification" of congressional leaders.[59] Instances of presidential administrations *informing* rather than *consulting* with Congress prior to the use of force abound. For example, prior to President Jimmy Carter's hostage rescue attempt in 1980, Carter met with Senator Robert Byrd (D-W.Va.). The meeting took place on the evening before the operation was scheduled to occur. Carter spoke with Byrd about the senator's expectations of proper consultation (Byrd noted "a sharp" distinction between notification and consultation), but the president stopped short of telling Byrd that the operation was going to take place one day later. When the mission was actually in progress the following day, Carter called congressional leaders to the White House and informed them of the hostage rescue attempt.[60]

Another case of notification and not consultation occurred in 1983 with the Reagan administration's intervention into Grenada. According to Secretary of State George Shultz's memoirs, President Reagan authorized the American military invasion of Grenada and then instructed his staff to invite congressional leaders to the White House to notify them of the forthcoming military action.[61] By Shultz's own recall, consultation with Congress was not even attempted, which is confirmed by other research on the actual decision-making process.[62] In

1986, President Reagan similarly called members of Congress to the White House only three hours before the American air strikes on Libya, when the operation was already in progress. Members of Congress felt they had little to no say in the "consultative" process. Likewise, in 1989 President George Bush notified members of Congress of the forthcoming military intervention "Operation Just Cause" in Panama only a few hours before the military action took place. President Bush authorized the invasion on December 17, 1989, yet the operation did not take place until December 20 at 1:00 A.M. Although members of Congress were on recess, clearly there was time to consult with Congress. In his address to the nation on the strikes, Bush himself indicated that he had *informed* the congressional leadership in advance but made no reference to consultation.[63]

Bush did request Congress's approval for the use of military force in Iraq, and his administration participated in a number of public congressional hearings on U.S. policy toward Iraq prior to the use of force. However, Bush, Secretary of Defense Cheney, and other administration officials were adamant that congressional approval was not required for military strikes on Saddam Hussein. In this sense, consultation meant "discussion," but for Bush, it never implied that Congress had the ability to force the president to reverse policy course and not use force. In practice, "consultation" has never been interpreted or implemented by presidents as an equal exchange of ideas or a balance of power.

The president and Congress have also differed over the definition of hostilities and whether American troops deployed abroad in any given case truly faced hostile conditions. In 1981, members of Congress challenged the presence of American military advisors in El Salvador, arguing that these troops were engaged in hostilities and subject to the requirements of the WPR. Not surprisingly, the Reagan administration argued otherwise, maintaining that the troops only served in a military advisory capacity.[64] In 1982, when the Reagan administration deployed American troops in a multinational peacekeeping force in Lebanon, where open conflict had been taking place, the administration again refused to acknowledge that U.S. troops were engaged in hostilities. Later, under pressure from both Republicans and Democrats, and after two Americans had been killed, the administration agreed that "significant hostilities" had taken place and set an eighteen-month withdrawal date for the operation.[65] After setting the withdrawal date, Reagan still argued that U.S. armed forces' being fired upon or even killed during a deployment does not automatically qualify as "actual or imminent involvement in hostilities."[66]

Another problem with the WPR stems from the sixty-day period in which the president is allowed to use force before he must gain congressional approval to continue with the military engagement. President Reagan's military invasion of Grenada began on October 25, 1983. All conflict ceased within one week, and all combat troops left the island by December 15, 1983.[67] President Bush's military invasion of Panama began on December 20, 1989. Manuel Noriega surrendered on January 3, 1990, and all American troops had departed by February 13, 1990.[68] If Congress truly enforced the WPR, it would prevent prolonged military engagements abroad. However, in the cases of Grenada and Panama, when the real armed conflict took approximately a week in both cases, the WPR did little to enhance Congress's role in checking the president.

In sum, the WPR was poorly written and has led to many disagreements between the Congress and the president. The resolution has largely failed to achieve the greater degree of shared governance that its authors intended, even though its application was intended to be broad.[69] As will be demonstrated, many of these same problems and semantical differences of interpretation surfaced again during the Clinton administration, which allowed Clinton to exercise wide leadership discretion as commander in chief. However, to dismiss the importance of the WPR without consideration does an injustice to the study of U.S. foreign policy making and the war powers interplay, which during the Clinton years in office, varied according to the domestic political environment, partisan interests at the time, and the agendas of key individual congressional leaders.

CONCLUSION

Although American history since World War II is replete with assertions of unilateral presidential war powers, it is Congress that, in the vast majority of cases, has the authority to determine when and if force should be used by the United States. The history of the Constitution demonstrates that Congress was the body granted the power to declare war and along with other military powers to effectively check the president. Strong evidence exists that the framers only intended the president to "repel sudden attacks." Similar sentiments were echoed in congressional chambers when the UN Participation Act was under consideration in 1945. By insisting upon specific language in Article 43 in the UN Charter, Congress demonstrated that it viewed itself as an equal player in determining how U.S. military force would be used, even in cases of collective defense. Inclusion of the phrase "constitutional process" in the UN Charter meant that Congress would have to approve American participation in UN-sponsored deployments. These same views were reiterated by the Senate in 1949 when considering U.S. membership in NATO. Before allowing the United States to join NATO, the Senate gained Secretary of State Dean Acheson's guarantee that Congress's fully recognized war powers were not changed through membership in the new military alliance. Finally, Congress reasserted its war powers vis-à-vis the president by passing the War Powers Resolution in 1973. Although flawed in many respects, it still provides a set of legislative tools to challenge the president when he uses force abroad unilaterally.

Despite the constitutional provisions and these statutory efforts, during the cold war the president asserted essentially unilateral powers as commander in chief. Congress allowed this executive omnipotence in foreign affairs because of the widespread acceptance that communism threatened American national security interests. Although the pattern of congressional deference and presidential perceptions of unilateral authority was the norm during the cold war, it was not unreasonable to suspect that Congress would break with this tradition and exercise its war powers when Bill Clinton entered the White House. In an era of strategic ambiguity, and given Clinton's limited foreign policy credentials and minimal international experience, coupled with a highly motivated Republican majority in 1995, an assertion of congressional war powers was quite possible during the Clinton presidency. This study now turns to President Clinton's first major military deployment abroad—an operation he inherited from President Bush. In Somalia, American troops used force and operated under UN endorsement. The political upheaval that ensued forced a constitutional battle over American participation in a UN operation that was only resolved with an expeditious move by the president.

2 Somalia

Somalia represented President Clinton's first real foreign policy challenge and crisis. By October 1993, the mission was a deep embarrassment for the United States, as American lives were lost in this peacekeeping and later "nation building" operation. When the troops were originally deployed, President George Bush had gained the support of the United Nations Security Council and Chapter 7 authorization to use "all necessary means to establish as soon as possible a secure environment for humanitarian relief operations in Somalia."[1] As broadcasted and illustrated by major television networks around the world, American troops also landed in Somalia "equipped for combat." Before the mission ended, American troops were using force against Somalian gangs and clearly involved in "hostilities" as specified in the WPR. Thus this deployment represented a real opportunity for Congress to test the president through a number of different legal and historical appeals on war powers.

Somalia and U.S. Foreign Policy

Like many African states, Somalia has a long and troubled history of colonial exploitation and internal repression, with a relatively short experience of American involvement. Somalia gained its independence from Italy and Britain in 1960 after nearly a century of various partitioning agreements. Prior to its independence, Ethiopia, France, and Kenya were also involved in divisions of Somalia with the Italians and the British. Although most Somalis speak a common language and have similar cultural origins, the most prominent group affiliation is local clans. In part because of these clans and historical land partitions, the development of a "national" identity, and consequently respect for a national government, was difficult to achieve.[2]

The Siad Barre regime set the stage for eventual intervention in Somalia by the United States and the United Nations in 1992. Barre took control of the East African state through a military coup in 1969. His rule amounted to little more than exploitative separations of the clans in order to maintain his power. However, with his socialist ideology and his diplomatic skills he attracted other communists' attention during the cold war, including the governments of the Soviet Union, Cuba, and East Germany. These allies provided Barre the necessary financial and military support to maintain control. Barre's communist backing, however, ended in 1977 when the Ethiopian government became communist and war between Somalia and Ethiopia ensued. In a stroke of realpolitik, Somalia's communist supporters—most importantly the Soviet Union—transferred their allegiances to Ethiopia; the United States moved in to fill the void. U.S. policy toward Somalia became codified in 1979, when the National Security Council directed the U.S. State Department to establish more formal relations with the Somalian government, with the goal of building a "military access agreement" between the two countries. Consequently, as the United States' new cold war partner, Somalia received American military assistance that eventually surpassed $750 million over the next decade.[3]

American assistance continued in the 1980s until cold war tensions dissipated and domestic developments within Somalia prompted the United States to reevaluate its alliance with Barre. When relations between the United States and the Soviets relaxed in the mid-1980s, Somalia's strategic significance to both states diminished. At the same time, observers of Somalian politics began to note that Barre's rule was "oppressive and corrupt," largely as a result of his widespread human rights violations. Congress became increasingly concerned about Barre's many human rights abuses and placed some pressure on President Ronald Reagan to cease U.S. foreign lending to Somalia.[4] By the end of 1988, U.S. financial support was cut dramatically. At the same time, many Somalis had grown weary of Barre's leadership, and domestic opposition groups were forming.

By 1991, Somalia was on the verge of breakdown. Clan allegiances were high, armed opposition groups conducted raids on villages, large-scale dissatisfaction with Barre's leadership existed, and widespread human rights abuses continued. By the year's end, the country had disintegrated into chaos, with no government, no police force, no functioning judicial system, and at least one million displaced persons. Some estimate that 30,000 people died during the year as a result of war and malnutrition.[5] The situation became so tenuous that both the American and Italian governments used military forces to extricate a number their nationals.[6]

From this chaos, Mohammed Aideed rose to become one of Somalia's strongest clan leaders. With a mixture of Somalian nationalism and occasional references to Islam but mostly a reliance upon violence, Aideed soared to the top rung of Somalian society as a prominent clan leader. Aideed was not a strong ideologue but was well supplied with weapons left over from the cold war era, which explains much of his ability to lead.[7]

By mid-1992 pressure was building in the United States to take action to prevent further starvation and instability. Human rights groups and some members of Congress called for an international humanitarian relief mission. A number of congressional committee hearings were held, most of which heard arguments in favor of a larger role for the United Nations at a minimum, with some members suggesting active American assistance and possible engagement.[8] The House Select Committee on Hunger was especially vocal in calling for U.S. leadership. A bipartisan group of eighty-eight members of Congress wrote President George Bush asking that his administration place its "highest priority" on Somalia.[9] These efforts eventually resulted in the Bush administration's support for the UN-supported humanitarian operation, United Nations Operation in Somalia (UNOSOM). In this operation, food and other necessities were provided to thousands of Somalis. Five hundred UN peacekeepers were initially deployed, which was soon increased by three thousand when the dimensions of the crisis became more obvious.[10]

As the graphic and disturbing pictures of starving Somalis continued to reach American viewing audiences, the pressure also grew in Congress for action. After its defeat to Governor Bill Clinton in the 1992 presidential elections, the Bush administration initiated and led Operation Restore Hope, or the United Nations Task Force (UNITAF), on December 3, 1992.[11] Using its Chapter 7 authority, the United Nations Security Council authorized U.S. troops to use "all necessary means" in the distribution of humanitarian aid. By December 9, twenty thousand troops were being deployed to Somalia, which eventually rose to approximately twenty-eight thousand. In the process, Bush received strong backing from Congress and high approval ratings from the American public.[12] Bush also received the blessings of President-elect Bill Clinton.

Foreign Affairs and a New President

When Bill Clinton took his inaugural oath, not only did he move into a position that was vastly different from his experience as governor of Arkansas, he also inherited a foreign policy gamble with Operation Restore Hope. Clinton was faced with the logistical difficulties of providing for a starving people and a dying state and was also confronted with important policy choices about how and when to extricate U.S. forces. Presumably, the Somalia mission fit into the foreign policy goals of President-elect Clinton. During the campaign, most of the campaign rhetoric centered on domestic issues. There was some indication that Clinton would give more attention to human rights in U.S. foreign policy, and the governor had been supportive of multilateral organizations and their potential to resolve world crises and conflict. At one point during the campaign, Clinton advocated the development of a UN rapid deployment force that would be readily available to address world crises.[13] However, as with any new president, there was still uncertainty about how Clinton would conduct foreign policy once in the White House. Much uncertainty also remained regarding the extent to which Congress would seek to influence or shape foreign policy in the post–cold war era.

CONGRESS AND THE WAR POWER

Both Clinton and Congress supported Operation Restore Hope when President Bush initiated the mission. The Senate approved of the mission on February 4, 1993, and the House voted on May 25, 1993, to support U.S. participation in the operation. However, these votes engendered different levels of controversy and guarded concern from individual members of Congress over the president's constitutional authority to conduct the operation and to use American forces abroad. Upon closer examination, however, presidential unilateralism, partisan politics, and congressional deference provide much insight on the war powers interplay.

The Senate

Before the Senate's vote in February 1993, support for the mission was strong. Although the UN Participation Act of 1945 clearly granted Congress a voice in whether to deploy American troops to Africa, and despite the United Nations authorization to "use all necessary means" in Somalia, any constitutional concerns the Senate may have had about the mission were not high on Washington's political agenda. Originally, when Bush deployed the troops under Security Council Resolution 794, the president noted that the troops would probably be home before Clinton's inauguration.[14] Although U.S. troops were authorized to use force, at the time of the initial deployment it seemed very unlikely that military combat would take place. However, some in the Senate expressed political and constitutional concerns about the mission as the Clinton administration took office. Senate Majority Leader George Mitchell (D-Maine) raised one skeptical voice regarding the president's constitutional authority to involve U.S. troops in Operation Restore Hope. Mitchell stated that Congress did have a role in peacekeeping decisions and that Congress had a responsibility to check the president when he deploys troops under a UN endorsement. In his most forceful remark, Mitchell argued, "UN Security Council resolutions are no substitute for congressional authorization."[15] Mitchell's statement is noteworthy in that it came from a distinguished and well-regarded member of the president's own party rather than a more partisan ideologue among the Republicans. In fact, the vast majority of Republicans said nothing on the constitutional implications of U.S. troop contributions to a UN operation. However, Mitchell's comment also speaks to broader exercise of congressional war powers. Mitchell's remarks as Senate majority leader came long after the deployment had taken place. Mitchell spoke assertively on congressional rights and duties *two months* after the deployment and had not raised the issue in December or in January over the congressional recess. No other evidence suggests that Mitchell saw the deployment as a crucial issue for the Senate to consider.

In a voice vote on February 4, 1993, the Senate approved the mission. Senate Joint Resolution (SJR) 45 stated that the mission was "consistent with" the War Powers Resolution (WPR). If hostilities were encountered, the WPR time mechanism would begin and the president would have to turn to Congress for authorization. SJR 45 also gave U.S. troops the authority to use "all necessary means" to fulfill their humanitarian objectives.[16] Because the resolution was reached by voice vote and was nonbinding, it meant little in terms of Congress's ability to exercise its war powers. Individual senators were not forced to take a formal position on the deployment and thus could not be held accountable for the mission if it failed. Thus the senate, led by the Democrats, took its first official step in deferring to the new president. While the resolution on its face looks assertive, in fact, the action represents a step of inaction and deference. When presidents first take office, they are typically granted some leeway in foreign policy making, especially by members of Congress from the president's political party.[17] In this case, the Senate Democrats closely followed this established practice.

After the vote, the Senate stayed relatively quiet on Somalia over the next month. However, as UNITAF proceeded, some interest began to develop. In a Senate Armed Services Committee meeting on March 25, 1993, Senators Sam Nunn (D-Ga.) and Carl Levin (D-Mich.) openly expressed their concern that the WPR requirements should be applied and that Congress was neglecting its duties by not forcing the president to gain full congressional approval for the deployment. About the president's actions in support of UNITAF, Nunn noted that "Congress is in the situation of sitting on its hands . . . while these commitments are being made, and not really taking any kind of responsibility under the Constitution. It seems to me we have some responsibilities here and we better start paying attention to them."[18] Senator Levin also stated that Congress's behavior demonstrated an "abdication" of its "responsibilities." He later argued that because of the strong possibility of hostilities and with the Pentagon's robust rules of engagement granted by the UN Security Council, the War Powers Resolution applied, and the president should seek authorization. Nunn also noted that because UN authorization fell under Chapter 7 of the UN Charter, congressional authorization for the operation was required.[19] These points echoed Mitchell's earlier remarks and came from another well-respected and senior member of the president's party. Nunn's and Mitchell's analysis correspond accurately with the legislative history of the UN Participation Act, which clearly specified Congress's role in UN deployments. Despite these pointed criticisms of Clinton's actions, however, the Senate pushed no further on this issue and remained content to criticize its own unwillingness to take further responsibility. Nunn and Levin also pressed no further on war powers issues, even though Nunn had previously introduced war powers legislation during the Reagan administration that called for greater consultation from the president.[20] In short, Nunn and Levin too were deferring to the freshman Democratic President, even though their public statements seemed to indicate otherwise. Senators of both parties essentially let the constitutional and legal issues rest, playing a "wait-and-see" game to determine their next move.

The House

The U.S. House of Representatives' behavior was similar to the Senate's in the first months of 1993. House Foreign Affairs Chairman Lee Hamilton (D-Ind.) stated in 1992 that Congress, and by implication the House Foreign Affairs Committee, would play a fundamental role in the deployment.[21] Collectively, however, the House was slow to act, and the Democrats made no serious effort to bring a resolution of support or a vote on the deployment to the floor. Like the Senate, some House members raised constitutional issues over the appropriate role for Congress with regard to the deployment. The discussion between Representative Harry Johnston (D-Fla.) and Clinton's deputy assistant secretary of state, Robert Houdek, at a House Foreign Affairs subcommittee meeting on February 17 provides some insight into the congressional-xecutive interplay. At the hearing, Johnston asked Houdek if the president needed congressional authorization to take further actions in Somalia. Johnston also inquired whether the WPR applied to Somalia. Houdek argued that a congressional resolution was not necessary and that the WPR did not apply in this case.[22] In the same hearing Houdek was pushed further by Alcee Hastings (D-Fla.), who questioned the deputy secretary on why the WPR did not apply. In response, Houdek returned to statements made by the Bush administration, arguing that since no intent to engage in combat existed and because no hostilities were being experienced, no authorization was needed. Hastings followed by asking Houdek for his views on Section 6 of the United Nations Participation Act, which provides for congressional authorization of U.S. participation in UN deployments. Although Houdek refused to comment at the hearing, he replied later in writing, "The President has constitutional and other legal authority to deploy U.S. troops in support of the UN efforts in Somalia."[23] These hearings demonstrated that some members of Congress were concerned about their constitutional responsibilities and did press the executive branch on these issues.

As in the Senate, most of the constitutional pressure on the president came from House members of Clinton's own party. However, as a body the Democratic majority was unwilling to place the operation in any political or constitutional jeopardy and thus placed no legal limitations upon their president, nor did they bring the issue to the floor for debate. As in the Senate, some members of the House were content to *assert* a constitutional role, but not to exercise it against the president. Houdek's response also was one of the first signals that the Clinton administration would assert wide powers as commander in chief, similar to other chief executives since the passage of the WPR in 1973.

On April 27, House minority discontent rose considerably at a House foreign affairs subcommittee meeting. At the time, the House was debating SJR 45, which had gained the Senate's voice vote approval for American participation in the operation. The resolution also authorized the operation for twelve months. At the subcommittee markup meeting for the House's consideration, Doug Bereuter (R-Nebr.) noted that the resolution and the House's actions to date were weak and open ended. He argued that the resolution being advanced violated the WPR and that U.S. troops should be returned immediately.[24]

Bereuter's concerns were indicative of a wider discontent, particularly among the GOP, that was soon expressed on the House floor. When the resolution reached the floor in May, a highly partisan debate ensued over Congress's role in dispatching troops under the United Nations. Many Republicans argued that the operation violated the WPR and that U.S. troops should be brought home. Some of this reaction was triggered by Clinton's and the United Nations' new policy on Somalia. On May 4, 1993, the UN Security Council ruled in Resolution 814 that control of the Somalia operation would shift to the United Nations Operation in Somalia II (UNOSOM II) and that Chapter 7 authorization still applied. Again, troops were authorized to engage in combat if the appropriate conditions arose in an effort to rebuild the governing structures of Somalia.[25] Because of these developments, House Republicans asserted that U.S. forces should not serve under a United Nations commander. Representative Bill Goodling (R-Pa.) argued, "We are authorizing the deployment of U.S. troops under foreign command. This in itself is a monumental event, unparalleled in our history. . . . I stand in opposition to the resolution before the House today."[26] To some degree, this position fits closely with a more traditional Republican foreign policy approach. As the mission became more multilateral in nature, the GOP went on the attack. Traditionally, Republicans have been more protective of national sovereignty and U.S. responsibilities in collective security organizations than Democrats. This position harkens back to the aftermath of World War I, when the Republicans, led by Senator Henry Cabot Lodge (R-Mass.), were instrumental in moving the Senate to keep the United States out of the League of Nations because of the feared loss of sovereignty. In 1993, the appearance of UN control of the military operations in Somalia became a catalyst for Republican activism.

Under the leadership of their ranking minority member on the House Foreign Affairs Committee, Benjamin Gilman (R-N.Y.), House Republicans fought for a shorter authorization period of six months and argued that Congress had not been appropriately consulted.[27] Representative Gerald Solomon (R-N.Y.) followed by noting that Congress needed to express its approval before U.S. troops were allowed to participate in the new Somalian operation.[28] Moreover, like the more vocal Senate Democrats, Gilman and Toby Roth (R-Wis.) claimed that Congress was avoiding its constitutional responsibility by giving President Clinton an operational blank check.[29] Furthermore, in written comments to the *Congressional Record*, Congressman Bereuter called for the operation's end and the immediate withdrawal of the U.S. troops.[30]

In the aftermath of Operation Desert Storm in Iraq, the Republicans' position on war powers and Congress's role in UN operations was, at times, quite striking. This was especially true of Representative Gilman, who was described by analysts as a "strong" supporter of President Bush after Saddam Hussein invaded Kuwait.[31] When the time came to vote on the use of force in Operation Desert Storm in 1991, Gilman was unwilling to limit President Bush's military powers and instead voiced his support for the United Nations. In discussing House Joint Resolution 658 on October 1, 1990, which expressed Congress's approval of President Bush's deployment of 200,000 American troops to the Middle East at that time, Gilman inserted these comments into the *Congressional Record:* "I think we must recognize that the unprecedented action of the United Nations Security Council gives us all hope that in an environment where east-west tensions are diminishing on a daily basis, multinational organizations such as the United Nations, will be able to play a constructive and productive role in maintaining law and order."[32] In 1991, Gilman made similar comments prior to Congress's vote on whether to support United Nations Security Council Resolution 678, which authorized UN member states to use force against Iraq. At that time Gilman again placed similar comments into the *Congressional Record:* "As the member of the United Nations with the most resources and the best ability to support the UN resolutions, the United States should not turn its back on Kuwait and the world. Rather, we should set the example for peace and security which will define our post cold war world."[33] About Desert Storm, another Republican, Paul Henry (R-Mich.), stated in more outspoken terms that "the US Congress ought not put itself at odds against the United Nations or question the considered opinion and actions of the Security Council. Turning against the United Nations in this instance would strike a blow against the struggle to refine and strengthen international peacekeeping institutions that will be so important in the post–cold war era."[34] These pro-UN comments from Henry and Gilman are striking compared to later Republican efforts to place legal restrictions on President Clinton in 1993 under the WPR. These more skeptical views on American participation in United Nations operations highlight how quickly some members of Congress reversed their positions on the relationship between Security Council decisions and Congress's role with respect to these resolutions.

The Republicans were not alone in their concern about war powers and United Nations operations. A small number of Democrats joined the Republicans in their constitutional concern. For example, in one of the more acute comments, Harry Johnston stated that "if we ever want this establishment, the U.S. Congress, to be relevant to the situation, then we [must] acknowledge the War Powers Act is the law of the land."[35] However, most Democrats wanted to grant the president greater latitude as commander in chief. House Democrats voted down the Republicans' attempts to limit further funding and to set time limits on the Somalia operation. In a highly partisan vote on May 25, the House voted 243–179 to continue support for the mission. Although it was a Democratic-led initiative that sought to restore the perceived imbalance of power during the Vietnam War with the WPR, in the constitutional arguments presented in 1993, most Democrats maintained that they had fully met their constitutional responsibilities by passing their nonbinding resolution. Alan Wheat (D-Mo.) noted: "Today's legislation fulfills our congressional obligation under the War Powers Act."[36] Foreign Affairs Committee Chairman Lee Hamilton stated that "By approving this resolution, the Congress shows that we are willing to step up to our responsibilities, I might say our constitutional responsibilities, and assume the proper role as a partner with the President in making the decision to commit U.S. troops abroad." He later added: "Congress here must play its constitutional role. Congress in my view should authorize whenever U.S. forces are sent abroad for potential use in combat. Such authorization is required by the constitution. It is required by the War Powers Resolution, and is required by the basic principles of sound policy-making."[37] Tom Lantos (D-Calif.), a longtime advocate of congressional war powers, noted similarly, "It is a constitutional and legal responsibility of the Congress to participate in decisions that commit our military forces. This resolution reflects a balanced approach to this issue."[38] Chairman Hamilton, who had earlier advocated a strong congressional role when the troops were originally deployed in December 1992, fought off Republican attempts to place more legal requirements on the president in May 1993. In a very partisan manner, House Democrats felt that they had met their "constitutional responsibility" by passing a nonbinding resolution in May—five months into Clinton's first year as President and six months after the original deployment.

Clinton and the WPR

Throughout the first months of his presidency, Clinton himself remained quiet on the legal specifics of constitutional war powers with regard to Somalia.[39] However, in different public forums, the Clinton administration took a somewhat different stand from its White House predecessors regarding the WPR. In April 1993, White House Communications Director George Stephanopoulous stated that Clinton was supportive "in theory" of the War Powers Resolution.[40] Moreover, in response to a letter from Representative Henry Gonzales (D-Tex.) Clinton recognized that tensions existed between the legislature and the chief executive over the WPR and that this was one area deserving examination.[41] Based on this letter and Stephanopoulous' statements, it is clear that the White House had not yet defined clearly what war powers responsibilities meant for its administration. Thus, some substantive congressional engagement on war powers appeared possible. It may be countered that any chief executive during the first few months of his presidency would respond similarly to a query from a curious member of Congress in order to foster good relations between the member and the president and between these two branches of government. With the exception of President Carter, however, no other president has expressed sympathy "in theory" with the WPR or recognized that some progress was needed in this area of presidential-congressional relations.[42] But even if the administration's official policy position on war powers was uncertain at the time, within the first months of the Clinton presidency the administration's actions fell closely in line with his predecessors. Deputy Secretary Houdek's legal arguments could have been used in nearly any presidential administration during the cold war to explain the executive branch's position on its war powers. In short, while some early remarks indicated otherwise, the stage was being set for a president who perceived his powers as commander in chief broadly. These patterns became codified as Clinton developed his position on American participation in UN operations.

A defining moment for President Clinton and the mission in Somalia came on June 10, 1993, with the president's official notification letter to congressional leaders about the mission in Somalia. In the letter Clinton stated that in order to be "consistent with the War Powers Resolution," he was informing Congress of the actions and progress in Somalia.[43] Clinton also noted the United Nations Security Council's decision to transfer control of the operational duties of the Somalia mission to the United Nations under UNOSOM II. Clinton noted that he had consulted closely with Congress and would continue to do so and that the deployment was constitutional under his power as commander in chief and under international law.[44] Clinton's position was very similar to President George Bush's prior to the Persian Gulf War, when he argued that through his powers as commander in chief and through the UN Security Council's support, the president had authority to use force against Iraq without specific congressional approval.[45] Clinton took a position that was in line with that taken by both Democratic and Republican presidents since World War II.

UNOSOM II and American Casualties

In August 1993 pressure on the Clinton administration resumed as Congressman Gilman again raised the deployment authority issue. The Congressman's written statement in the *Congressional Record* was entitled "Death of the War Powers Resolution in Somalia." In his statement, he argued that because sixty days had passed since combat had broken out in Somalia on June 5, 1993, both Congress and the president were at fault for not enforcing the WPR. Included in Gilman's statement was a letter he had sent to Secretary of State Warren Christopher, cosigned by Senator Jesse Helms (R-N.C.), ranking minority member of the Senate Foreign Relations Committee. They asked whether American troops faced "hostilities" as defined by the WPR in Somalia.[46] In a written response from Assistant Secretary of State Wendy Sherman, the administration's position was well articulated and provides much insight on the president's interpretation of war powers.

Sherman remarked creatively that, regardless of whether the WPR was constitutional, it was intended for American troops in "sustained hostilities" and followed by noting, "This is not the situation we face in Somalia." Further, she added that the American use of force had been undertaken with a United Nations mandate and noted that both the House and the Senate approved of U.S. participation in the Somalia peacekeeping operation by approving SJR 45. However, echoing George Bush's position on Congress's vote on Operation Desert Storm, she stated, "We do not believe that specific statutory authorization is necessary."[47] These statements are reminiscent of President Ronald Reagan's effort to redefine "hostilities" during his U.S. troop deployment to Lebanon in a multilateral peacekeeping operation. Reagan, too, sought to avoid congressional legal limitations on his deployment, arguing that "there is no intention or expectation that U.S. Armed Forces will become involved in hostilities in Lebanon." In Reagan's view, the War Powers Resolution did not apply.[48] Like Reagan, the Clinton administration's legal claims rested on semantical differences with Gilman over what was meant by "hostilities" and the authority granted to the president in previous United Nations Security Council decisions and congressional resolutions.

Sherman's position is also notable considering that UN forces had come under fire on a number of occasions prior to her letter. On June 4, twenty-three UN peacekeepers from Pakistan were killed by Somali gangs. In the weeks that followed, three Italian peacekeepers were killed, and French and Norwegian peacekeepers also came under fire. The United States was also involved in "retaliatory raids" for the clans' aggression.[49] It is difficult not to conclude that American troops were engaged in "hostilities."

By August, with Congress in summer recess, 4,028 U.S. troops were still deployed in Somalia. On August 8, four American troops were killed by a Somalian land mine. This calamity became the principal catalyst for congressional action among Democrats. When members of Congress returned to Washington, the national debate on Somalia became quite intense. One of the most vocal advocates of policy change was Senator Robert Byrd (D-W.Va.). Prior to this public effort by the senator to check the president, Byrd had earlier shown interest in defining the legal responsibilities of the White House and Congress by urging the president to gain full congressional approval for the Somalia operation.[50] After the American casualties, Byrd proposed a resolution that would have eliminated funding for the Somalia operation if the president did not gain full congressional approval within one month. Byrd argued that the president had not consulted appropriately with Congress after the mission changed under UNOSOM II. Byrd stated, "The United Nations' mandate to disarm the warlords and rebuild a civil society in Somalia, approved by the UN Security Council, was never addressed, never debated, or never approved by this body."[51] As a senior senator in the majority party, with the power to filibuster and focus debate in the senate chamber, Byrd could easily have raised his concerns publicly much earlier if he had wanted. By going public at this time, Byrd placed considerable pressure on the White House.

Byrd's aggressive public effort to check the president was tempered by his Senate colleagues. In a nonbinding resolution, the Senate approved a measure that called for Clinton to consult with Congress by October 15 and to obtain Senate approval for the mission by November 15. The vote, which Byrd supported, was 90–7.[52]

Although the House let the Senate lead in August, it did not stay quiet for long, especially after three more American troops were killed on September 26.[53] The House responded by voting to set a November 15 deadline for Clinton to gain full congressional approval for the operation. In a bipartisan manner, this nonbinding resolution was cosponsored by Richard Gephart (D-Mo.) and Benjamin Gilman. The 406–26 vote in favor of the resolution demonstrated its widespread support.[54] However, the most significant development in the congressional-executive interplay occurred with the death of eighteen U.S. Army Rangers and the wounding of eighty other Americans in a battle with General Aideed's forces. One American soldier's body was dragged through the streets of Mogadishu, and the scene was broadcast to American living rooms. As the coverage reached American viewing audiences, public reaction against the deployment was strong.[55]

After the atrocity, many members of Congress vigorously attempted to limit the American role in UNOSOM II. Senator Russ Feingold (D-Wis.), a new but legally oriented senator, pushed the president and his colleagues to accept their full legislative responsibility. In a statement on the Senate floor, Feingold noted, "It has been my position that the troops should not have been there past 90 days after President Bush sent American soldiers there in December without a congressional resolution of approval."[56] Other Democrats, such as Peter DeFazio (D-Oreg.), called for the invocation of the War Powers Resolution, arguing that Congress had neglected its duties, and the president needed to bring the issue to Congress. He asserted, "It is time for the President and the Congress to face up to their constitutional responsibilities."[57] Most Democrats called for a reevaluation of the current Clinton policy, but some cautioned against an immediate withdrawal. Senators Nunn, John Warner (R-Va.), and Jim Exon (D-Nebr.) made similar remarks.[58] Thus Democrats in both the House and Senate were willing to question the president's deployment authority openly.

The Republicans, some of whom had earlier made efforts to restrict the president, spoke together against the president. Representative Bud Shuster (R-Pa.) remarked:

> Our troops are in combat. I call upon the President to invoke the War Powers Act. It is the law of the land.
>
> If the President does not invoke the War Powers Act, I call upon the Congress to see to it that we can take action. It is the law of the land, and it is an impeachable offense for any President to violate the law.[59]

One hundred forty-two House Republicans also sent a letter sent to President Clinton calling for the immediate withdrawal of U.S. forces.[60]

Many members of Congress also became increasingly concerned about the issue of proper command of forces and whether American troops were serving under U.S. or UN leadership. Senator Helms, whose career is marked by efforts to limit the United States' role in the United Nations, was vocal on this issue: "The United States has not constitutional authority, as I see it, to sacrifice U.S. soldiers to Boutros-Ghali's vision of multilateral peacemaking. . . . I do not want to play any more UN games. I do not want any more of our people under the thumb of any UN commander—none."[61] Despite Helm's vehemence, his version of the military command structure in Somalia grossly misrepresented the role played by the United States. In all situations in Somalia, U.S. troops served directly under U.S. leadership. The United States was also the principal author of all UN resolutions that dealt with Somalia. Specifically, when the eighteen Army Rangers were killed by Aideed's forces, these troops were serving directly under U.S. command.[62] However, this anti-UN position resonated with many members of Congress, especially Republicans, who later recalled these events in crafting their foreign policy positions in the "Contract with America" (see chapter 4).

The perception that U.S. troops were killed while under UN command can be attributed in part to the Clinton administration, who used the UN as a scapegoat to avoid criticism. Ignoring his administration's role in sponsoring previous Security Council resolutions on Somalia and U.S. command of the Army Rangers in Somalia, Clinton argued, "We cannot expect the United Nations to go around the world, whether it's in Cambodia or Somalia or any of the many other places we're involved in peacekeeping, and have people killed and have no resolution for it."[63] Thus, the United Nations was used by both parties either to shift the blame for the disaster or exploit the issue for a partisan advantage.

With congressional pressure building after the attack, Clinton responded by setting a March 31, 1994, mission departure date. At the same time the president sent 1,700 more troops to Somalia and reported that 3,600 troops would be stationed offshore.[64] The president's actions were persuasive enough to members of Congress to prevent any legal challenges from the Democratic majority in either chamber but were not enough to quell Congress's public displeasure with the operation, as expressed in the hearings that were to follow. However, Congress's efforts were never assertive enough to fully develop a collective legal challenge to the president, despite some members' apparent wishes.

After Clinton announced the American departure date, Congressman DeFazio still criticized his party's chief executive by again bringing his legal qualms with Congress and the president to the House floor. Noting that there was some confusion about the responsibilities of "the President as Commander in Chief and the constitutional obligation of the Congress and its war making authority," DeFazio pushed for Congress to take responsibility:

> There is no declaration of war. This body nor has the other body authorized the deployment of troops to Somalia.
>
> There is no national emergency. President Clinton must meet his obligation under the War Powers Act and submit a written request for authorization to the Congress defining the scope, duration and, most importantly, the objectives of our military operation in Somalia.
>
> Congress, we must stop ducking our responsibilities and vote to authorize this deployment or bring the troops home.[65]

DeFazio was not the only member of Congress to seek a legally binding role for Congress after Clinton's withdrawal announcement. In the Senate, a resolution offered by Senator John McCain (R-Ariz.) called for a "prompt withdrawal" of troops from Somalia, but the Senate voted down this measure in a 61–38 mostly partisan vote.[66] Most Democrats were again willing to grant the president the benefit of the doubt and accepted his withdrawal date. Thus, despite the willingness of some individual members to assert congressional authority, the Senate and House Democratic leadership was appeased by Clinton's withdrawal date. They avoided defining the proper legal role for Congress concerning the Somalian deployment and were unwilling to invoke a legally binding position for themselves or against the president.

On October 19 and 20, 1993, the Senate Foreign Relations Committee held hearings on the U.S. role in Somalia. At the hearings, Feingold again pushed for the invocation of the War Powers Resolution and stated that he opposed this mission on "its merits." There was also some disagreement over the level of consultation between the White House and Congress. Senator Frank Murkowsi (R-Alaska) speculated that when the mission went from UNOSOM to UNOSOM II, "it might have been more prudent had the administration sought some consultation with Congress." Senator Paul Simon (D-Ill.), however, argued that he had been in contact with the administration and that "there clearly was consultation."[67] Whether Simon's comments accurately reflected the majority of Democrats at the time is not clear, but it was clear that many Republicans felt as Murkowski did. At least some Democrats felt as Simon did, both in the Senate and the House, again reflecting partisan interpretations of war powers in practice.

During these hearings, most senators turned to other issues, including the financial costs of the operation and the level of allied cooperation. The question of authorization for the use of force was not the central issue. The hearings also provided little insight into the executive branch's position on Congress's role, but since most members were not calling for greater constitutional articulation, the administration had few political incentives to put forth such statements. Clinton's ambassador to the United Nations, Madeleine Albright, stated that Congress and the president must "work together to establish . . . consensus" and that the executive branch would continue in its consultations with Congress.[68] Other than these remarks, the executive branch offered no reevaluations or new definition of its position on division of powers.

Soon after these hearings, Senator Claiborne Pell (D-R.I.) called for further clarification of the administration's position with respect to Article 43 of the UN Charter. In his view, the United Nations Participation Act of 1945 and Article 43 provided Congress with the ability to exercise its war powers, and the president could not act unilaterally in United Nations enforcement activities.[69] While his position accurately reflected the debates held in the U.S. Senate in 1945, Pell stood alone in his references to Article 43. Nonetheless, even in light of the statements from Pell, Feingold, and DeFazio, the Democratic majority avoided placing further restrictions on the president's powers in foreign affairs. During this period of assertiveness, Senator Byrd was successful in passing a resolution to cut funding for the operation on March 31, 1994. Some individual senators made references to the WPR, but most did not pursue legal arguments concerning UN Security Council authorization.

The House Democrats' deference to the president was further highlighted by their resistance to proposals from the House GOP leadership to return American troops sooner. Under the leadership of Congressmen Gilman and Floyd Spence (R-S.C.), the ranking minority member of the House Armed Services Committee, the Republicans sought to force the troops' return two months prior to Clinton's March 31 withdrawal date. Gilman's resolution was barely defeated in the House Foreign Affairs Committee by a vote of 22–21.[70] Though three Democrats, Robert Andrews of New Jersey and Sherrod Brown and Eric Fingerhut of Ohio, voted with the unanimous Republican minority, these Republican efforts died under the weight of the Democratic majority as Congress accepted President Clinton's March 31 deadline and the Democrats prevented any further limitation of Clinton's foreign policy in Somalia.[71] Members of the majority party were much more interested in finding a short-term political solution to the immediate crisis in Somalia than solving any long-term constitutional or legal issues and thereby embarrassing their democratic colleague in the White House.

CONCLUSION

Somalia was the first real foreign policy test for the new president and Congress in 1993. With a new president who had little experience in foreign affairs, in an era replete with strategic ambiguities for the United States, Congress seemed to have an excellent opportunity to assert its war powers. U.S. troops were deployed under a UN peacekeeping operation, which by definition, allows for congressional approval and oversight. The American troops were also originally deployed with the authority to use force under Chapter 7 of the UN Charter and were "equipped for combat." Moreover, as early as June 1993, when Pakistani troops experienced casualties, American forces were involved in what the WPR describes as "hostilities," or at the very least, "imminent hostilities." Congress had the legal and constitutional authority to check the president but to a large degree followed its old patterns with regard to war powers, even though the actors were new. A number of factors explain this interplay between the White House and Congress.

Congress: Partisanship, Leaders, and the Domestic Context

One of the principal elements of the interplay is the importance of partisanship. The Democrats worked hard to protect the new Democratic president. Prior to the deaths of American troops in Somalia, most members of Congress did not take an active role in trying to force the president to bring the troops home. The Democrats in particular chose to grant Clinton considerable leeway in UNITAF and UNOSOM II until American casualties served as the catalyst for Congress's assertion of war power. Some House Republicans, such as Congressman Gilman, tried to keep pressure on the president to change course, citing the WPR in their efforts. Under Gilman's leadership in the House, the Republicans were strongly unified in their opposition against the Democrats, who vigorously fought against legal restraints on Clinton's actions. This chapter illustrates that Republican views of the United Nations Security Council decisions contrasted with the GOP's support of the UN under President George Bush. Many Republicans actively argued against UN missions and mandates, despite their seemingly "internationalist" leanings prior to Congress's vote on U.S. participation in Operation Desert Storm. Yet, among all players, House Republicans were the most adamant in their critiques of Clinton's unilateralism as commander in chief, while Democrats worked to prevent Gilman and others from restricting the president.

Once Americans were killed in combat, as a body Congress rose to force a change in Clinton's foreign policy though partisan differences remained. The deaths of four American soldiers to a Somali land mine in early August sparked a new level of congressional assertion. The intensity of legislative activism reached new heights after three additional American soldiers were killed and was further exacerbated by the deaths of 18 U.S. Army Rangers. Although Democratic Senator Robert Byrd led the Senate in these efforts, most House and Senate Democrats deferred to the president during the operation and accepted his withdrawal date in the aftermath of the casualties. The Democrats only *threatened* the invocation of the WPR. The Democratic leadership prevented all efforts to reduce funding or to bring troops home prior to the date established by the president. The influence of those Democrats who would assert Congress's constitutional powers was kept to a minimum. In an interesting twist of political fate, Congressman Lee

Hamilton, who had argued in December 1992 for a meaningful congressional role in UN deployments, later contended (in response to Republican efforts) that Congress should not micromanage foreign policy.[72] Like Gilman, Hamilton too played partisan politics in his application of war powers. Thus, in this case, partisan politics explains much of the war powers interplay, with Democrats protecting their new president and the Republicans applying standards to the commander in chief that ran counter to their previous behavior toward Republican President George Bush.

The absence of assertive individual leaders is another aspect of this war powers interplay. Congressional leaders, especially Senate Majority Leader George Mitchell and Speaker of the House Tom Foley, protected their president and resisted constitutional assertions of congressional war powers. While a few members of Congress, including Senators Pell, Byrd, and Feingold, made constitutional claims of congressional war powers, these voices were kept to a minimum. Mitchell and Senator Nunn, among others, were willing to raise constitutional questions rhetorically but were unwilling to exercise their legal powers. When Senator Byrd became too aggressive for his colleagues, he was reigned in by his party's leaders. Thus, not only the Democratic majority as a whole but individual leaders preferred deference.

An additional factor related to the Democrats' as well as individual leaders' protection of Clinton is the domestic circumstances in which the interplay took place. Bill Clinton was the Democrat's first president in twelve years, and he was in the first year of his presidency when the crisis developed. As noted, presidents are often granted some foreign policy leeway when they first enter office, and this held true in the Democratic Party's deference to Clinton. After the casualties and Clinton's establishment of a withdrawal date, congressional Democrats again returned to protecting their president against any constitutional assertions by the Republicans. Thus, the fact that there was a new president provides additional insight into why Congress avoided its war powers responsibilities. Deference remained the norm, but the reasons for this behavior cannot be explained simply by appealing to Congress's institutional preferences.

Presidential Leadership

President Clinton's position remained consistent throughout the entire Somalia experience: Congress had no formal authority to limit or restrain this deployment. The president responded to Congress when it pressured the administration to bring the troops home, but Clinton never acknowledged that Congress had a legal decision-making role in this process. Like all other chief executives since the WPR's passage, Clinton stated that he would continue his "consultation" with Congress, but no evidence suggests that the president felt Congress had the power to force the troops' return.

As the Reagan administration did in deploying troops to Lebanon and "military advisors" in El Salvador, the Clinton administration also employed a flexible definition of "hostilities" in order to avoid legal restrictions stemming from the WPR. Despite U.S. participation in military raids, Clinton officials argued that hostilities did not exist in Somalia and thus the WPR was not applicable.

Clinton also used United Nations authorizations to justify his actions, just as George Bush did prior to Operation Desert Storm, even though the legislative history of U.S. membership in the United Nations requires congressional approval for American participation in such operations. Thus despite the vast ideological differences between himself and Presidents Bush and Reagan, Bill Clinton used arguments almost identical to those of his predecessors to justify his conduct and his assertion of broad authority as commander in chief.

3   Haiti

The United States' military deployment to Haiti represents another occasion when U.S. armed forces were used abroad by the Clinton administration. As was the case in Somalia, American participation in this peacekeeping operation was approved by the United Nations Security Council under Chapter 7 authorization and entailed the use of American troops in a situation that allowed application of the WPR. In the end, in remarkable fashion, Congress chose to defer to the commander in chief, as Clinton asserted essentially unilateral military powers as chief executive. A full understanding of the congressional-executive interplay surrounding this use of force demands a comprehensive analysis of the domestic political factors that shaped the interplay of war powers.

U.S. Foreign Policy and Haiti

Unlike the United States' more limited history with Somalia, there is an extensive record of U.S. intervention in Haitian politics. Under the leadership of revolutionary Toussaint L'Ouverture, Haiti gained its independence from France in 1804. During its first century of freedom, however, the country was ravaged by corrupt politicians, wide divisions in wealth, and general instability.[1] With the U.S. victory in the Spanish-American War and with President Theodore Roosevelt's amended version of the Monroe Doctrine, or the "Roosevelt Corollary," American hegemonic aspirations in Latin America grew considerably in the first years of the twentieth century. Roosevelt implemented and enforced export and import duties on neighboring Santo Domingo in order to rectify its debts to the United States. Approximately a decade later, in 1915, President Woodrow Wilson deployed 350 U.S. troops to Haiti. Historians contend that Wilson acted in response to fears of a

German intervention into Haiti, Haiti's poor economic condition, the Haitian government's "slaughter" of 167 people, and the United States' increasing willingness to assert its power in the region. This occupation lasted until 1934, when the United States left behind its ally, President Stenio Vincent.[2]

Following the American withdrawal, Haiti endured a series of leaders after Vincent, who tried to maintain power through attempts to alter Haiti's constitutional one-term presidency. From 1934 to 1956, government repression was also widespread, and grassroots democratic groups were tyrannized. From this repression and instability, Francois Duvalier rose to prominence. Duvalier had earned a medical degree and practiced medicine throughout rural Haiti, endearing himself to many natives in the process. He also opposed the various corrupt regimes in power and for some time had been hiding from the government. In 1957, Duvalier, or "Papa Doc," came out of hiding and gained power initially through elections that many analysts believe were tainted with corruption.[3] Despite the corruption, Duvalier's election was the beginning of a dynasty that lasted until 1986. During his tenure as president, Duvalier used a combination of dictatorial policies supported by his own secret police force, his public use of voodoo to generate fear, and his popular appeal to solidify his rule. In the 1957 election, the United States gave most of its backing to another candidate, Louis Dejoie, although Duvalier apparently had some American assistance.[4] In the years that followed, American support for the regime varied. There are some reports that the Kennedy administration may have tried to assassinate Duvalier. However, U.S.-Haitian relations improved noticeably during the Nixon administration, as demonstrated by a visit by Vice President Nelson Rockefeller in 1970.[5]

Upon his father's death in 1971, Jean Claude Duvalier, or "Baby Doc," took over as Haiti's new ruler. As a nineteen-year-old president, Duvalier was welcomed by the United States. American support continued despite his repressive government, his looting of the government's treasury, and his wife's lavish expenditures of government funds. By 1986, Haitian domestic opposition had grown so much that, at the United States' urging, Duvalier was exiled to France with assistance from the U.S. Air Force.[6]

After Duvalier's rapid departure, a series of rulers occupied Haiti's presidency, all of whom came to power through either a coup d'etat or corrupt elections. However, in an election judged to be free and fair by outside observers, Haitians elected former Catholic priest Jean Bertrand Aristide president in 1990. Aristide had gained prominence from the pulpit by preaching his own version of liberation theology against past Haitian rulers. In the process he developed a strong following among the poor. Yet democracy lasted for only eight months. On September 30, 1991, Aristide was expelled from office in a coup orchestrated by his top military officials, particularly Lt. General Raoul Cedras.

After Aristide's ousting, the United States strongly condemned the Cedras regime. President George Bush stated that although he was reluctant to use military force to help return Aristide to power, he fully supported the restoration of democracy.[7] Bush also supported the economic sanctions imposed on Haiti by the Organization of American States, and he froze the American financial assets of Haitians involved in the coup.[8] Members of Congress were also livid about the coup. Both the House and Senate, with strong bipartisan support, passed resolutions calling for the restoration of democracy in Haiti.[9] The coup also resulted in a flood of Haitians seeking refuge in the United States, primarily in Florida.

As Cedras' rule became increasingly oppressive, Haitians continued to seek entry into the United States. The Bush administration's Haitian refugee policy was essentially a systematic rejection of these people. In 1992 Democratic presidential candidate Bill Clinton took issue with Bush's policy, stating: "If I were President, in the absence of clear and compelling evidence that they were not political refugees, I would give them temporary asylum here until we restored the elected government of Haiti. I would turn up the heat and try to restore the elected Government of Haiti and meanwhile let the refugees stay here."[10] Soon after Clinton criticized Bush's refugee policy, many congressional Democrats began to push the administration to place more attention on these Haitians' human rights. Human rights activists and religious organizations also put pressure on the administration for policy change.[11] By the summer of 1992 Bush faced considerable opposition from candidate Clinton, an increasingly vocal Congress, and many human rights organizations to give greater respect to Haitian refugees. Despite the criticism, Bush resisted these pressures and remained steadfast in his policy throughout the rest of his presidency.

President Clinton and Haiti: 1993

Upon becoming president-elect, Bill Clinton made one of the first of his foreign policy reversals that would come over the next two years. One week prior to his inauguration, Clinton retracted his campaign promises on the Haitian refugees and decided to continue with Bush's rigid policy. His decision received much criticism from human rights organizations and later became the target of fierce congressional reproach.[12] Following the announcement of his change in position and throughout the first few months of his presidency, Clinton's policy remained essentially the same, as Democrats allowed their president to enjoy his honeymoon months in office. Clinton expressed his support for a restoration of Haitian democracy at a joint appearance with Aristide, but overall no new developments came from the executive branch in the first few months of Clinton's presidency.[13] Much of this political tranquility was due to the diplomatic success experienced at Governor's Island in the summer of 1993. At Governor's Island, former Argentinean foreign minister Dante Caputo, who acted on the United Nations' behalf, negotiated an agreement between Cedras and Aristide. The settlement had ten points, with the key decision being Cedras' agreement to depart from Haiti and allow Aristide's return as president on October 30, 1993.

Although the Clinton administration supported the agreement, the president continued his diplomatic pressure and economic sanctions. On July 16, the Clinton administration voted in favor of United Nations Security Council Resolution 841, which placed a global oil and arms embargo on Haiti. Clinton stated that the United States was leading the effort to place further sanctions on Haiti and had earlier noted that he believed at some point a multinational peacekeeping force would have to be deployed there in order to restore democracy.[14]

As 1993 progressed, it remained unclear whether Cedras would keep his promises. The Clinton administration took a step toward using force on September 23, 1993, when it voted in favor of Security Council Resolution 867. The resolution allowed for twelve hundred policy and military advisors to enter Haiti under the terms of the Governor's Island agreement in order to ensure a peaceful leadership transition. After Resolution 867 passed, the Clinton administration was deeply embarrassed on October 11, when the USS Harlan County, loaded with 250 U.S. military engineers, linguists, and medical specialists, was turned away from a Port-au-Prince dock by chanting and ostensibly hostile Haitian gangs. Moreover, the protestors had the support of Haiti's police forces, who did little to prevent the chaos.[15] These developments coincided with the debate in Congress over the American casualties in Somalia and Congress's proper role in UN operations. In response to the mood of the times, Clinton's embarrassment over the USS *Harlan County* incident, and the growing role of United Nations Security Council resolutions in American foreign policy, Senator Don Nickles (R-Okla.) introduced legislation to prevent U.S. participation in UN military operations abroad.[16] These were the first steps taken by Congress that demonstrated some willingness to limit and challenge the president's perceived authority in foreign policy.

Clinton reacted firmly by writing that he was "fundamentally opposed to amendments which improperly limit [his] constitutional duties as Commander-in-Chief." Clinton did indicate that he remained committed to "consultation" with Congress as required by the WPR, yet nowhere in his letter did he state Congress's proper role in such deployments or acknowledge any legitimacy to the claim that Congress had any decision-making authority in troop deployments.[17] In essence, the letter implied that the president could act independently when necessary because the commander in chief's powers were so broad.

Two days later Clinton exercised his perceived broad powers when he deployed six U.S. naval ships to Haiti to enforce the new UN embargo. Although the UN Security Council had not given UN member states the authority to deploy the ships, the Clinton administration made the precarious claim that authority had been gained by previous Security Council decisions. In a hearing before the House Committee on Foreign Affairs, Undersecretary for Policy at the Department of Defense Frank Wisner stated that the ships were "enforcing a UN Security Council decision." With regard to the use of force, Wisner remarked, "The President has not ruled out options, but that option is not one we are considering."[18] What Wisner clearly implied was that the Clinton administration felt it had authority to act without either the United Nations' or Congress's approval in his naval deployment. The administration also noted that it had not ruled out the option of force, insinuating that it had authority to use force if necessary.

Congressional and executive relations worsened on October 21, 1993, when the United States fired two warning shots across the bow of a

Turkish merchant ship that was in violation of the Security Council embargo. The ship was later searched and turned back to sea after the Turks would not allow all of its cargo to be examined.[19] On the same day, Senator Jesse Helms (R-N.C.) introduced an amendment calling for prior congressional approval before any appropriations could be made for military operations in Haiti. The vote failed, 19–81, but demonstrated some Republicans' willingness to challenge the commander in chief. However, in a vote that achieved nearly unanimous approval, the Senate supported a resolution by Majority Leader George Mitchell (D-Maine) stating that Congress must give prior approval to use force in Haiti unless vital national security risks were at stake. The resolution was adopted 98–2.[20] While the vote implied that the Senate wanted a role in the deployment process, in reality the language of the resolution gave great military leeway to the president. The Senate wanted to assert its war powers but also granted the president independent authority to use force if "national security interests" were threatened. The vote demonstrated nearly complete acquiescence to the president but allowed Congress to criticize the Clinton administration later if further problems developed or if the president independently deployed troops.

After the naval deployment and once the troops retreated from an aborted entry at Port-au-Prince, Republican opposition to American participation in a Haitian intervention and the increasing role of the United Nations in American foreign policy continued. For example, in the House, Congressman John Doolittle (R-Calif.) said, "I have been very concerned about our mission in Haiti, this UN mission which the President approved and was trying to move troops into support of that. Thank goodness, under pressure for the Congress, he reversed his decision."[21] On a larger scale, many members were unwilling to push for intervention into Haiti after the Somalia debacle and were very critical of President Clinton's foreign policy in general. Reflective of many Republicans' mood at the time, House Minority Whip Newt Gingrich (R-Ga.) stated, "I think it is very important for this President to understand that he has a deep, serious foreign policy crisis and that he needs to thoroughly overhaul his defense and foreign policy establishment and he needs to find a way to calmly and consistently lead Americans in a way that we can support and follow."[22]

Part of the reason for Congress's lack of support for a Haitian intervention came from conservative senators' questions on Aristide's mental stability. Senator Helms, who helped wage an all-out battle against Clinton's Haitian policy, cited Central Intelligence Agency reports that raised questions about Aristide's psychological balance. Helms referred to Aristide as a "psychopath"[23] and called Aristide a "demonstrable killer."[24] Democrats contested these summaries of the classified committee briefings, but these new claims about Aristide provided another element to the intervention debate and another reason for more in the GOP to oppose an intervention.[25]

While Helms mounted his challenge to the administration, some members of Congress pushed vehemently for a Haitian intervention. One of the most vocal advocates was Congressman Major Owens (D-N.Y.)—one of the chief spokesmen for the congressional Black Caucus. During the 103rd Congress, the Black Caucus had grown to become a particularly strong political faction. With thirty-nine members in the House and an influential and articulate leader in Kweisi Mfume (D-Md.), the caucus represented an important coalition of votes for the president and his future domestic legislation. Most of the members were liberal democrats and generally sympathetic to President Clinton's policy proposals.[26] Thus Clinton could not ignore the caucus. Owens had the following remarks inserted into the *Congressional Record*: "Without further waiting the United States must do whatever is necessary to support the majority of the people of Haiti. Democracy in Haiti is definitely a vital interest of the United States."[27] The Black Caucus later became an even more vigorous advocate of military force and through its recommendations implicitly gave the president wide authority as commander in chief to use force in Haiti.

Throughout the rest of 1993, Clinton remained on a foreign policy tightrope with Congress, and after Congress's reaction to Somalia and the naval deployment to Haiti, no more military actions were taken. Yet even in the aftermath of the Somalian tragedy, Senate Democrats were still unwilling to limit their president's military powers and could only muster a symbolic vote against Clinton with George Mitchell's resolution. In short, the Senate was willing to assert a role for Congress in deployment decisions, but when it came to limiting the president, as Jesse Helms' resolution would have done, it shied away from any *required* decision-making role for Congress in advance of a deployment. Clinton kept open the option of using force in Haiti, but it seemed that after the Somalia fiasco the use of force in the Caribbean was not high on the president's priority list.[28]

THE DEPLOYMENT TO HAITI: 1994

Presidential Decision Directive 25

Throughout 1993 and into 1994, the Clinton administration continued to claim the option of using force in Haiti.[29] However, Clinton was well attuned to the political dynamics of the Somalia debate and the new assertiveness that had developed in the House and Senate on Haiti. During 1994, the Clinton administration adapted to these developments by reformulating its policy on UN peace operations in a way that, on paper, was much more cognizant of Congress and, ostensibly, its war powers. The president's new policy, Presidential Decision Directive (PDD) 25, provided a set of guidelines for future participation in multilateral military enforcement operations.[30] The paper made several major points that reflected many of the concerns raised previously by the UN operation in Somalia.

PDD 25 reiterated that the United States would never allow foreign command of U.S. troops, that it would only participate in missions in which there is a strong likelihood of success, that U.S. expenditures on peace operations would decrease, and that the United States would push for reforms at the United Nations. The new policy also recognized the importance of Congress's role in American foreign policy making. A summary of the decision stated: "Traditionally, the executive branch has not solicited the involvement of Congress or the American people on matters related to UN peacekeeping. This lack of communication is not desirable in an era when peace operations have become more numerous, complex and expensive. The Clinton administration is committed to working with Congress to improve and regularize communication and consultation on these important issues." More specifically, the paper stated that the president would continue to consult on a bipartisan basis with congressional leaders, have monthly staff briefings, keep Congress informed of all UN activities, and support the repeal of the War Powers Resolution in favor of "some sort" of required consultative mechanism.[31] On paper, Clinton could not have gone much farther in recognizing the political and constitutional significance of Congress in UN operations. With the exception of President Truman in 1945, no other president had recognized Congress's role vis-à-vis the United Nations to this degree. At the same time, PDD 25 granted no legal authority to Congress and was still vague about Congress's specific authority. There was also no reference to Section 6 of the UN Participation Act or Article 43 of the UN Charter. Thus, although the president reached out to Congress politically, legally little changed, as the president still maintained his perceived right to act independently from Congress in multilateral military operations.[32]

The United Nations Security Council and Haiti

Throughout the rest of 1994, the United States continued to pressure Cedras through UN Security Council resolutions that condemned the Haitian regime. In a series of threats, the Clinton administration approved of UN Security Council Resolution 905, which reiterated the United States' support for implementing the Governor's Island agreement. The United States also approved of Security Council Resolutions 917 and 933, which placed further economic sanctions on the Haitian government and called for the implementation of the Governor's Island agreement.

The key UN Security Council decision came in Resolution 940. Made under Chapter 7 of the UN Charter, the resolution authorized member states to use "all necessary means" to remove the Haitian dictatorship. The president and others in the administration used this as an ultimatum to Cedras, warning him that the United States was committed to using force to restore Aristide. Congress did not automatically accept the UN authorization as constitutional, however, and a number of efforts were made in 1994 to restrain the president.

The House

In 1994, Congress's attention to Haiti grew considerably. The legislative year began with heightened scrutiny of the United States' involvement in UN military deployments and the lack of consultation with Congress.[33] As the year progressed, most members of Congress were hesitant to support an American deployment to Haiti. Other members, notably the congressional Black Caucus and some members of the Florida delegation, pushed Clinton to restore Aristide to power.[34]

By mid-spring, congressional pressure for a new refugee policy rose considerably. A House foreign affairs subcommittee held hearings on the humanitarian aspects of the economic sanctions on Haiti in which a number of members were critical of Clinton's continuation of Bush's policy. In a more public display of concern and protest, on April 21, Congressman Joseph Kennedy (D-Mass.) and five members of the congressional Black Caucus were arrested for civil disobedience in protest of Clinton's policy.[35] Moreover, activist Randall Robinson, who had lobbied extensively against U.S. policy toward South Africa over apartheid, began a fast that brought considerable attention to the refugees' cause.[36] The day before Robinson's fast began, he stated that the Clinton administration's policy was "cruel, patently discriminatory and . . . profoundly racist." Adding to the pressure on Congress, Aristide used the millions of dollars of frozen assets from the Haitian dictators to lobby for his cause.[37]

Clinton reacted to these new developments by slightly amending his refugee policy with a more liberal examination process for the refugees, which appeased liberal Democrats in the short term. As Clinton's policy evolved, congressional interest in the War Powers Resolution increased. In May 1994, Representative Tom Lantos (D-Calif.), chairman of the Subcommittee on International Security, International Organization, and Human Rights, called for all relevant documents and correspondence between the president and Congress over the War Powers Resolution.[38] Meanwhile the GOP initiated a number of other important political and potential legal challenges. On May 24, 1994, Representative Porter Goss (R-Fla.) led a successful effort in the Committee of the Whole to require Clinton to gain congressional approval prior to a Haitian intervention, which also included a measure to create new refugee safe havens.[39] The vote passed, 223–201.[40] However, on June 9 the resolution was rejected on the House floor by a vote of 195–226. Approximately twenty-five House Democrats switched their positions before the final vote, demonstrating the importance of partisanship in war powers interpretation, as the congressional Democrats scrambled to avoid placing restrictions on the president.[41]

Thus for the first half of 1994, House Democrats prevented the passage of any major legislation that would limit the president's perceived powers and in effect kept the House out of deployment decisions. Although Democrats were concerned about the use of force abroad, most did not want to substantially limit the president and his military options. However, as in Somalia, there were a few exceptions. In a House Foreign Affairs Committee meeting, Robert Torricelli (D-N.J.) questioned former member of Congress and newly appointed special advisor to the president on Haiti William Gray on the WPR's relevance to Haiti. Torricelli asked Gray if the president intended to seek legal authorization "before or simultaneously with the military invasion of Haiti." Gray responded that the administration would remain in consultation with Congress, but he would not indicate whether a vote would be sought prior to the use of force. Gray and Torricelli also could not come to an agreement on whether or not the WPR required congressional approval in every instance in which force was used.[42]

As the year progressed, the Democrats' rejection of the Goss amendment did not discourage Republicans from raising other challenges to the president. In July, Benjamin Gilman (R-N.Y.) sent a letter to the president with 102 House signatures asking that he seek prior congressional approval before troops were introduced to Haiti.[43] Moreover, in a July foreign affairs subcommittee meeting, Chairman Torricelli reiterated his concerns on the WPR. Although he did not press Clinton administration representatives extensively on the issue, he stated: "I trust that the Clinton Administration consistent with the precedents established by the Bush Administration, in the Persian Gulf war and consistent with the legislative responsibilities as envisioned in the War Powers Act, will come before this Congress before proceeding militarily. It is in any case our intention to have it do so consistently with our responsibilities."[44]

Similar sentiments were expressed in August, soon after UN Security Council Resolution 940. In response to Clinton's support of Resolution 940 and the seemingly inevitable deployment of American troops, Congressman David Skaggs (D-Colo.) said:

> Unfortunately, there is no indication that the President will seek authorization from the only body the Constitution vests with the power to grant it: The U.S. Congress. . . . When President Bush made the case for expelling Saddam Hussein from Kuwait, the Congress gave its approval. The debate in Congress, and the decision by Congress, strengthened the President's hand. Following the Constitution worked as the founding fathers intended. We now have a similar constitutional challenge, and I urge my colleagues to join in affirming our constitutional duty. It would be a bad

bargain indeed if we damaged democracy in America while attempting to restore it in Haiti.[45]

About Security Council Resolution 940, Jim Cooper (D-Tenn.) also said: "It is not enough to get UN approval as the administration has done. UN approval has nothing to do with U.S. approval. American interests must come first."[46] Representatives Skaggs, Sherwood Boehlert (R-N.Y.), and Dick Durbin (D-Ill.) introduced legislation calling for prior approval for the use of force in Haiti in light of UN Security Council Resolution 940.[47] Congressman Goss also remained steadfast in his opposition to a "Haitian invasion."[48] Thus by the end of August members of both parties expressed strong concerns about the constitutionality of a U.S. deployment to Haiti. Ostensibly, the environment in the House of Representatives existed for a constitutional showdown.

The Senate

Like the House, throughout 1994 the Senate made its own efforts to influence U.S. foreign policy. The year began with Senator Bob Dole (R-Kans.) introducing the Peace Powers Act. The legislation, cosponsored with twelve other Republican senators, sought a more prominent role for Congress in UN military operations. His resolution required that no U.S. troops serve under foreign command and that an outside inspector must examine UN expenditures. The proposal also called for a reduction in U.S. monetary contributions to peacekeeping operations. On the Senate floor, Dole argued that there should be "no U.S. forces for a UN army without congressional approval" and that Congress should be "in the loop" concerning U.S. participation in UN operations.[49]

Specifically on Haiti, the Senate quickly took up the issue of the refugees' human rights. At a foreign relations subcommittee meeting, Tom Harkin (D-Iowa) noted in a prepared statement that Clinton's policy had been "embarrassing and shameful." At the same committee hearing, a number of humanitarian and human rights groups, including the Catholic Relief Services, Oxfam America, and Human Rights Watch, all criticized the Clinton administration's policy on the refugees.[50] More direct legislative pressure for policy change came in April, when six senators introduced the Haitian Restoration of Democracy Act, which called for stiffer sanctions against the Haitian regime, more international support for the sanction's efforts, and a new refugee policy.[51] However, it did not provide specific support for the use of force in Haiti, completely avoiding the war powers issue.

At the same time, many senators were uncomfortable with deploying U.S. troops to Haiti. The Senate's key vote came on August 3, 1994, when Bob Dole and Judd Gregg (R-N.H.) introduced a resolution stating that UN Security Council Resolution 940 would not be sufficient authorization for the president to deploy troops to Haiti under the WPR. The vote on the resolution was unanimous, indicative of the bipartisan sentiments that UN approval did not qualify as legal authorization for a deployment.[52]

In the floor discussion leading up to the vote, additional concerns about the United Nations and Congress's constitutional role surfaced. For example, Senator Gregg noted:

> You cannot have the United States agreeing with the U.N. Security Council on sponsoring an amendment of the U.N. Security Council which essentially calls for war without having the Congress of the United States alter the process and the people of the United States involved in the process. . . .
>
> I do not wish to be perceived as bashing the United Nations here, because I am not trying to. . . . But the fact is that that does not mean that the role of the United Nations can be allowed to usurp, to exceed, or to in any way replace the role of the Congress of the United States and the role of the people of the United States in relationship to the Presidency and the President's authority to declare war.[53]

On the same day, Senator Dole added, "International support is fine, but it is no substitute for the support of Congress and the American people."[54] The passage of this resolution was a rare statement from this chamber, especially with a Democratic majority that had earlier been content to criticize President Clinton's deployment under UNOSOM I but remained generally deferential to the freshman president prior to the American casualties in Somalia. The Senate took a clear stand on UN resolutions and the legal relevance of the WPR.

However, the Senate's assertiveness did not go so far as to require an automatic role in force deployment decisions. Senator Arlen Specter (R-Pa.) offered an amendment that introduced language requiring the president to gain approval from the Senate prior to the use of force in Haiti.[55] But Senator John McCain (R-Ariz.) countered with a motion to kill Specter's amendment, noting his fear that Specter's initiative would unconstitutionally extend Congress's role vis-à-vis the commander in chief. Although McCain was opposed to an American intervention, he still sought to protect the notion of a strong commander in chief, stating:

> My problem with the Specter amendment is that it exceeds the authority of the Congress of the United States. . . .
>
> [I]t is impossible for legislative bodies to anticipate world events. That is why our Founding Fathers put those responsibilities, enormous responsibilities—the lives of American service men and women—within the authority of the President of the United States of America.[56]

McCain's interpretation of the founding fathers' intent and the legislative histories surrounding the UN Participation Act is grossly inaccurate, yet his motion gained support from thirteen Republicans and fifty Democrats, enough to defeat Specter's proposal. Among the Democrats, only Paul Wellstone (D-Minn.) and war powers advocate Russ Feingold (D-Wis.) voted against McCain's motion.[57]

In short, the Senate was clear in its belief that United Nations Security Council resolutions alone did not give the president authority to use force abroad, but it remained unwilling to require the president to gain prior approval before using force in Haiti. Like the House, the Senate expressed strong concern about a Haitian deployment, but resistance from the Democratic majority and some Republican presidential power advocates prevented a vote on requiring prior Senate authorization.

International Diplomacy: The South American Dynamic

While concerns brewed in the House and Senate, Clinton faced other international political pressures surrounding UN Security Resolution 940. With the United States' long history of intervention in South and Central America, and Latin American states' traditional apprehensions about and resistance to U.S. intervention in the region, the Clinton administration went to some lengths to seek approval from foreign states south of the U.S. border. Quiet diplomatic efforts with members of the

Organization of American States had been in progress during the year but became much more public after Resolution 940.[58]

Two Latin American countries sat on the UN Security Council when it voted on Resolution 940: Argentina and Brazil. Argentina approved of the resolution, while Brazil abstained from the vote and later expressed its opposition. On the day of the vote, Mexico also expressed its opposition, and Cuba soon echoed the Mexican position.[59]

The United States responded by trying to lobby these states (with the exception of Cuba) to switch their vote. Clinton's first major effort came at a Caribbean Community (CARICOM) meeting in which member states unanimously adopted a resolution in support of Resolution 940 and its "all necessary means" provision. CARICOM's endorsement of the "all necessary means" clause, however, has dubious international legal standing. CARICOM was formed primarily to enhance the economic integration process that had already begun under the Caribbean Free Trade Association, its precursor formed in 1967. Although CARICOM does support foreign policy coordination of its members, this coordination has centered on common export and tariff policies. Yet Clinton's Deputy Secretary of State Strobe Talbott stressed at a State Department press conference that "CARICOM, as a group, unanimously endorsed the action,"[60] suggesting that some sort of legal endorsement had been gained through CARICOM's vote.

Clinton officials were also present at a Rio Group meeting held in Brazil. Assistant Secretary of State for Inter-American Affairs Alexander Watson met with the foreign ministers from fourteen states to lobby again for troop contributions for a multinational peacekeeping force in Haiti. However, Watson was unsuccessful in his efforts. Argentina announced that while its support for Resolution 940 had not changed, it was unwilling to send troops to Haiti in support of the resolution.[61]

Clinton's international lobbying efforts may have been due in part to congressional pressure and well-informed members who raised he concerns of Latin American states on the chamber floor. Senator Gregg noted his diplomatic concerns about Brazil's abstention and Latin American apprehensions: "It is important to note that one of the nations who abstained from the vote was Brazil. I think it is equally important to note that some of our sister nations expressed extreme concern and outright opposition to the concept."[62] Gregg recognized that Latin American opposition could be an important diplomatic stumbling block for U.S. policy, and as someone who opposed an invasion, he raised an important diplomatic issue for the Clinton administration.

Clinton's diplomatic efforts demonstrated that the administration clearly placed some importance on Latin America's prior approval of a Haitian invasion. The administration went to some lengths to gain these states' political endorsement, even though their endorsement would have no legal merit or constitutional relevance to war powers. Despite these efforts to gain Latin American approval, the Clinton's administration's formal position regarding its authority to deploy troops did not change. After the CARICOM endorsement and prior to the Rio Group meeting, Strobe Talbott stated, "UN Security Council Resolution 940 authorizes the international community—the member states of the United Nations—to use all necessary means to bring about the departure of the dictators from Haiti and to establish the conditions that allow the restoration of democracy in Haiti."[63] According to Talbott's analysis, since the Security Council endorsed the resolution, no further multilateral legal approval was necessary. Yet in practice the administration did not discount the political importance of Latin American support and thus made serious lobbying efforts to gain further regional approval. These efforts would also possibly appease well-informed members of Congress.

The Deployment

As President Clinton gave further signals that the United States was readying for a Haitian intervention, heated debates occurred in Congress over the issue of proper "consultation" between the president and Congress. Anti-UN rhetoric also resurfaced and figured prominently in the debate. These sentiments were most visible in the House. Dana Rohrabacher (R-Calif.) asked, "Why is it that the President of the United States has sought guidance and permission from the United Nations, and from many, many other countries around the world in terms of policy for Haiti, but we haven't bothered to have any type of consultation ourselves, either a hearing or any type of a vote on whether or the U.S. government should be invading Haiti?"[64] Representatives Henry Hyde (R-Ill.) and Donald Manzullo (R-Ill.) made similar remarks about the perceived lack of consultation.[65] Democrats took exception to these claims. Southern Florida Democrat and Black Caucus member Alcee Hastings (D-Fla.) argued that the consultation requirement had been met and that it was time to support the president.[66] However, Hastings and the Black Caucus were in a small minority in Congress that supported intervention. The vast majority was unwilling to advocate publicly the use of force. Yet even though opposition to a Haitian intervention was intense, the Democrats' willingness to support the president also remained strong. Efforts were made in both the House and the Senate to vote again on a Haitian deployment. In both cases, the Democratic leadership used legislative stalling tactics to prevent a vote from taking place.[67]

On September 15, President Clinton said in a nationally televised address, "The message of the United States to the Haitian dictators is clear: Your time is up. Leave now, or we will force you from power."[68] Clinton also characterized the current regime in Haiti as the "most violent regime in the western hemisphere." He also noted that the United States was prepared "to stop brutal atrocities that threaten tens of thousands of Haitians" and to "end the reign of terror."[69] Some hope for a diplomatic solution arose the following day when, in a last-minute diplomatic effort, Clinton dispatched Senator Sam Nunn (D-Ga.), former Joint Chiefs of Staff Chairman Colin Powell, and former President Jimmy Carter to negotiate with the Cedras regime. During late-hour negotiations with Cedras, Clinton sent sixty-one American warplanes on a flyover mission of Haiti in preparation for an air assault.[70] Soon after, Cedras gave in. On the following day, Clinton deployed 1,500 U.S. troops, which eventually rose to approximately 10,000 in the following weeks in "Operation Uphold Democracy." In a letter to Congress, Clinton justified the invasion with a reference to UN Security Council Resolution 940, and invoked his perceived constitutional powers as commander in chief and his authority as chief executive to conduct foreign relations.[71]

Although public opinion prior to the deployment was against an invasion, in polls taken after the deployment the president's approval ratings increased. One poll indicated that Clinton's overall job approval rating raised nine percentage points, and with regard to Clinton's handling of Haiti specifically, public opinion jumped twenty-two points.[72] Past presidents have received similar boosts in public opinion after military deployments, and Clinton was no exception. Congress too responds to public opinion, which was quite clear in the days immediately following the deployment.

Congress's Response

Once American troops reached Haitian soil, both the House and the Senate passed resolutions supporting the president and the troops. At the same time, neither chamber explicitly approved the deployment, and both called for withdrawal as soon as possible. Both resolutions were sufficiently vague to gain widespread support from both parties.[73]

In the two weeks following Congress's innocuous resolutions of support, both congressional chambers revisited the Haitian issue. In the Senate, there was widespread criticism of the deployment. Senators of both parties expressed their disapproval of the president's actions, including key senior senators with experience in foreign policy such as Jesse Helms, Joseph Lieberman (D-Conn.), Max Baucas (D-Mont.), Hank Brown (R-Colo.), Robert Byrd (D-W.Va.), and Dirk Kempthorne (R-Idaho).[74] Other senators deferred to the president using a logic reminiscent of Congress during the Vietnam War. Sam Nunn said, "I wasn't in favor of invading Haiti. . . . But now that we're there I think if we're going to avoid having American interests over the world challenged . . . then we better make up our mind we've got to make this one succeed."[75] Senator Bob Smith (R-N.H.) asserted, "I adamantly oppose the occupation of Haiti by American troops, and I oppose the policy of sending them there. . . . But they are there—they are there, and they need our unequivocal support. We do not need another situation as we had in Vietnam."[76] And Senator Slade Gorton (R-Wis.) added, "I have expressed my strong objections to our mission in Haiti on a number of occasions, but those objections in no way reflect upon my admiration for the troops we have there today. They have done a remarkable job, and they certainly have my full support and I believe that of all of the Members of this body."[77] Thus members who vigorously opposed an intervention caved in to the president's policy by giving their support to the troops and were content merely to criticize the president.

The Senate's more restrained response was attributable in part to the domestic political environment and the many Republican presidential aspirants in the Senate at the time. Senators Bob Dole, Richard Lugar (R-Ind.), Arlen Specter, and Phil Gramm (R-Tex.) were all organizing presidential campaigns and thus may not have wanted to appear as unpatriotic or partisan obstructionists to the president when troops were deployed abroad in a dangerous mission. It was much easier to wait for public opinion to weigh in as the operation progressed than to take a formal constitutional position on the deployment. Thus, constitutional issues and war powers responsibilities were not central to the vast majority of members' critiques of the deployment.

One exception to the norm was Russ Feingold. Just as he had done previously in response to the Somalia tragedy, Feingold pushed for the application of the WPR and a congressional role in deployment decisions. He noted that Congress never approved of the Haiti mission and that UN authorization alone was not legal authorization to take action. He described the situation as "a sloppy and ineffective approach to war powers" and argued that "Congress should have a central role in authorizing the Haiti mission because it is a large military operation where our troops may face imminent hostility."[78] In his Senate floor statements, Feingold shared with the Senate printed correspondence from the Clinton administration's legal counsel, Walter Dellinger. In Dellinger's letter, the Clinton administration provided the most legally articulate defense of its position that it had offered throughout the entire deployment, and in this sense the letter was similar to Assistant Secretary of State Sherman's defense of Clinton's deployment to Somalia.

Dellinger used three arguments to support the administration's claim that Operation Uphold Democracy was an entirely legal deployment. In his first argument, Dellinger wrote that in 1993, Congress only required that the president report to Congress about any planned deployment in Haiti, a stipulation with which the president had fully complied. In this argument Dellinger referred to Senator Mitchell's resolution, which had been passed into law.[79] Second, he asserted that the deployment satisfied the WPR. Dellinger's position was that, because the WPR does allow unilateral deployments in national emergencies, and because the president did notify Congress about the deployment, the WPR had not been violated. Finally, he claimed that the Haiti deployment did not fit the definition of a "war." Because the nature, scope, and duration of the deployment were not tantamount to "war," congressional approval was not needed.[80] Perhaps considering partisan sentiments at the time, Dellinger made no reference to United Nations authorization. Dellinger also made no reference to Dole's successful resolution stating that UN approval was not legal authorization for a deployment. Nor did he address or seek to define "consultation" between the branches as required under the WPR.

Dellinger's arguments also failed to address the fact that the WPR refers not only to "war," but also to troops being deployed in "hostilities" or "imminent hostilities." American troops were being deployed in a potentially dangerous situation, where the rule of law was quite precarious. American troops were certainly at risk, having been deployed under Chapter 7 of the UN Charter, which allows for the use of force and therefore suggests that the possibility of "hostilities" clearly existed. In his address to the nation, President Clinton admitted that these conditions existed in Haiti only days before the U.S. deployment was initiated. To suggest that conditions had become peaceful and risk-free overnight was to deny the reality of the situation in Haiti.

As expected, Dellinger's arguments did not satisfy Senator Feingold, one of the only senators to raise constitutional and legal questions of this nature after the deployment. As a body, the Senate had only passed a resolution that required nothing more than written reports and updates on the deployment. The resolution did include a recognition that the president should have come to Congress for approval prior to the deployment, but the Senate took no position on the actual legality of the deployment and placed no time limits upon the operation itself. In essence, the president was given free reign in Haiti as long as reports were filed with Congress, despite the many earlier efforts to oppose such a deployment.

In the House, the challenges made to the president were much more substantive in nature. Both House Republicans and some Democrats tried to place limitations on the deployment but were unsuccessful. As with Somalia, most vocal among the GOP was again Benjamin Gilman. Gilman introduced a resolution calling for the "immediate withdrawal of American troops" from Haiti. In a very partisan vote, the resolution failed, 205–225, with only one Republican, Jay Dickey (R-Ark.), voting against Gilman. After this attempt, the House voted for reports on the mission but placed no time limits on the deployment and avoided any constitutional judgments.[81] The resolution stated after the fact that Congress should have been asked for prior approval.

Even though the resolution that passed was sponsored by the Democrats, not all majority members were pleased. Lee Hamilton (D-Ind.), who voted in favor of the resolution, stated: "We have not approved of the policy, we have not disapproved of the policy. We simply default. We do not take a position on the gravest decision a government can take—whether to commit forces abroad."[82] He stated that the resolution provided "retroactive authorization" for the deployment, and "unlike the Persian Gulf, the President acted without Congressional approval."[83]

Racial tensions over the deployment also rose in the House. Members of the congressional Black Caucus made accusations of racism against those members who opposed the intervention. For example, Charles Rangel (D-N.Y.) noted that the invasion of Grenada had been conducted to save "20 white students," implying that because most Haitians were black, the same standard in American foreign policy was not being upheld.[84] Congressional Black Caucus member Representative Gary Ackerman (D-N.Y.) also noted: "I think it is also interesting to note how partisan we can suddenly get when it comes to protecting democracy for a bunch of people whose skins are slightly darker and colored in comparison to how nonpartisan we can be when it comes to preserving democracy for a bunch of other people whose skins are lighter and provide us with gasoline and our oil."[85] Thus the political tone in the House was anything but congenial, both from partisan and racial perspectives but, again, did not focus on the legal or constitutional issues.

In the end, the House voted with the Senate to approve a policy that only required the president to submit reports to Congress on the mission's progress. The Democratic House leadership avoided bringing substantive legal or constitutional issues to the floor and prevented GOP leaders from placing restrictions on the commander in chief.

CONCLUSION

Like the deployment of American troops to Somalia, Operation Uphold Democracy provides an example of presidential assertiveness and congressional deference in American war powers. As with the Somalian intervention, in the American deployment to Haiti the support of the United Nations, the domestic political conditions at the time of the deployment, the choices made by individual leaders in Congress, and strong partisan protection of the president explain why the congressional-executive interplay proceeded in the manner it did.

Presidential Unilateralism

President Clinton provided a number of arguments to justify his deployment to Haiti. As in the Somalian operation, the Clinton administration relied heavily upon a United Nations Security Council resolution to avoid Congressional "intrusions" upon his perceived authority. In addition, like President Bush in Operation Desert Storm, Clinton used the United Nations Security Council endorsement to legitimize his foreign policy and to supersede domestic debates about the Constitution. Because of the negative reactions toward the United Nations after the American deaths in Somalia, however, the president also used other unilateral assertions of constitutional authority by appealing to wide powers as commander in chief and chief executive. Clinton also maintained that Haitian instability represented a direct threat to U.S. national security interests. These arguments appeased many members of Congress who were content to let the full political responsibility for Haiti rest with the president.

Just as State Department official Wendy Sherman did to explain the Somalian deployment, Clinton legal counsel Walter Dellinger also employed semantical strategies to evade application of the WPR and any legal decision-making authority for Congress. Although U.S. troops were prepared and authorized by the UN Security Council to use "all necessary means" to bring down the Haitian dictatorship—in a potentially risky and militarily precarious environment—Dellinger still maintained that Congress had no authority to prevent this operation. However, the WPR was meant to be applied to any cases, including those short of "war," in which U.S. armed forces were "equipped for combat." Although U.S. forces did not come directly under fire in Haiti as they did in Somalia, Clinton signaled some willingness to use force by ordering the flyover of Haiti by sixty-one aircraft during the diplomatic negotiations, which is covered by Section 4(a)(2) of the WPR, since armed forces were introduced into "airspace" of a foreign nation. The troops were ready and authorized to use force if necessary when they arrived in Haiti, a country that had experience much instability, and there was a real possibility of hostilities, as the president himself acknowledged. Clinton described the situation in Haiti only days before the deployment as a "reign of terror," clearly insinuating the potential for hostilities. Thus, although the Clinton administration argued otherwise, the WPR clearly applied.

Clinton kept Congress informed of his actions in Haiti, but like other recent presidents, he never granted or accepted any claim or role for congressional decision-making authority, and Congress was not consulted prior to the flyover. Whether the purpose of the flyover was only to threaten Cedras or actually to use force is not clear, yet no evidence indicates that Congress had any role in the decision, and thus the action was a violation of the WPR's consultation requirement.

Clinton's practices also demonstrated that his new policy on peacekeeping operations, PDD 25, meant very little to the war powers interplay. In contrast to the document's guidelines, Clinton never reached out to Congress for its approval and continued with traditional executive claims of war powers autonomy as commander in chief.

Finally, regional diplomacy played a much more prominent role in the Clinton administration's military endeavors in Haiti than it had in the Somalian deployment. The administration sought regional approval for the deployment. Although CARICOM's endorsement had little legal foundation, Clinton officials aggressively sought it to gain regional support in order to shield itself from domestic and international criticism that another "Roosevelt Corollary" was being enacted.

Congress: Partisanship, Domestic Politics, and Leadership

The Haitian case represents another example of congressional deference to presidential unilateralism. Congress allowed Clinton to deploy U.S. troops, authorized by the United Nations to use force if necessary, without its formal approval. These actions violated the intent of the UN Participation Act of 1945 and Article 43 of the UN Charter. Because of the manner in which the operation was conducted and the conditions under which the troops were deployed, the WPR also applied. Nonetheless, with the exception of occasional hints of constitutionally assertive behavior, Congress deferred to the president's leadership.

As with Somalia, partisan politics, leadership decisions, and domestic political conditions again explain much of Congress's deference. In the House, the Democrats were content to criticize the president individually but would not restrict his perceived broad powers as commander in chief. Its leadership was unwilling to schedule any votes on Haiti during the buildup to the deployment in September 1994. Many liberal Democratic members went on record in favor of an intervention but never raised concerns over the constitutional implications of Clinton's use of force. This behavior differs notably from the conduct of many liberal Democrats during the Bush and Reagan administrations, and certainly from many during the Vietnam era, when Democrats openly challenged presidents on the authority to use force abroad. The House Republicans, led by Benjamin Gilman, were unified in their efforts to limit and restrict President Clinton's asserted powers in Haiti. However, these efforts were defeated easily by the Democratic majority.

Regarding the domestic political conditions, House members who challenged the president also faced a well-organized and vocal congressional Black Caucus, which may have served as a deterrent for some Democrats who opposed a deployment. In this sense, the domestic political conditions created an additional incentive for Democrats to defer to the president. Some conservative columnists maintained that the Black Caucus, spurred by Randall Robinson's efforts, directed Clinton's policy toward Haiti.[86] One can only speculate about the caucus's influence on the Clinton administration, but Clinton also certainly had important legislative incentives to keep this group as a dedicated political ally. Members of Congress also had political interests in not being branded as "racist" by some caucus members for opposing a deployment.

Such intense partisanship was not present in the Senate, which may have been influenced in part by the many senators who were seeking the presidency at the time and probably did not want to appear "unpatriotic" during this crisis. Moreover, with House Republicans applying a good deal of partisan challenge to the president, presidential aspirants presumably saw little political advantage in engaging in an all-out political assault. Had the intervention been conducted at a different time with fewer aspiring presidential candidates, perhaps the Senate's assertiveness would have been greater. However, since Clinton was willing to take legal and political responsibility for this risky deployment, Senate Republicans and these candidates had clear interests in deferring to Clinton in case the mission encountered trouble.

At one point, it appeared that the Senate would be constitutionally aggressive, especially when it unanimously asserted that UN approval alone was not adequate authority to deploy troops to Haiti. However, the political reality was different. In the days immediately preceding the deployment, Senate Democrats did not allow constitutionally aggressive legislative proposals to be voted on. Senate Majority Leader George Mitchell prevented votes on Haiti during the deployment's September build-up stage, despite some checking efforts made in the Senate chamber. Senator Dole's Peace Powers Act also ostensibly introduced a new measure to check the president at the beginning of 1994. However, in practice, Dole did not vigorously pursue this legislation, and it is highly unlikely that Senate Democrats would have supported it anyway. Thus, even some in the Senate's Republican leadership shied away from a substantive decision-making role when the opportunity existed.

Congress could have asserted its war powers through a number of legal and constitutional means but chose not to. For all the congressional posturing that took place, including the Senate's vote on American participation in UN operations, in the end Congress deferred to the president. Despite the presence of a new and seemingly assertive GOP majority that was elected in the 1994 congressional midterms, Congress behaved similarly in response to the United States' participation in NATO air strikes in Bosnia in 1994 and 1995 and in the eventual peace-enforcement deployment in the Balkans.

4 Bosnia

The United States military action in Bosnia was the third major deployment of American armed forces under President Bill Clinton. Like the operations in Somalia and Haiti, this U.S. deployment involved a peace-enforcement operation authorized by the United Nations Security Council and Chapter 7 of the UN Charter. However, this case is considerably different from those considered in the previous two chapters, in that the American military intervention in Bosnia occurred under the auspices of the North Atlantic Treaty Organization as well as the UN. For the first time in its history, NATO conducted military strikes and oversaw and directed a major peacekeeping operation. In 1994, the Republicans also won a sweeping victory in the congressional midterm elections, giving them majority status in the House and Senate. Although there are some similarities with the deployments to Somalia and Haiti, the domestic political conditions in 1995 as well as the legal and constitutional questions in play were considerably different, resulting in a complex congressional-executive struggle over war powers.

U.S. Foreign Policy and Bosnia

In the aftermath of World War I under the aegis of Woodrow Wilson's Fourteen Points, the state that came to be known as Yugoslavia was created in accordance with the principle of "self-determination" by the allied victors.[1] The newly formed state previously existed as the Kingdoms of Montenegro and Serbia within the Austro-Hungarian Empire. Wilson and the European leaders justified its creation by arguing that a new Balkan state would serve as a buffer between Austria and Serbia —the initiators of World War I—and would produce regional stability in an area inhabited by many different ethnic and religious groups. In the newly established Kingdom of Serbs, Croats, and Slovenes (renamed

Yugoslavia in 1929), the Serbs came to dominate key leadership positions during the 1920s and into the 1930s. Serb dominance did not sit well with many other Yugoslavs, particularly the Croats. During the first two decades of the country's existence, discontent developed over the lack of autonomy within the various provinces.[2] Many non-Serbs viewed their country's government as a foreign-imposed political arrangement and detested the Serbs' control. Consequently, in 1941, the Croats moved to secede from the state, resulting in military conflict between the Serbs and Croats. However, soon after these events, all major groups in Yugoslavia became engulfed in World War II as the various factions paired with either the Nazis or the Allies.

From World War II until 1980, Yugoslavia existed as a relatively peaceful state. Much of this stability can be attributed to the communist leadership of Josip Broz Tito. During World War II, Tito solidified his power in the state's communist party and after the war rose to become president. As leader, Tito allowed a mild form of national self-determination among the differing populations and provinces. Power was shared between the national and local governments, and people were encouraged to identify with the historical and ethnic traditions of their homelands. Tito's constitution also called for multiethnic tolerance, and the government actively promoted equality among the various groups.[3] In many ways, Tito's model of socialism, coupled with his policies of regional political tolerance, managed to transcend the differences between the various Yugoslav factions and to keep the nation at peace. Internationally, Tito practiced a policy of neutrality during the cold war. Tito was not included in and did not seek an alliance with Stalin's communist bloc, but neither was he a puppet of the American government. As an advocate for the less-developed world, Tito was instrumental in leading the Nonaligned Movement against the western economic powers in the United Nations, while boldly asserting his country's independence from both superpowers. Yet in its first years after World War II, Tito's Yugoslavia benefitted greatly from financial assistance from the International Monetary Fund, the World Bank, the United States, and other private banks abroad.[4]

Upon Tito's death in 1980, the country's government underwent significant decentralization. Under a new constitution, the chief executive position rotated among six Yugoslav republics, with each republic temporarily occupying the presidency. These republics included Bosnia-

Herzegovina, Croatia, Macedonia, Montenegro, Serbia, and Slovenia. Kosovo (see Chapter 6) remained a part of Serbia. In this new polity, hostilities fomented when Serbian leader Slobodan Milosevic called for a greater Serbian nationalism and argued that Serbs were being discriminated against in southern Yugoslavia (Kosovo) by its Albanian majority. In 1987, his campaign rhetoric gained strong support from many Serbs who felt that they had historically been discriminated against and politically underrepresented.[5] Tensions were also building over the relative economic differences between the republics and the deep-rooted historical religious and ethnic divisions. Slovenia and Croatia were more developed financially than the rest of Yugoslavia, and cross-national ties between the provinces had not solidified during Tito's reign.[6] As president of Serbia, Milosevic attempted to centralize his power by trying to gain formal control of each republic. In doing so, he reached out to fellow communists and Serbs throughout Yugoslavia. Instead of increasing his national support, however, his efforts resulted in heightened fears among other Yugoslavian republics and greater nationalism elsewhere in the country. Two preliminary steps toward secession were initiated in 1990 in Croatia and Slovenia. Milosevic reacted by stating that no republic would be allowed to secede under his rule. In 1991, domestic anxiety intensified when Serbia and Montenegro blocked the appointment of Stipe Mesic, a Croat who was due to take over the rotating presidency. Armed conflict soon followed when Croatia and Slovenia declared their independence on June 25, 1991. The atrocities commenced when Milosevic sent troops to both provinces but did not continue for long, in part because of the widespread support for both independence movements. Combat spread in 1992 when Bosnia-Herzegovina followed Slovenia and Croatia by declaring its independence.

From the conflict's earliest days, the Serbs practiced a policy of "ethnic cleansing." The Serbs targeted for destruction the cultural, religious, and historical structures of its non-Serb neighbors, particularly in Bosnia. The Serbs bombed mosques, centuries-old historic buildings, and libraries in the first months of the conflict in Bosnia. Reports of mass killings, systematic rapes, tortures, and other gross violations of internationally recognized human rights began to emerge, the vast majority of which were committed by the Serbs.[7]

As the conflict escalated, U.S. President George Bush's attention was focused firmly on Operation Desert Storm. Yugoslavia was not high on the American foreign policy agenda in late 1990 and early 1991. Prior to the conflict's outbreak in 1991, U.S. Secretary of State James Baker met individually with each province leader in an effort to prevent war. In his memoirs Baker wrote that he firmly expressed the United States' opposition to violence in the region but noted that Milosevic and Milan Kucan, Slovenia's leader, had little interest in diplomatic initiatives for peace or negotiation.[8] However, Baker's visit to the region also included a visit to Albania and meetings with Soviet leaders, demonstrating that Yugoslavia at this time was not occupying the center position in U.S. foreign policy.[9]

Once the violence began, Bush and other high-ranking U.S. administration officials spoke out against the inhumanity and violence, but from the outset they viewed Yugoslavia's problems as regional or "European," and not in the U.S.'s vital national interests.[10] An assertive or vigorous use of force, such as the deployment of ground troops, was simply not an option. Baker noted, "[W]e don't have a 'dog' in this fight."[11] The administration was operating under the principles of Chairman of the Joint Chiefs of Staff Colin Powell, or the "Powell Doctrine." Powell maintained that force should only be employed to protect America's vital interests and would only be used "overwhelmingly" once initiated. Since Bosnia did not fit this criterion, Baker notes that within the administration both Powell and Secretary of Defense Dick Cheney resisted the use of force. Their unwillingness to use force was supported by the Central Intelligence Agency's estimates that massive bloodshed would occur in Yugoslavia's civil war, and U.S. troops would be at great risk if placed on the ground.[12]

Despite the hands-off approach, the Bush administration was active in the United Nations on Bosnia. The United States supported UN Security Council Resolution 713, which enacted an arms embargo on Yugoslavia. The Bush administration also supported UN Security Council Resolution 757, which placed an economic embargo on Serbia and Montenegro. In 1992, the administration backed UN Security Council Resolution 770, which authorized the use of "all measures necessary" to ensure the safe delivery of humanitarian aid.[13] However, at the same time the Bush administration remained steadfast in its belief that the conflict was European in nature and that the United States would not serve as the "world's policeman."[14] Bush later backed the creation of the United Nations Protection Force (UNPROFOR), which aided principally in the delivery of humanitarian supplies to Bosnia-Herzegovina, but was unwilling to commit U.S. troops in any sort of peace-enforcement deployment.[15]

In the early stages of the conflict in Bosnia, reaction from Congress was mixed, although members were not advocating the deployment of ground troops. Most of the reaction came from the Senate in 1992, when a bipartisan faction called for policy change. On April 29, 1992, the Senate called for Serbia to halt its aggression in Bosnia and to withdraw its forces from Bosnia, Croatia, and Kosovo. Later, on May 21, the Senate voted unanimously to place economic sanctions on Serbia and Montenegro, but these had little effect on the Serbs. The Bosnian Serbs responded by bombing Sarajevo, killing twenty and wounding one hundred Bosnian Muslims who were waiting in line for bread.[16] After the attack, a number of senators, including Bob Dole (R-Kans.), Richard Lugar (R-Ind.), Claiborne Pell (D-R.I.), and Joe Biden (D-Del.) called for a limited use of force against the Serbs. Their efforts resulted in the approval of a Senate resolution encouraging the United Nations Security Council to consider the use of force.[17]

In August 1992, the Senate increased its pressure on Bush by expressing its support for armed assistance if necessary in the delivery of humanitarian aid to Bosnia. This decision came after the Senate Foreign Relations Committee issued a report entitled "The Ethnic Cleansing of Bosnia-Herzegovina," which criticized the Serbs' conduct during the war. Near the end of Congress's session, the Senate also gave the president authority to lift the arms embargo on Bosnia and to supply the Bosnian military with up to $50 million in military assistance. While these resolutions received strong support, there still remained considerable opposition in the Senate to any U.S. armed intervention.[18] The House also approved a measure to revoke Yugoslavia's most-favored nation status and supported the use of force if necessary in the delivery of humanitarian aid.[19] Thus both congressional chambers had grown restless with the Bush administration's approach throughout 1992. The opposition was bipartisan, yet neither chamber ever argued for the deployment of U.S. ground troops.

Bush's hands-off Yugoslavian policy eventually became an issue in the 1992 presidential election. Candidate Clinton openly criticized the president on his resistance to engage U.S. troops in a combat role and focused on the many human rights violations in Bosnia as an affront to traditional U.S. values. The Arkansas governor claimed confidently that he "would begin with air power against the Serbs to try to restore the basic conditions of humanity." Clinton also hinted that a new arms embargo policy should be considered, which ran counter to Bush's current policy.[20] As the ethnic cleansing continued and the November elections approached, Bush elevated his diplomatic pressure for peace by supporting a no-fly zone banning certain types of military flights over portions of Bosnia.[21] After his defeat in the 1992 elections, Bush also supported a naval blockade in support of the arms embargo.[22] Thus by the end of 1992, the United States was slowly becoming engaged in the war-torn region, but most in Congress were hesitant about further involvement for U.S. troops.

CLINTON AND THE 103RD CONGRESS

President Clinton

Like Somalia and Haiti, Bosnia presented yet another serious foreign policy issue facing the novice president from Arkansas. Regarding Bosnia, Clinton also had very explicit campaign promises to keep. One of Clinton's first statements as president on Bosnia was his pledge to provide up to 25,000 U.S. ground troops to a multilateral peacekeeping operation in the event that a comprehensive peace settlement was reached.[23] Clinton reiterated this commitment in March at a joint press conference with French President Francois Mitterrand.[24] However, in his first year in office, despite his tough campaign rhetoric, Clinton's policy in general varied little from President Bush's. The continuation of the previous administration's policy was signaled and perhaps best illustrated by Secretary of State Warren Christopher, who during his Senate confirmation hearings referred to the problem in Bosnia as a "European situation."[25]

Throughout 1993, Clinton made a number of other policy changes that have relevance here. One of his earliest initiatives was the support of a war crimes tribunal for the former Yugoslavia. The court was established in an effort to punish those who had violated human rights, and supporting it achieved the Clinton administration's political objective of appearing to address Americans' concerns about the situation in Bosnia.[26] Along with the war crimes tribunal, Clinton also supported the development of UN safe enclaves under Security Council Resolution 824 and initiated airdrops of humanitarian aid to Bosnia.[27] The administration also voted in favor of UN Security Council Resolution 816, allowing for the use of "all necessary measures" to police UN no-fly zones. The president's policy exhibited the implicit belief that he had adequate constitutional authority to use force in the former Yugoslavia without congressional approval. The United States also supported Security Council Resolution 836, which authorized all UN member states to use "all necessary measures" to protect UNPROFOR forces. The president also backed United Nations Security Council Resolution 842, which called for a peacekeeping force on the Yugoslav-Macedonian border in order to check the conflict's expansion into Greece and provide a deterrent to Serbian expansionism to the south. Clinton deployed three hundred American troops to this operation. Notably, the American troops stationed in Macedonia were deployed under Chapter 7 of the UN Charter and were given the authority to use force in self-defense if necessary.[28] Again, Clinton's position was clear: he felt he had the authority to allow troops to use force in Macedonia if necessary without Congressional approval. Article 43 of the UN Charter and the UN Participation Act of 1945 received no recognition in the public policy debate over Bosnia.

Congress, a New President, and Bosnia

Throughout 1993, most members of Congress did not encourage the president to take an active role in Bosnia. A few members, most notably Senator Joe Biden actively lobbied for a more assertive policy, but most agreed with the administration that Bosnia was a "European problem" and that the United States should stay out.[29] Some members protested Clinton's peacekeeping deployment to Macedonia by making an analogy with the Vietnam War; that is, once troops were deployed to the region, they would be difficult to extricate.[30] However, the vast majority raised no objections to the mission but rather were in favor of participating in this cautious manner in southern Europe.[31] Many members also supported the humanitarian airdrops.[32]

Much of Congress's action concerning Clinton's Bosnia policy, however, came after the fiasco in Somalia. As demonstrated in Chapter 2, Clinton's relationship with Congress during the fall of 1993 became very tense as some Democrats and many Republicans made efforts to limit his perceived authority as commander in chief. This situation spilled over into policy questions on Bosnia. Consequently, many members voiced their opposition to a European deployment.[33] The Senate supported a nonbinding resolution introduced by Majority Leader George Mitchell (D-Maine), which called on the president to gain prior congressional approval before sending troops to Bosnia. The House also approved of this resolution in a voice vote as part of a defense appropriations bill that Clinton eventually signed into law.[34] With many in Congress fuming about the eighteen American casualties in Somalia and with considerable opposition to a U.S. deployment to Bosnia, it would have made little political sense for Clinton to enact any serious policy change or propose a deployment in the final months of 1993.

On the war powers interplay, what is most interesting in 1993 is what Congress did not do. Bill Clinton promised NATO allies that he would provide 25,000 troops to Bosnia if a peace was reached, yet at no time did he imply that congressional consent was required. Clinton also authorized U.S. troops to use "all necessary measures" to enforce Bosnia's no-fly zones, and he deployed U.S. peacekeepers to Macedonia under Chapter 7 of the UN Charter. A few voices in Congress expressed dissent over these moves, but as a body Congress did not try to alter Clinton's deployment policy even slightly and did not question his legal authority to make these decisions. Congress was certainly wary of any further peacekeeping deployments, and Clinton surely recognized the thin political ice he was on. Yet when it came to the legal and constitutional specifics, Congress avoided consideration of these issues.

1994: NATO Strikes

In 1994, human rights violations persisted as civilians were the target of many attacks. In a sharp policy change from 1993, and in a historic first, President Clinton implemented past decisions of the UN Security Council by working with NATO to conduct air strikes against Bosnian Serb targets. On five occasions, U.S. planes and soldiers acted with NATO to conduct limited or "surgical" attacks against primarily Bosnian Serb military outposts. These "pinprick" attacks remained the pillar of U.S. foreign policy until August 1995. The Clinton administration outlined a number of constitutional justifications for these strikes.

Clinton sent four official notification letters and reports to Congress after U.S. troops participated in the NATO attacks. In a letter to Congress prior to the first strike, Clinton stated that NATO had accepted the request of the UN secretary general to conduct air attacks upon all unauthorized flights in the no-fly zones and that he had made available sixty U.S. aircraft for this purpose. He justified these actions as "pursuant to [his] constitutional authority to conduct U.S. foreign relations and as Commander in Chief."[35] In this case, Clinton asserted his authority well in advance of NATO's first attack on February, 28, 1994. Congress was fully informed about what could take place and under what constitutional grounds the action would be conducted. In two other letters after the NATO bombings, Clinton restated that he was fully authorized to order U.S. troops to participate in NATO combat operations. Both letters maintained that the president was fully authorized to use U.S. troops in NATO based on his powers as commander in chief and under his responsibility to conduct the nation's foreign affairs.[36]

In public statements about the NATO bombings, the administration noted its concern for the UN's success and for the people working in these operations. After the second series of bombings on April 10 and 11, U.S. Ambassador to the United Nations Madeleine Albright noted that the operation was, "according to the UN resolution, to protect the UNPROFOR personnel."[37] This theme was echoed in Clinton's April 12 letter to Congress, in which he stressed that because of threats to Gorazde (a "safe enclave" established by the United Nations protection force) and because UNPROFOR and United Nations High Commission for Refugees personnel were in grave danger from the Bosnian Serbs, NATO was fully justified in conducting its bombing raids.[38] The September 22 NATO attack also came in the aftermath of an attack on French peacekeepers in UNPROFOR, which prompted strident calls from NATO allies for retaliation.[39] Clinton also increased the number of U.S. troops deployed to the Macedonia peacekeeping mission to approximately five hundred and repeated his claim that American participation in this deployment was constitutional.[40]

While Clinton followed the reporting requirements of the WPR, he never acknowledged that U.S. participation in NATO's activities fell under the resolution's requirements. American aircraft, by participating in these NATO military operations, were entering foreign airspace, were clearly engaging in "hostilities," and by definition were "equipped for combat." Nonetheless, Clinton viewed these activities as part of his constitutional powers as commander in chief.

1994: Congressional Response

For the Congress, 1994 began with a challenge to President Clinton from Senate Minority Leader Bob Dole when Dole introduced the Peace Powers Act.[41] As noted in the previous chapter, the bill did not go far in the Senate but was a precursor for what was to come with the Republican majority in 1995. Dole was a leading Republican challenger for the presidency, and the midterm elections were approaching, so Dole's efforts may have been undertaken as an early attempt to position himself and his party politically against Clinton's foreign policy and to identify Republicans as stronger defenders of U.S. sovereignty and national security. After the American casualties in Somalia, Congress in general was skeptical and wary of peacekeeping operations, and motions had been made to cut back substantially on U.S. funding for UN peacekeeping.[42] Dole's support of this policy trend made for good partisan politics during an election year.

Prior to the NATO bombings, the House conducted hearings on NATO's future. In the hearings, Undersecretary of Defense Walter B. Slocombe testified before a subcommittee chaired by Lee Hamilton (D-Ind.) that one condition to be met before placing U.S. troops on the ground was "the support of Congress."[43] However, Slocombe did not specify what "support" from Congress meant, and the issue was not pressed further by the subcommittee. Once the bombings began, Congress said little about the constitutionality of U.S. participation in the NATO operations. More often than not, the policy debate centered on whether the Bosnian operations addressed the United States' national security interests rather than on questions of constitutional authority. In February 1994, Senator Joe Biden and Representative Frank McCloskey (D-Ind.) strongly encouraged NATO attacks, implicitly suggesting that the president had authority to order such attacks without congressional approval.[44] More reactions, especially from GOP leaders, came after NATO's bombings in April, as some members responded to the air strikes apprehensively. Many felt that the bombings would not produce the long-term peace that the United States sought.[45] Members were unquestionably concerned about the utility of NATO air strikes but expressed almost no interest in the history of the North Atlantic Treaty or war powers. The promises gained from Secretary Acheson and President Truman in 1949 about congressional authorization for American participation in NATO operations had essentially no relevance in the discussion.

Other members, particularly key leaders in Congress, strongly supported the air strikes and encouraged the president to do more. Among those advocating NATO air strikes were Senator Dole and House Majority Whip David Bonior (D-Mich.).[46] Bonior stated: "It is time, Mr. Speaker, to use the full weight of United States and NATO warplanes in Bosnia. If the Bosnian Serbs continue to practice genocide and continue to dishonor the cease-fires, it is time to pound the Bosnian Serbs into submission. And if the Serbs continue to hit targets in Bosnia, then selected targets in Serbia itself ought to be hit in return."[47] Senator Dianne Feinstein (D-Calif.) added her support for the president and NATO, as did Senator Orrin Hatch (R-Utah).[48] Thus, Clinton had bipartisan backing from key congressional leaders in both the House and Senate. It is notable that in all the key statements supporting an escalation of the bombings, nowhere did a member note a constitutional concern about Congress's role in the use of force. By 1994's end, after NATO had used force on five different occasions, Congress took no official stand on NATO's actions. This silence is all the more interesting in light of congressional hearings held in May 1994 addressing Presidential Decision Directive (PDD) 25, in which the administration welcomed Congress as a real player in U.S. foreign policy and multilateral peacekeeping operations, even though no formal recognition of its status was given. Ostensibly, Congress did not consider NATO's use of force constitutionally relevant to PDD 25 and thus deferred to presidential judgement within the military alliance.

To paint Congress as a completely deferential body is not entirely accurate. Many members of Congress were critical of President Clinton's support for the United Nations arms embargo on Bosnia. Their concerns eventually resulted in nonbinding resolutions that called for the United States to end its participation in the embargo and begin arming the Bosnian Muslims.[49] But with the political ramifications of the Somalian tragedy in mind, Congress also expressed strong opposition to a ground deployment. Clinton probably understood the political limits of his Bosnian policy and thus did not press for deployment of ground troops. At the same time, the war powers interplay changed little. Throughout 1994, Clinton's assertions of power were based principally on United Nations Security Council Resolutions and NATO's support as well as his perceived broad powers as commander in chief and his perceived "authority to conduct foreign relations." Undersecretary of Defense Walter Slocombe's promise to House Foreign Affairs Chairman Lee Hamilton that the president would gain Congress's "support" was the only recognition from the executive branch that Congress had a military decision-making role. PDD 25, in practice, also had little legal impact on congressional-executive relations. Clinton kept Congress informed about his Bosnian policy with letters to congressional leaders as the WPR requires but still asserted essentially unilateral powers as president, which Congress did not resist. However, after the 1994 midterm elections, the prospect for a fundamental change in the war powers relationship appeared to be at its highest level ever.

The "Contract" and the Republican Majority

The Contract with America was formulated during the 1994 midterm election cycle. It sought to provide voters with a clear issue platform identifying what the House Republicans stood for. If the House Republicans became the majority party, they promised to vote on the Contract's ten issues within the first one hundred days of the 104th Congress. In the area of foreign policy, the Contract promised a "National Security Restoration Act," which called for "No U.S. troops under UN command" and would restore "the essential parts of our national security funding to strengthen our own national defense and maintain credibility around the world."[50] After the House Republicans gained majority status in the historic election, they took their pledges seriously. Even though very few American voters actually knew exactly what the Contract stated, House Republicans claimed that their victory over the democrats—their first in forty years in the House— defined a policy mandate for change.[51] Under the new Republican leadership of Senate Majority Leader Bob Dole and Speaker of the House Newt Gingrich (R-Ga.), it appeared that the Republicans were going to seek a new role in the foreign policy making process, especially regarding U.S. peacekeeping operations. Moreover, at the time, President

Clinton was still perceived as weak on foreign policy, which lent further credence to the idea that Congress had an opportunity to restore a balance with the commander in chief.[52] Perhaps as a recognition of the possible new relationship to come with the new Congress, Clinton's national security advisor, Tony Lake, expressed a new willingness to rework the war powers relationship: "What is needed is a war powers mechanism and system of consultations that work. Next year, we will hold serious discussions with Congress on amending the War Powers Resolution in an effort to ameliorate a struggle between these branches of government that has lasted two centuries."[53] Thus even the Clinton administration appeared to be setting a foundation for an improved war powers interplay as the new Republican majority was about to take its seats.

The Republican Revolution?

The newly elected Congress appeared quite unlike the deferential body that existed during the cold war and the first two years of the Clinton presidency. Republican discourse on Clinton's foreign policy and American participation in United Nations peacekeeping was quite critical. Although this was not the first time a president had faced a hostile Congress over U.S. relations with the United Nations, congressional vehemence aimed at U.S. foreign policy was striking.[54] For example, on whether the Contract was a true "mandate" from the people, new House Majority Leader Dick Armey (R-Tex.) averred, "It's a statement by the Congress that we, too, have heard the voice of the American people. . . . The nation has gone too far in the direction of globalism."[55] Later in 1995 Representative Dana Rohrabacher (R-Calif.) said that the UN is "a collection of tin-pot dictators and corrupt regimes from around the world. . . . Everything done through the United Nations can be better accomplished on a bilateral basis."[56]

With this sentiment resonating among Republicans, the National Security Revitalization Act was introduced on January 4, 1995. With this bill, Republicans hoped to achieve a number of goals. Most relevant to this study is the reassertion of Congress's powers regarding UN peacekeeping deployments. Titles 3, 4, and 5 of the bill dealt specifically with Congress's role vis-à-vis the UN Security Council. As stated in a House committee summary of Title 4, the new proposals required that any agreement between the president and the UN Security Council regarding international peace and security would have to be approved by Congress.[57] This stipulation differs little from the statutory language of the UN Participation Act of 1945 and Article 43 of the United Nations Charter.

Other key provisions of the bill demanded that any U.S. forces serving in a United Nations operation must serve under a U.S. commander and that Congress must be informed fifteen days in advance of any UN Security Council vote on requests for additional funding to peacekeeping missions. The House also wanted to restrict the transfer of U.S. intelligence to the United Nations by requiring prior congressional approval before any information could be shared with the United Nations.[58]

About these proposals, Dana Rohrabacher noted: "This is America comes first as policy. . . . Americans have sacrificed their lives and well-being for an ungrateful world for far too long."[59] Representative Toby Roth (R-Wis.) added: "The reason we have a Contract with America is because we want to put Congress back into the loop in the decision making process when it comes to peacekeeping."[60] The bill later passed on the House floor in a 241–181 vote, with nearly unanimous support from Republicans.[61] Thus, in the first month of the House Republicans' tenure, tremendous efforts were devoted to limiting peacekeeping appropriations to the United Nations.[62] These were clear signs that a period of congressional ascendency had begun in which the president would be checked by the House—especially with regard to deployments sanctioned by the UN Security Council. Ostensibly, the House was going to exercise its war powers.

In the Senate, members were also reevaluating presidential powers and the use of force abroad. On the first legislative day of the 104th Congress, Senate majority leader and aspiring presidential candidate Bob Dole along with nine cosponsors reintroduced the Peace Powers Act. Dole had originally supported the WPR in 1973 but now maintained that it had led to greater tensions between the White House and Congress. He argued that the president needed greater flexibility as commander in chief, citing the need to "untie the President's hands in the use of force to defend U.S. interests."[63] Yet Dole's proposal also noted that greater limitations on the president's ability to deploy troops in UN operations were needed: "The President in every possible instance shall consult with Congress before introducing United States Armed Forces into hostilities or into situations where imminent hostilities are clearly indicated by the circumstances, and after every such introduction shall consult regularly with the Congress until United States Armed forces are no longer engaged in hostilities or have been removed from such situations."[64] His bill also restated the language employed by the United Nations Participation Act regarding Congress's role in UN military operations: "Any special agreement or agreements negotiated by the President with the Security Council providing for the numbers and types of United States Armed Forces . . . to be made available to the Security Council for the purpose of maintaining international peace and security in accordance with Article 43 of the United Nations Charter shall be subject to the approval of the Congress by Act or joint resolution."[65]

The Peace Powers Act did nothing to solve the longstanding problem of defining "consultation" as stipulated in the WPR, nor did Dole's proposal offer a novel legal interpretation of Article 43, yet Dole and his cosponsors certainly asserted a new and much more assertive legislative posture for Congress in peacekeeping deployments. By offering the bill on the first legislative day of Congress and by repeating the WPR's consultation requirements and the relevant sections of the UN Participation Act, Dole appeared genuine in his commitment to giving Congress a greater say in American troop deployments under the United Nations.

In a rare move for a Senate majority leader, Dole appeared before a Senate Foreign Relations Committee hearing on the proposed Peace Powers Act and the National Security Revitalization Act in March 1995 to make his case. He repeated his desire to repeal the War Powers Resolution but also argued that "we need to reign in the blank check on UN peacekeeping."[66] Senator Rod Grams (R-Minn.) also referred to Congress's "peace powers" oversight and argued that with Dole's legislation some congressional responsibility would be restored.[67]

Despite the committee attention given to Dole's and the House's legislative initiatives, the Senate acted on neither of these proposals. Recognizing that Clinton would have vetoed Dole's legislation, and doubtful of a two-thirds majority in the Senate to override the president's veto, Senate leaders apparently decided to avoid embarrassing one of their stronger Republican presidential challengers and simply dropped the issue. However, the Republicans undeniably demonstrated a willingness to redefine the legal specifics of war powers, with Congress positioning itself as a meaningful player in troop deployment decisions.

In the summer of 1995, when discussing the American Overseas Interests Act, Representative Henry Hyde (R-Ill.) offered an amendment to repeal the WPR. It kept the consultation and reporting requirements of the WPR but eliminated the sixty-day clock that required troop withdrawal if Congress had not yet approved of the mission. Speaker Gingrich supported the bill by arguing that the presidency needed to be strengthened in foreign affairs and national security, which seems contradictory to the House's overall reassertion of congressional war powers. However, Hyde's proposal did not specifically address the issue of UN peacekeeping and did not reflect Congress's feelings on U.S. participation in UN operations, and thus the measure failed by a vote of 217–201.[68] While many Republicans theoretically wanted a powerful commander in chief, they did not want the president to have unchecked power to involve American troops in UN deployments. Congressman Hyde's primary motive was to strengthen U.S. foreign policy via-à-vis an enemy who might seek to exploit the sixty-day clock. Republicans who voted against Hyde's amendment noted that with a potential deployment to Bosnia looming, it made little sense to vote for a repeal because of the WPR's remaining value as a legislative and symbolic tool to check the president's powers as commander in chief.[69] Given the presence of a highly cohesive and well-disciplined new Republican majority, Gingrich's support of the measure seems questionable. Had Gingrich considered the bill a legislative priority, it is safe to assume that he could have garnered the necessary votes.[70]

Clinton, Bosnia, and the New Congress

During the first months of the 104th Congress, Clinton reacted sharply and worked to prevent any limitations on his perceived constitutional powers. In a letter to Speaker Gingrich, Clinton argued that the National Security Revitalization Act harmed U.S. interests by limiting his constitutional power. He claimed that the Republicans' proposal unconstitutionally limited his authority to place U.S. troops under temporary foreign command and wrote that required consultations with

Congress would limit his ability to respond "swiftly and proportion-ally" to protect U.S. interests abroad.[71] In another letter to congressional leaders, the president lobbied members to accept a strong role for the United Nations in American foreign policy.[72] Clinton also began to la-bel those who sought a reduced role for the United States in the United Nations as "new isolationists."[73]

Despite the new pressures from Congress, the Clinton administra-tion stayed the course in 1995 with two NATO bombing raids on Bos-nian Serb targets. NATO strikes occurred on May 25 and 26 and again on July 11. On neither occasion did Clinton file a letter with congres-sional leaders notifying them of the attacks, nor did the new Republi-can majority react with constitutional concern over his decision. There was virtually no congressional challenge to Clinton's legal authority to conduct the bombings.

In early May, there was some indication that the Clinton ad-ministration's policy was evolving when the United States stationed 3,500 troops off Italy's coast in the event that a massive evacuation pro-gram for UNPROFOR was needed.[74] In a National Public Radio inter-view, Clinton stated: "We have obligations to our NATO allies and I do not believe we can leave them in the lurch, so I must carefully re-view any request for an operation involving temporary use of ground forces." Similar sentiments were repeated on the same program by Sec-retary of Defense William Perry and National Security Advisor Anthony Lake.[75] The Clinton administration's appeal to NATO and cooperation with American allies was a particularly good political strategy. Many members of Congress, including well-respected senior Republicans, had urged Clinton to define a new strategy for NATO in the post–cold war era.[76] Now that Clinton was leading NATO in a new direction that was obviously backed by the European allies, it became much more diffi-cult to criticize his policy.

Clinton's policy change however, did not sit well with all Republi-cans. House International Relations Committee Chairman Benjamin Gilman (R-N.Y.) reiterated the necessity for consultation between Con-gress and the White House prior to the deployment of any ground troops. Doug Bereuter (R-Nebr.) likewise expressed the importance of "real" consultation, which in his view went beyond mere committee hearings.[77] Republican House leaders were clearly posturing themselves for a battle with the president if ground troops were to be deployed.

There is no reason to think that House rank-and-file members, especially freshmen with public promises to support the Contract with America, felt any differently.

By mid-summer, Clinton's Bosnia policy was in deep trouble, as UNPROFOR was in dire need of help. The Bosnian Serbs had embarrassed the United States and the United Nations when they overran Srebrenica, a UN "safe enclave," and took thirty Dutch peacekeepers hostage in mid-July. U.S. Air Force Captain Scott O'Grady's plane was also shot down while enforcing the UN no-fly zone, prompting a strong reaction from Congress. Congressional concern escalated significantly in August, when both the House and Senate passed another resolution requiring the president to end U.S. participation in the arms embargo.[78]

In late August, President Clinton responded to these developments by authorizing substantial air strikes against the Bosnian Serbs.[79] Under NATO auspices, 3,500 sorties occurred, including 2,318 by U.S. bombers.[80] In his legal defense, Clinton said he "authorized these actions in conjunction with our NATO allies to implement the relevant UN Security Council resolutions and NATO decisions." He also relied upon claims, "pursuant to my constitutional authority to conduct the foreign relations of the United States and as Commander in Chief and Chief Executive."[81] Congress's response, just as it had been earlier in the year to NATO's bombings, was virtual silence. Both chambers were quite passive, considering the gravity of NATO's conduct.[82] Congress was willing to reprimand the president verbally when he was not taking action, but members did not place themselves on record in an up or down vote on whether to support NATO's actions. By declining to endorse the bombings, Congress could reserve criticism for a later date if they resulted in American deaths. Thus Congress employed a wait-and-see approach and avoided any constitutional responsibility for American participation in the NATO attacks. The promises the Senate had secured from Secretary of State Acheson and President Truman in 1949 had no bearing on Congress's behavior.

"Consulting" with Congress

After the August NATO bombings, a cease-fire arrangement was signed between the three main factions in Bosnia, and it looked as if there was a strong possibility for a more comprehensive peace agreement for the region. If this came about, the United States would be called upon to honor the president's previous promise of support for peacekeeping operations.

Prior to the peace talks that would occur soon in Dayton, Ohio, the Clinton administration began its public relations effort to appease Congress by suggesting the constitutional importance of the Congress in the deployment that might come in the future. Chief of Staff Leon Panetta indicated on NBC's *Meet the Press* that if a peacekeeping force were to be deployed, the president would consult with Congress. Yet Panetta also stated that the president would not give up his constitutional powers as commander in chief.[83] Secretary Christopher also stated, "We want Congress's approval. . . .We consult very much with them."[84] Moreover, the president himself indicated that he would consult with Congress over a possible deployment. He stated: "The United States will not be sending its forces into combat in Bosnia. We will not send them into a peace that cannot be maintained. But we must use our power to secure that peace. I have pledged to consult with Congress before authorizing our participation in such an action. These consultations have already begun."[85] While the peace talks were in progress, Vice President Al Gore also told some members of Congress that the president would not act unilaterally and that Congress would have the opportunity to debate the deployment.[86] And Clinton sent a letter to Gingrich indicating that Congress would be consulted after the negotiations were complete.[87]

However, once President Clinton addressed the nation on November 26 after a comprehensive peace accord was reached, in many ways the decision to send troops to Bosnia appeared to have been made. In the address, the president stated: "I want you to know what is at stake, exactly what our troops will be asked to accomplish, and why we must carry out this mission. . . . In Bosnia we can and will succeed because our mission is clear and limited." Clinton's remarks implied that the mission was approved. However, Clinton also said that if the NATO plan of action met his approval, he would "immediately send it to Congress and request its support."[88] With this statement, the president did not necessarily appear committed to sending troops abroad without congressional support and left an opening for the legislative deliberation.

Clinton's behavior contrasts with George Bush's political posturing prior to Operation Desert Storm. At no time did Bush recognize any legal authority for Congress in the deployment in the Persian Gulf War. Yet before, during, and after the Dayton Peace Accords, the Clinton administration publicly acknowledged the importance of Congress in peacekeeping deployments. Although Clinton never articulated what the administration meant by "consultation," it was clearly part of the administration's strategy to openly recognize Congress as a more prominent political player in the deployment. This strategy was new to the war powers interplay and demonstrated that Clinton felt some political necessity to appease Congress with promises of consultation.

After Clinton's address to the nation, however, it soon became clear that the comments made by Panetta, Gore, and Clinton had only limited value. On December 6, 1995, prior to the key congressional vote on Bosnia, Clinton sent a letter to congressional leaders stating that he was sending 1,500 U.S. troops to Bosnia and Croatia to begin laying the groundwork for the Dayton Peace Accords NATO Implementation Force (IFOR). Clinton noted that these decisions were made "in conjunction with our NATO allies" and that his decision met the requirements set forth by the U.S. Constitution.[89] On December 21, Clinton sent another letter to Congress indicating that twenty thousand U.S. troops were on their way to Bosnia and Croatia. Clinton again noted that his constitutional authority and Security Council authorization allowed the deployment.[90]

Congressional Deference, Gingrich, and the Budget

After the August 1995 NATO bombings, efforts were made in the House to limit Clinton's perceived authority as commander in chief. The most substantial effort came two days prior to the Dayton peace talks. In a proposal introduced by Steve Buyer (R-Ind.) and Paul McHale (D-Pa.), the House passed a resolution stating that the president should not assume he could send troops abroad without authorization from Congress. This "Sense of the House" resolution passed by a vote of 315–103. Only two Republicans voted against the measure.[91] Although the Speaker had been critical of Clinton's foreign policy in Bosnia, soon after the vote, Gingrich maintained that NATO's and America's leadership credibility could be at stake without American participation. He thus appeared willing to follow Clinton's leadership on the issue with some reservations.

Other high-ranking Republicans were not as open to the deployment. For example, Rules Committee Chairman Gerald Solomon (R-N.Y.) said, "Heart-wrenching as . . . this tragedy has been, and as despicable as the Serb aggression has been, this conflict does not justify putting one single American solider in combat."[92] Journalistic accounts of the House Republican Conference meeting on November 8 also indicate that Republicans "overwhelmingly" called for immediate action to prevent the proposed peacekeeping deployment.[93]

At the same time that the Bosnia issue was under House scrutiny, the House Republicans were in an intense battle with the White House over the national budget and had threatened to shut down the federal government if Clinton did not meet their demands. One of the foremost policy objectives of the 104th Congress was a balanced budget. For the Republicans, the political problem was that polls indicated that most people would blame the GOP for a shutdown if one occurred.[94] Their predicament was complicated by the fact that it was now time to live up to the promises Clinton had made American allies in 1993 to provide U.S. support for a comprehensive peace plan. By opposing Clinton on both support for the peace plan and the budget, the Republicans risked being viewed as obstructionists.

In the short term, on November 17, the House passed a measure originally sponsored by Joel Hefley (R-Colo.) stating that the president would not be allowed to use federal funds for the Bosnian mission unless appropriated and approved specifically by Congress.[95] However, shortly after Clinton's national address, it became increasingly apparent that Clinton was strongly committed to the operation. The House Committee on International Relations did hold hearings on U.S. policy toward Bosnia on November 30, 1995, but this time it was fairly clear that Clinton's intent was to proceed with the deployment mission. While the House Republicans complained about the process, they seemed resigned to the fact that Clinton was going ahead with the operation regardless of their views. The committee debate centered on the logistical specifics of IFOR and avoided any constitutional questions about a deployment. Senior House Republican Henry Hyde expressed his frustration by saying that "the dye is cast, now we have to fall in line." But after noting the futility of his complaints, Hyde followed with logistical questions about IFOR.[96] Doug Bereuter stated that he felt that Clinton had presented IFOR as a "fait accompli" and there was little that Congress could do to prevent the deployment.[97] So in a symbolic stand against the president, 186 Republicans and 15 Democratic members of the House signed a letter sent to the president that stated unequivocally: "We urge you not to send ground troops to Bosnia."[98]

Despite the large-scale opposition and some members' belief that the president was acting in an unconstitutional manner,[99] the House acquiesced on December 13, 1995. In a 287–141 vote, the House voted to support the U.S. troops but also expressed its opposition to Clinton's policy.[100] In effect, the House admitted defeat and demonstrated that it was unwilling to test Clinton on constitutional war powers issues. Without Gingrich's strong support and with their battle over the budget soon to come, the political timing was not right to challenge the president on the Bosnian deployment. When the budget issue developed in November and December of 1995, the GOP appeared to place a higher priority on tax and spending issues than on war powers questions and Bosnia. The vote crafted by the House also gave the Republicans the political cover to justify their votes in their congressional districts. By supporting the troops and not the policy, they could appear patriotic and supportive of America's soldiers in Bosnia but could also remain critical of Clinton. Thus the vote allowed the Republicans to hold contradictory positions. They could avoid blame if the mission went badly, but if it went well, the could take credit for having supported the troops.

The Senate acted similarly. As a body, the Senate was less adversarial than the House, although a number of members were particularly vocal in their concern about a deployment. Senator Dole initially led the charge against the president by noting that Clinton should not assume Congress's automatic support for an American deployment to Bosnia and that Congress had not been fully consulted on the issue. In September 1995 Dole had sent a letter to the president expressing his reservations about a potential deployment.[101] Soon after Dole's comments, the Senate passed a "Sense of the Senate" resolution, calling for the president to gain prior approval before a deployment ensued. Introduced by Senator Judd Gregg (R-N.H.), the measure passed 94–2.[102] This mood continued into the next month, when the Senate Foreign Relations Committee held hearings on Bosnia. At one of the hearings, one telling interchange came between Senator Chuck Robb (D-Va.) and

Secretary of State Christopher. Robb asked Christopher what the administration's view would be if the Senate passed a resolution requiring congressional approval prior to a deployment. Christopher responded: "From a fundamental standpoint, the President would have to say that he is not bound by such a resolution. I do not think he can give away his constitutional authority as commander in chief any more than President Bush was willing to do so. As you know, right up to the last, he said that if there was a resolution, he would welcome it. But if there was a resolution, he would not feel bound by it."[103]

Christopher offered these statements before the Dayton peace talks had even begun, even in light of other comments he made indicating Congress's importance. While the Clinton administration was promising consultation, at the same time it felt it could deploy troops independently of Congress. Senator Robb did not follow Christopher's remarks with any rebuttal in favor of a congressional role, and in fact he had prefaced his question by stating that he did not support or encourage a resolution of "that kind."[104] His comments are telling in that congressional acquiescence to the president already was at work, especially among the Democrats. Senator Jim Exon (D-Nebr.) later noted that even in the event that Congress had voted against the president's deployment, he still felt the president most probably had the constitutional authority to deploy the troops, adding that military deployment decisions are "judgement calls" and the president's powers as commander in chief are broad.[105]

Not all members were resigned to the fact that the mission appeared to be proceeding without a congressional vote. Senator Feingold (D-Wis.) stated: "The President has in effect rendered Congress's role meaningless. . . . Congress is not simply supposed to be consulted on such matters or just be a rubber stamp for such actions. Congress is supposed to be an active partner in this process."[106] However, most senators were not interested in the legalities of the deployment.

By late November, Dole was willing to support the president on the Bosnia mission. Dole's position was a crucial factor in the Senate's deference. Because Dole was the leading Republican contender to topple the Clinton administration in the 1996 president elections, his decision to support the president placed other Republicans in a precarious position; if rank-and-file Republicans challenged Clinton, they would also be challenging their own leadership—and the Republicans' best hope to unseat Clinton. Like the House Republicans, Dole too had political incentives not to be viewed as an obstructionist during a period of near crisis in American foreign policy.[107] During the Vietnam War, many members of Congress who opposed the president were seen as divisive, which is a label that Dole was probably unwilling to risk heading into the first presidential primaries.

In the end, the Senate like the House voted to state its support for the troops but expressed reservations about the policy in a 69–30 vote.[108] The vote demonstrated that, like the House, the Senate Republican majority did not want to take legal responsibility for any casualties that might occur. From a public relations standpoint, both chambers sought to wash their hands of the policy and remain patriotic at the same time. Despite all the policy initiatives sought in the 104th Congress, and in the cold war's aftermath when Congress theoretically would stand up to check the president more readily, the Republicans remained unwilling to exert their constitutional powers, even in light of another UN-endorsed peacekeeping operation that a majority of Americans opposed.[109] Because of the priority they placed on achieving a balanced budget and the risk of being viewed as obstructionists and unpatriotic, the Republican leadership decided to avoid its constitutional war powers and defer to the president, choosing instead to assume a cautiously crafted political position of supporting the troops but not the policy.

CONCLUSION

Bosnia is an especially interesting and telling case with regard to the congressional-executive interplay over war powers. In this post–cold war peace-enforcement operation sanctioned by the United Nations and NATO, a number of conditions existed that appeared conducive to a reassertion of congressional powers: a new and seemingly assertive Republican majority in both the House and Senate, public opinion suggesting a majority in opposition to an American deployment to Bosnia, and a president whose policy on Bosnia seemed confused and uncertain. Yet in the end congressional deference remained the rule, to a great extent because of domestic political considerations and the positions taken by key congressional leaders.

Clinton, International Organizations, and "Consultation"

The Clinton administration's position on war powers authority in Bosnia remained consistent from the beginning. Clinton stated in 1993 that a peacekeeping force would be deployed if a comprehensive peace settlement was reached. Once the Dayton Peace Accords were signed, Clinton fulfilled his promise. Clinton also had Chapter 7 authorization to participate in NATO's enforcement of the no-fly zones and later the bombing campaign on the Bosnian Serbs. However, what is noteworthy about President Clinton's rhetoric and strategy with Congress prior to the IFOR deployment was the extent to which he remained publicly willing to "consult" with Congress—implying that Congress would have a real opportunity to contribute to the deployment decision. Clinton, Vice President Gore, Chief of Staff Leon Panetta, Secretary of Defense William Perry, and Secretary of State Warren Christopher all indicated that Congress would be consulted *after* the Dayton Peace Accords' conclusion. With Republican opposition so strong, especially in the House, the Clinton administration recognized the need to use the WPR's language of consultation and went to great lengths to have top administration officials appear at House and Senate committee hearings to defend the policy. With a new Republican and ostensibly assertive Congress, Clinton could not afford to bypass Congress without taking some measures to appease the GOP. In this case the domestic political conditions demanded that Clinton at least talk about consultation in a manner that had not been witnessed before. In practice, however, the Clinton administration only paid lip service to the idea of consultation, since the decision to participate in IFOR was made well in advance of the hearings.

Like President Bush in 1990 and 1991 before Desert Storm, Clinton officials also expressed on different occasions that the president had authority to deploy troops without Congressional authorization. However, Clinton's strategy with Congress was different from the one adopted by Bush, who maintained that UN Security Council Resolution 678 gave him full authority to expel Saddam Hussein from Kuwait. Bush recognized the political value in turning to Congress to request its support, but his language was different from Clinton's, both before and after Congress's vote on Operation Desert Storm.

The domestic political conditions were also much different than they were at the time of the Haitian and Somalian deployments. In those cases, Clinton could rely upon Democratic majorities to protect him from Republican challenges. This was not the case in 1995, and as a result the war powers interplay was different. What was similar for President Clinton, however, was his appeal to the authority granted to him by the United Nations Security Council and, in this case, NATO. Clinton appealed to these endorsements during the bombings to insulate himself from congressional objections to his uses of force, which appeared to work to the president's advantage. His appeal to NATO's authority was a particularly useful political strategy, in that it placed him on the side of fifteen allies at a time when NATO's mission was evolving to meet post–cold war challenges. In effect, criticisms of Clinton's actions also were de facto challenges to all NATO allies, and thus the domestic political dynamic was favorable to Clinton's policy direction.

Congress and Domestic Politics

In many respects, the 104th Congress acted very much like all other Congresses in recent history. The 104th Congress did not question the president on the constitutionality of U.S. participation in NATO's bombings, which is noteworthy considering that the bombings in the former Yugoslavia represented NATO's first military strikes ever and were substantial uses of force. Despite the history surrounding the North Atlantic Treaty of 1949 and its protection of Congress's war powers, Congress avoided a constitutional debate with the president when NATO policed the no-fly zones and when it bombed the Bosnian Serbs in 1995. Congress also could have raised a host of questions over the WPR, including the American troops' participation in "hostilities." However, Congress sat on its hands and did not exercise its authority regarding U.S. participation in these activities.

When it came to the IFOR deployment, both the House and Senate expressed reservations over U.S. participation. Yet even with the opposition votes made earlier and other well-articulated statements of opposition from members of Congress, both chambers yielded to the president and preferred not to place constitutional limits on the operation. Republicans gave themselves safe cover politically in their decision to support the troops and not the policy, making deference an acceptable option. The Senate and House votes were reminiscent of the predominant attitude demonstrated by Congress during the Vietnam War. Once troops were stationed abroad, even those members who opposed the war were reluctant to vote against wartime appropriations for fear of not supporting "our boys." In 1995, a similar attitude pervaded Congress. To avoid appearing unpatriotic, members of Congress evaded their war powers legislative tools with a politically expedient vote. With the Republican priorities set on the looming battle over the budget in December 1995, and without key leadership opposition to the president from either the Speaker of the House or the Senate's Majority leader, Congress remained acquiescent to the president.

It may be argued that upon becoming the majority party in Congress, the Republicans were really not seriously committed to fundamental change in the U.S.-UN relationship and that the Contract with America and Dole's Peace Powers Act were actually cases of political maneuvering designed to be received well by the electorate rather than real, substantive efforts to check the president. For a number of reasons, this argument runs counter to the evidence.

The House Republicans took their seats with a deep commitment to check the president's ability to use U.S. troops in UN peacekeeping operations. In the aftermath of the U.S. deaths in Somalia, and with the misgivings surrounding the deployment to Haiti, the new Republican majority had little interest in allowing the president to deploy troops again in another controversial UN mission. The House quickly passed the National Security Revitalization Act with nearly unanimous support from the Republicans, indicative of their design to rein in the United States' role in United Nations. Statements from GOP Congressmen Armey, Rohrabacher, and Roth also demonstrate the Republicans' serious commitment to checking presidential war powers. Speaker Gingrich did make a case for the expansion of presidential war powers when Congressman Hyde attempted to repeal the WPR. However, no evidence exists to suggest that the Speaker showed any commitment to rallying his party on the bill's behalf. In a time when House Republican Party cohesion was at its apex, Gingrich could easily have marshaled the rank and file in the amendment's behalf. That he did not demonstrates the Speaker's weak commitment to expanding the commander in chief's powers. The vast majority of the House Republicans appeared ready to challenge the president over participation in IFOR as late as the House Republican Conference meeting on November 8, 1995, and with Congressman Hefley's proposal on November 17. In the end, the House leadership concluded that politically its best battle would be over budgetary politics rather than Bosnia. Without support from the leadership to oppose the president, the GOP rank and file fell in line behind Gingrich and voted to support the troops but not the policy.

Just as the House Republicans' Contract with America appeared to sincerely reflect GOP beliefs, Bob Dole's commitment as majority leader to a stricter application of Article 43 of the UN Charter and Section 6 of the UN Participation Act also appeared genuine. Dole had introduced his Peace Powers Act in the previous year and took the unusual step as Senate majority leader of appearing at a Senate committee hearing to lobby for the bill's passage in 1995. Moreover, Congress's discussion of Article 43 is significant in that although the article had largely become a moot point after 1945, its invocation demonstrates the GOP's unfeigned support for its application. Never before had these past legislative decisions consumed so much attention from members of Congress. Thus, to argue that the Republicans sought only to make popular political waves through the Peace Powers Act and the National Security Revitalization Act ignores the many substantive legislative GOP legislative efforts to limit U.S. participation in UN deployments. In the end it was Congress's GOP leadership that chose not to exercise its war powers, largely due to domestic political considerations.

Postscript: The Campbell Resolution

For the duration of Clinton presidency, American troops remained in Bosnia in support of the peacekeeping operation. In 1996, as IFOR became the NATO Stabilization Force (SFOR), Congress continued to appropriate money for the operation. The most substantive challenge to Clinton's authority as commander in chief with regard to the deployment in Bosnia came through the efforts of Congressman Thomas Campbell (R-Calif.). On March 18, 1998, Campbell introduced a resolution entitled "Removal of United States Armed Forces from the Republic of Bosnia and Herzegovina." Although the resolution failed in a 193–225 vote, the political dynamics surrounding the debate tell a great deal about the status of war powers in the House of Representatives.

Campbell's resolution called for "a court of competent jurisdiction" to determine the constitutionality of his bill. The bill required the president to remove U.S. forces from Bosnia in sixty days unless Clinton gained congressional authorization. Campbell's resolution was written specifically to test the WPR's constitutionality. He maintained that because there had been no declaration of war and no congressional authorization for the American deployment to Bosnia even though U.S. troops had experienced "hostilities" during the deployment, Clinton was in violation of the WPR and needed congressional approval to continue the mission. Campbell's resolution, however, stated that it was not meant to judge the policy in Bosnia, nor did it necessarily reflect any disagreement with the policy.[110] If the court found his resolution constitutional, Clinton would be required to abide by the WPR and ask for congressional approval.

When the House floor debate commenced, most Republicans presented legal and political arguments in favor of the resolution. Many who supported Campbell did so primarily on policy grounds, arguing that Clinton's deployment was not in the nation's interest.[111] In response, Campbell rose twice to argue that the vote was not about "policy" but the validity and applicability of the War Powers Resolution.[112] What is notable about the House floor debate is the absence of the Republican Party leaders. The highest-ranking GOP member who rose to speak was Judiciary Committee Chairman Henry Hyde. Speaker Gingrich, Majority Leader Dick Armey, and Majority Whip Tom Delay (R-Tex.) did not participate in the floor debate.[113] Although Armey and Delay voted for the measure, they made no visible effort to advance the legislation.[114]

The Democrats presented legal and policy arguments to oppose the bill. Representative Lee Hamilton, ranking minority member of the House International Relations Committee, led the resistance. He was joined by Minority Whip Bonior, among other Democrats. Most Democrats maintained that Campbell's measure was an effort to end the American troop's presence in Bosnia, despite the policy disclaimer attached to the resolution. In closing the debate, Chairman of the House International Relations Committee Benjamin Gilman sided with the Democrats, stating: "Perhaps in law school classrooms that argument might have some merit, but in the real world, the vote we are about to exercise concerns our nation's policy in Bosnia."[115] Of the forty-three Republicans who voted against the measure, a number mentioned that

they had been to Bosnia and now felt that the United States was making measurable progress in the mission. In their view, to pull the plug
on the operation would not have been wise at that time.[116]

This short but telling debate has many implications with regard to
congressional war powers. One implication stems from the language
of the resolution, which stated that Congress never consented to the
actual policy of placing troops in Bosnia. In some respects, this was
accurate. In Congress's key votes on the deployment in December 1995,
the House opposed the policy and the Senate expressed its concern.
However, Congress ultimately deferred to the president in these resolutions rather than raising any constitutional challenge. As the operations progressed, the Republicans could have refused to grant Clinton
the funds needed for IFOR and SFOR but instead decided not to block
the president. If the Republicans sincerely felt that they never granted
President Clinton the authority to conduct IFOR and SFOR, they apparently suffered some degree of collective amnesia. The Republicans'
actions demonstrate the danger of their politically expedient and constitutionally ambiguous votes in 1995. By not taking a clear position
when it had the opportunity to do so, Congress granted Clinton tremendous powers as commander in chief.

The voting behavior of the Campbell resolution also illustrates the
strong partisanship that exists with regard to war powers. Only thirteen Democrats crossed party lines to vote with the Republicans. Some
Democrats who had been strong advocates of congressional war powers in the past—including Don Edwards (D-Calif.), who had taken a
strong stance on Panama;[117] and Sherrod Brown (D-Ohio) and Robert
Andrews (D-N.J.), who opposed the president on Somalia[118]—voted
against Campbell's resolution. On the Republican side, Henry Hyde's
vote was perhaps one of the most partisan votes made, considering his
past efforts to repeal the WPR and his intense criticism of it. Hyde tried
to justify his vote on the Campbell measure by arguing that although
he did not like the WPR, it was still "the law." He argued that if Campbell's resolution was the only means of bringing the troops home from
Bosnia, he would hesitantly back it.[119] Thus, like other war powers votes
during the Clinton administration, the Campbell resolution was also
treated in a politically partisan fashion, rather than in the serious legal
manner its author intended.

The absence of public endorsement from key GOP leaders also limited Campbell's ability to get the support he needed to control the more maverick rank and file within the party. Although the party leaders did not formally say as much, they had incentives to see the resolution fail. With their knowledge as floor leaders that the Campbell measure did not have the necessary votes to win, GOP leaders such as Delay and Armey could vote in favor of the resolution, knowing that they would not have to accept any formal legal responsibility for the mission because of the bill's preordained failure. Thus, political incentives remained to let the president have full responsibility for the mission in Bosnia rather than risking the possibility that their party would be forced to take some measure of responsibility for either ending or continuing the mission.

As the senior member and chairman of the International Relations Committee, Benjamin Gilman dealt the resolution a death blow through his public objection to the bill. Again, the position of an individual senior leader in Congress had a fundamental impact on the exercise of congressional war powers. Gilman helped to ensure that Campbell's measure failed.

In sum, the war powers interplay over Bosnia was often influenced by the actions of key leaders in the House and Senate. In the 1995 vote on Bosnia, and later in the Campbell resolution, Congress's leaders chose not to use their legislative powers to check the president, even though these powers are well documented in Congress's history with NATO in 1949 and articulated in the WPR. Other domestic political conditions at the time, including budgetary politics and the desire to appear not as obstructionists, but as patriotic, help explain why Congress continued to defer to the president. Deference remained the norm in part because of domestic political conditions favorable to the president, but also not without the efforts of a few key Republican leaders.

5   Terrorism:
Usama Bin Laden

Bill Clinton's strikes on Usama Bin Laden represented a very different sort of military action than the other uses of force considered thus far. The president had multilateral support from either the United Nations or NATO prior to the use of force in Somalia, Haiti, and Bosnia. The responsibilities of the president and Congress in carrying out the "constitutional processes" required for American military participation in such operations were clearly articulated in the 1945 and 1949 treaties addressed in Chapter 1. In the cases discussed so far, the WPR also applied because of the presence of "hostilities," because American troops were "equipped for combat," or because of the UN Chapter 7 authorization to use force.

When the WPR was created, however, its authors obviously could not anticipate the many different types of threats that exist today. For example, the WPR does not speak specifically to the constitutional duties of either branch of government in response to acts of "terrorism" directed against the United States. The WPR does grant the president the right to use force when there is a declaration of war, specific statutory authorization, or a "national emergency created by attack upon the United States, its territories or possessions, or its armed forces."[1] According to the last exception, a terrorist strike on the United States would allow for an immediate military response from the president according to the WPR. This position corresponds with James Madison's notes, which indicated that the president should be allowed to respond defensively to aggression against the nation. Yet, as specified by the WPR, presidential consultation with Congress is required in "every possible instance," regardless of the enemy.[2] Although the WPR does not specifically say so, it follows that if any uncertainty exists about the identity of a terrorist perpetrator, or in the event that there is not an immediate need to retaliate against a terrorist, it would be "possible" to consult with Congress, and therefore it should be consulted. In sum, the president does have unilateral authority to respond to terrorism if the nation's "territories or possessions" have been attacked, but this authority may be slightly tempered depending on the particular circumstances.

During the Clinton administration, the threat of terrorism became a more prominent security concern for Americans, as reflected in numerous public opinion polls.[3] This was especially true in the days prior to the New Year's celebrations for the year 2000, when worldwide "terrorist alerts" were issued by the U.S. State Department. Two years earlier, President Clinton's decision to strike the alleged terrorist outposts of Usama Bin Laden was one of the most important steps taken against a terrorist actor during his presidency and thus presents a useful case to examine regarding the role of war powers and the use of force against terrorists. This strike was also conducted unilaterally, without the approval of either the United Nations or NATO. Because of the close similarities with President Ronald Reagan's 1986 strikes against Libyan leader and widely recognized terrorist supporter Muammar Qaddafi, this chapter also presents a comparison between these two uses of force, which is helpful for understanding Clinton's interplay with Congress and the relevance of the WPR during his presidency.

U.S. Foreign Policy and Terrorism

When the Clinton administration took office, terrorism was not considered one of the central security threats to the nation. By the end of Clinton's first term, however, the federal building in Oklahoma City had been bombed; Japanese terrorist Aum Shinruki had killed twelve and injured five thousand others on a Japanese subway; and in 1993 New York City's World Trade Center had been victimized by terrorists. Moreover, in 1996, nineteen American servicemen were killed in Dahran, Saudi Arabia, when terrorists exploded a car bomb near an American military complex.[4] These events among others exposed the United States and the world to new levels of terrorism.

The importance of terrorism in American national security has evolved considerably over the last twenty-five years. In 1979, terrorism reached new heights during the American hostage crisis in Iran, when loyalists of the Ayatollah Khomeini overtook the American embassy in Tehran and held fifty-two Americans captive for 444 days. In the mid-1980s, terrorism again gained prominence among perceived threats to the United States as a result of the state-sponsored terrorism of Libyan leader Muammar Qaddafi and the activities of Palestinian extremist groups. In 1983, the deaths of 243 U.S. Marines killed in Lebanon by a suicide bomber were particularly painful for the United States. During the late 1980s and early 1990s, with the notable exception of the bombing of PanAm flight 109 over Lockerbie, Scotland, terrorism moved off the American political agenda temporarily, but it resurfaced midway through Clinton's first term.[5] Although the empirical record suggests a reduction of terrorist incidents in the post–cold war era, policy experts contend that terrorists now represent a much greater threat to the United States because of their increased access to weapons of mass destruction and the growing technological vulnerabilities of industrialized countries.[6]

The Clinton administration, like its predecessors, made a number of policy efforts to address terrorism. During the Clinton presidency, the U.S. State Department noted that it dealt with terrorists in four ways: by providing "no concessions" to terrorists; by bringing to justice those who support or conduct terrorist activities; by working to "isolate" and "change the behavior" of terrorists; and by working with other countries to advance their counterterrorist efforts.[7] The United States also operated an Anti-Terrorism Training Assistance Program, which assisted foreign states with airport security, hostage rescue, bomb detection, and other counterterrorist measures. The United States is also party to eleven different multilateral conventions to combat terrorism.[8] The Clinton administration also used the Counter Terrorist Center (CTC), which was created in 1986 and reports directly to the director of the Central Intelligence Agency on terrorism intelligence gathering. The CTC is a joint effort of the National Security Agency, the Defense Intelligence Agency, the CIA, the FBI, and the State Department, all of which also conduct their own antiterrorist activities.[9]

Despite these efforts, in a clear act of terrorism on August 7, 1998, forces struck the American embassies in Kenya and Tanzania. These attacks were soon attributed to Usama Bin Laden. The antiwestern Muslim fundamentalist Bin Laden has long been a security challenge for the United States. Bin Laden was born in Saudi Arabia, the son of a wealthy contractor. His father accrued great wealth through his many construction activities in the Middle East, including the rebuilding of Muslim holy sites in Mecca and Medina. As a young man, Bin Laden's first and most pivotal experience in world affairs came with the Soviet Union's intervention in Afghanistan, a state with a majority Muslim population. Bin Laden viewed the Soviet's actions as a direct and unforgivable assault on Islam; it disturbed him profoundly and motivated him to travel to the country to support the Islamic Mujahideen resistance. During the war, Bin Laden's religious zeal and political extremism against the west developed. His vast financial resources—estimated at $200 million—allowed Bin Laden to develop and oversee a wide network of Islamic terrorist organizations by the late 1980s. In the ensuing years, this network was linked to an assassination plot on Pope John Paul II, the 1993 bombing of the World Trade Center, a 1993 bombing in Yemen, a 1995 truck-bombing in Saudi Arabia, and various other high-profile terrorist acts around the world.[10] On February 22, 1998, as tensions between the United States and Iraq reached new heights over Iraq's refusal to comply with the United Nations Special Commission on weapon inspections, Bin Laden publicized a fatwa, or religious decree, calling for strikes against all U.S. citizens and military personnel anywhere in the world. Bin Laden had announced a similar edict previously, in August 1996.[11] Thus Bin Laden was no stranger to those in the intelligence community, nor was his willingness to take extreme measures to achieve his goals.

Before examining the war powers interplay over the United States' response to Bin Laden, a useful comparison can be made with Ronald Reagan's decision to use force against the government of Libya for its alleged ties to a terrorist act. This case is not perfectly analogous in that terrorism had not achieved the heightened saliency that it now commands, and unlike Usama Bin Laden, Qaddafi is a *state* leader. Yet Reagan's 1986 air strikes provide perspective for better understanding the interplay between President Clinton and Congress, and the very different strategy that Clinton employed.

Qaddafi, Reagan, and the WPR

Muammar Qaddafi came to power in 1969 after a bloodless coup against Libyan King Idris. A flamboyant and often self-righteous leader, Qaddafi was inspired by the leadership of Egypt's Gamal Abdul Nasser and viewed himself as the leader of a pan-Arabic revolution.[12] Qaddafi had managed to improve social conditions for Libya, but he ruled in an authoritarian manner and employed international terrorism to achieve his foreign policy objectives. His terrorist activities have been most closely connected to Palestinian extremist groups but have extended beyond Africa and the Middle East to Europe. By 1979, the Carter administration considered his regime a serious national security threat. Qaddafi drew the Reagan administration's attention in its first year by threatening America's naval presence in the region, and in response the United States shot down two Libyan aircraft. Tensions mounted in 1986, when the Reagan administration led a worldwide effort to place and implement tight economic sanctions on Qaddafi for his terrorist connections. By this time, the U.S. State Department maintained that the Libyan regime had been involved in fifty-nine different terrorist acts around the world.[13]

In early 1986, viewing the waters of the Gulf of Sidra as part of Libyan territory, Qaddafi stated that any ship or aircraft that crossed the "line of death" in the gulf would be fired upon. Although Qaddafi's territorial claim was not accepted by most countries, the Reagan administration chose to test it by placing U.S. ships and aircraft in the contested waters and airspace. Libya responded with antiaircraft missiles, prompting the United States to fire on missile sites and patrol boats in the area near the Libyan city of Sitre. Approximately two weeks later, a bomb exploded in a German dance club frequented by American serviceman. One U.S. soldier and one German woman were killed. Two hundred others were injured, including sixty Americans. In the following days, with the assistance of French and German intelligence sources, the bombing was attributed to the Libyan regime. Reagan responded on April 14, 1986, with air and naval strikes on Libyan military sites, which probably resulted in the death of Qaddafi's adopted daughter.[14]

In his address to the nation, Reagan asserted that Qaddafi's links to the terrorist bombing in Germany were "conclusive" and that the evidence was "direct," "precise," and "irrefutable."[15] In his notification letter to Congress, which is required by the WPR, Reagan wrote that he conducted these strikes pursuant to his "authority under the Constitution, including [his] authority as Commander in Chief of United States Armed Forces." He also noted that his actions were allowed under Article 51 of the United Nations Charter, which permits member states of the United Nations the right to self-defense.[16]

Three hours before the attack, Reagan asked congressional leaders to come to the White House to be consulted. Although the administration later argued that any member of Congress could have stopped the operation there, some members present at the meeting maintained that they had merely been informed of what was going to happen. While the bombings were well received by the American populace,[17] many Democrats and some Republicans contended that the WPR had been violated, in that proper consultation had not taken place. Senator Sam Nunn (D-Ga.) noted that in order for "consultation" to occur, many options had to be open to consideration. He argued that these conditions did not exist at the Reagan administration's ad hoc meeting. Another senior senator, Robert Byrd (D-W.Va.), likewise noted that proper consultation had not taken place and that Congress had merely been "notified" about the attack.[18] In response to Reagan's conduct, Senator Alan Cranston (D-Calif.) introduced a bill requiring better consultation with Congress when the president seeks to use force.[19] Others in the Senate, most importantly Senate Majority Leader Bob Dole (R-Kans.), argued that Congress was trying to micromanage foreign policy and that the president should be given more latitude in using force against terrorists.[20]

In the House, Democrats went a step further by holding hearings on Reagan's actions and the perceived violation of the WPR. At a meeting of the House Foreign Affairs Subcommittee on Arms Control, International Security, and Science, led by Foreign Affairs Chairman Dante Fascell (D-Fla.), Democrats pushed the administration on what they perceived as a lack of compliance with the WPR. Through its legal advisor, Abraham Sofaer, the Reagan administration argued that with regard to counterterrorism, the executive branch had unilateral authority to use force, due to the need for secrecy and because these actions fall short of total war.[21] While the hearings produced much discourse on war powers and counterterrorism, in the end Congress let the constitutional issues rest and made no formal challenge to the president.

In retrospect, the war powers interplay produced much tension and controversy. Contrary to Senator Dole's position, many members of Congress, particularly Democrats, argued that the WPR had been violated and that greater consultation was necessary in order to meet the WPR's requirements. Even though the target of the president's strikes was widely considered a terrorist state, guilty of terrorist acts against Americans and others, many in Congress felt that Reagan had overstepped his powers as commander in chief and ignored his obligation to consult with Congress. Qaddafi's convincing "credentials" as an international terrorist made little difference to the war powers advocates on the Hill. In the case of Usama Bin Laden, however, the interplay was much more unconventional and produced very different results.

Usama Bin Laden and the WPR

When the United States embassies in Kenya and Tanzania were bombed, nearly three hundred people were killed, including twelve Americans, and five thousand others were injured in the blasts. One week after the attack, on August 14, CIA Director George Tenet presented information to Clinton's top national security officials that Bin Laden was responsible for the strikes.[22] Six days later, the Clinton administration responded by launching seventy-nine tomahawk missiles on alleged Bin Laden outposts in Afghanistan and the Sudan. When the president addressed the nation on the strikes, he provided essentially four justifications for his actions. He noted that Bin Laden had publicly called for a terrorist war against the United States; that his network of extremist Islamic organizations had been involved in other major terrorist attacks in the 1990s; that there was "convincing evidence" that Bin Laden was behind the embassy bombings in Kenya and Tanzania; and that "compelling information" suggested Bin Laden was planning another attack on the United States.[23]

In his notification letter to Congress, Clinton, like Ronald Reagan, also noted that under Article 51 of the United Nations Charter he was entitled to act in the nation's self-defense. He also stated that his actions were undertaken pursuant to his "constitutional authority to conduct U.S. foreign relations and as Commander in Chief and Chief Executive." Included in this letter was the statement that he had kept Congress "fully informed, consistent with the War Powers Resolution."[24] His justification was nearly identical to Reagan's legal arguments for his overt strike on Qaddafi. Clinton's letter also differed little from his own past constitutional claims when unilateral military force had been used.[25] While the substance of his legal argument was essentially the same as Reagan's, Clinton's political strategy with Congress prior to the attack was considerably different and in fact was quite dissimilar to that of any president since the WPR's passage.

After the embassy bombings, U.S. investigations in Kenya and Tanzania began immediately. Speaker of the House Newt Gingrich (R-Ga.) indicated that in the days prior to the attack the Clinton administration had shared intelligence with the Speaker himself.[26] On the night before the strikes, Senate Majority Leader Trent Lott (R-Miss.) and Gingrich were also both called by National Security Advisor Sandy Berger before Clinton gave the formal approval of the strikes, which was done at approximately 2:00 A.M., Thursday morning, August 20. Because House Minority Leader Dick Gephardt (D-Mo.) was traveling abroad and unable to get to a secured phone line, Berger spoke with members of his staff. Senate Minority Leader Tom Daschle was also phoned by Berger on the morning before the strikes occurred.[27] This is a marked contrast to the three hours' notice given to congressional leaders in 1986.[28]

Clinton's efforts to bring the leadership more closely into the decision-making process produced high dividends for the president. In the immediate aftermath of the strikes, almost no negative reaction or skepticism surfaced in Congress. The vast majority in Congress was highly supportive from the beginning. Senator Lott noted that the information on Bin Laden's connection to the bombings was "very compelling." Gingrich stated that his consultation with the White House had been "done in a methodical, professional way" and that he strongly supported the actions taken by the Clinton administration.[29] Gingrich also informed the Republican caucus that it would be wise to stand behind the president against Bin Laden and to give strong support to Clinton for his actions. Gingrich instructed his close partisan ally and political operative Rich Galen to contact all major Republican media personalities and radio talk shows to reiterate Gingrich's support for the president on this measure.[30] Congressman Norman Dicks (D-Wash.), ranking minority member of the House Permanent Select Committee on Intelligence, noted that the evidence against Bin Laden was "compelling." Even the sometimes acerbic Clinton antagonist House Majority Leader Dick Armey (R-Tex.) backed the president.[31]

Research in the aftermath of these strikes illustrates that some in the Clinton administration, especially Assistant Secretary of State Phyllis Oakley, felt that the evidence linking Bin Laden to an alleged chemical weapons plant hit in Sudan was questionable. The doubts centered on the soil sample taken from the area surrounding the Sudan plant, which contained higher than normal levels of Empta, a chemical used to create nerve gas. While the samples showed possible links to chemical weapons, some in the Central Intelligence Agency and State Department apparently called for more samples to confirm the linkages. Others also apparently felt that a Bin Laden relationship with the plant was plausible but had not been established conclusively.[32] At the time that the Clinton administration's intelligence was shared with congressional leaders, however, no concerns were raised. The intelligence was accepted as convincing by all leaders of Congress who were consulted.[33]

On the day of the strikes, two members of the Senate, Arlen Specter (R-Pa.) and Dan Coats (R-Ind.), expressed reservations about the bombings by questioning the political timing of the attacks. Only three days before, the president had admitted to his affair with Monica Lewinsky. However, Specter's and Coats' reservations quickly subsided the following day after discussions with their leadership and Clinton officials. Thus, nearly all members of Congress gave strong support to Clinton at a time when his public trust, as indicated by public opinion polls, was in question.[34] Approximately 40 percent of Americans believed that Clinton's military strikes were influenced by his domestic problems with Ms. Lewinsky.[35] Congress, however, raised no constitutional objections and no concerns regarding violations or exploitation of the WPR. In sum, the interplay between the White House and the Congress was unprecedented.

In contrast to Reagan's strike on Libya, for which there was only cursory notification rather than consultation, in the case of Clinton's strikes on Bin Laden, there was an early dialogue with the Speaker of the House, which later included, albeit at a lesser degree, the Republican Senate Majority Leader. When Clinton deployed troops to Somalia, Haiti, and Bosnia, debates surfaced in Congress over Clinton's WPR responsibilities and his authority to conduct thee operations. Although Congress ultimately deferred to the president in these cases, there was at least some rhetorical challenge to the president, at least within the Republican Party. But for his strikes against Bin Laden, Clinton had essentially universal support from both legislative chambers and political parties on his constitutional authority and his adherence to the WPR. In contrast to their negative reactions to past uses of force, members of Congress were quite satisfied with their relationship to and their role with the White House in this case. Even noted advocates of congressional war powers such as Senators Joseph Biden (D-Del.) and Russ Feingold (D-Wis.) raised no constitutional qualms with the president.[36] Those members who doubted the president in the first few hours after the strike quickly refrained from any more challenges.

Based on one interpretation of the Constitution, one could make a case that the president had authority to use force without congressional consent. If one accepts President Clinton's claim in his national address that Bin Laden was planning a second attack on American citizens (which was never refuted or challenged by any of the Congressional leaders), the president was justified to act on behalf of the country's defense to repel the attack. Intelligence officials had established that Bin Laden supporters had attacked the United States' "possessions," that he had openly declared war on United States citizens and military personnel, and that evidence existed that he was about to strike the United States again. Thus, the president could have made a case for a unilateral strike because Bin Laden ostensibly represented an immediate danger to the United States.

Another practical security concern is that an open debate on the House and Senate floor over the wisdom of striking Bin Laden would have given him time to hide or move his terrorist camps, which would have rendered strikes against him militarily futile. The founders could never have anticipated today's rapid flow of information, which allows terrorist actors and others to monitor current developments in American politics. Thus, it may be concluded that the founding fathers might have granted some leeway to the president in such situations.

The WPR also allows the president to use force if United States "territories or possessions" are attacked. The bombings of the American embassies in Kenya and Tanzania clearly meet this criteria. At the same time, the WPR still requires consultation in "every possible instance," and the constitution is still a document based on the principle of checks and balances, with distinct responsibilities for the president and Congress. Because there was a considerable time lag between the actual intelligence gathering process and the eventual strike, a "possibility" for consultation existed, and the president had some responsibility at least to consult privately with members of Congress in advance in order to protect constitutional principles.[37]

Even with the constitutional interpretations and the WPR's exceptions in his favor, Clinton still reached out to Congress in advance and thus met the most minimal standard of consultation. If a president shares intelligence information with a Speaker of the House from the opposing party days prior to the strikes and talks with the Speaker and the Senate Majority Leader before the final decision to use force has been made, some degree of "consultation" has occurred. Perhaps this is not exactly what the creators of the WPR intended, and this may point to the inherent difficulty of defining what "consultation" means, but in this case it appears that Clinton took steps, albeit small ones, to include congressional leaders in the process. By comparison, Clinton's dealings with Congress before the attack on Bin Laden certainly met the WPR's requirements better than Reagan's communications with the legislative branch before the strike on Qaddafi. In the case of the Libyan attack, many in Congress felt that Reagan had violated the WPR. Moreover, as noted in Chapter 1, when President Carter deployed forces in an attempt to rescue American hostages held in the U.S. embassy in Iran, his administration likewise never consulted with Congress.[38] Although these uses of force are not entirely analogous to the attack on Bin Laden, the Clinton administration's war powers behavior was striking compared with that of past presidents, who either did not even attempt consultation or did so in only a superficial way hours before the strikes. Explaining this phenomenon, the interplay, and this markedly different behavior entails analysis of a number of political factors.

Domestic Political Dynamics: The Lewinsky Factor

On August 17, 1998, President Clinton announced in an address to the nation that he had "misled" the public regarding his extramarital affair with Monica Lewinsky.[39] While Clinton's admission had little impact on how the public felt about the president's job performance, it immediately affected the public's trust in him. Polls showed a rapid decrease in the president's credibility with the people.[40] Having denied the affair for months and now openly admitting to infidelity, the Clinton administration no doubt understood that there would be major political, partisan, and possibly legal fallout. This recognition placed the White House in a crisis state, with tremendous political ambiguities and uncertainties for the president.

With the new dynamic of this scandalous revelation introduced into the political environment, the president had strong incentives to share with congressional leaders all intelligence gathered on the embassy bombings. In the days immediately prior to Clinton's public admission of his relationship with Ms. Lewinsky, Clinton had incentives to be cooperative with the Speaker of the House in the event that he would be forced to confess publicly. Thus, breaking with the tradition of presidential unilateralism, the president briefed Gingrich (and later Trent Lott) on the available intelligence regarding Bin Laden. It seems probable that Clinton understood that if he was forced to admit to his "inappropriate relationship," it would be essential to have congressional leaders behind him in undertaking any military action that could involve the loss of American lives. Had Clinton used force without consultation only hours after admitting that he lied to the public, many in Congress and the media would have waged an all-out assault on him, accusing him of diversionary tactics and a lack of substantive "consultation." Such a reaction was quite possible from House GOP members, particularly those who had entered the House in 1994, many of whom had waged anti-Clinton campaigns to win their seats.[41] While other presidents have easily survived congressional scrutiny after the use of force, Clinton's situation was unprecedented, uncertain, and extremely volatile. One can easily imagine the serious reservations and constitutional qualms many members of Congress would have about supporting the president in such circumstances without some degree of advance consultation. Thus, Clinton had strong political motives to work with congressional leaders and wisely sought a minimal level of advance consultation with the Republican leadership.

As a consequence of Clinton's decision to acknowledge that he had "misled" the public, the entire administration was placed in a very precarious position. Cabinet members who had publicly defended the president against the Lewinsky charges learned that they had been lied to. Because the use of force always entails political and military risks and because the administration's political stature had become so perilous, members of Clinton's cabinet also had strong interests in bringing

Congress "into the loop." If force had been used without real dialogue, the cabinet too would have faced additional scrutiny for its decisions. It made good political sense for top administration officials to work closely with congressional leaders. Their historic record and level of success with Congress are inextricably tied to the president's ability to lead. With the commander in chief's dubious status at the time, there were strong incentives for some level of consultation.

The way in which Usama Bin Laden was portrayed provides additional insight into this extraordinary interplay. During the cold war, Congress granted presidents considerable leeway when force was used against communists.[42] The same held true for President Clinton when he had either threatened or used force against Saddam Hussein, who is widely accepted as a threat to U.S. national security (see chapter 6). In Bin Laden's case, the intelligence provided was ostensibly excellent. Even though other evidence surfaced later indicating that the United States was possibly mistaken in targeting the Sudanese pharmaceutical plant, in the days before the attack all top foreign policy makers, including congressional leaders, agreed that the evidence was compelling. Moreover, Clinton had not "provoked" Bin Laden, as some suggested about Reagan's actions in Libya. Bin Laden also publicly declared war on American citizens on more than one occasion. From a political perspective, all of these factors made Bin Laden a safe target for the Clinton administration. No member of Congress wanted to be accused of preventing the president from using force against a Muslim fundamentalist linked to embassy bombings who had also declared war on the United States.

Campaign considerations may also have played a role, as the 1998 midterm elections were only three months away. Traditionally, the president's party loses seats at the midterm election of his second term, and now with the new dynamic created by the president's admission of misleading the American people, the Democrats were faced with the possibility of a significant political defeat. While the president could no longer hide from his personal lie, he could work to ensure that no further harm was done to his party. As Clinton had thrived on elections throughout his life, it is not unreasonable to assume that he understood that his lie could potentially threaten the party as it moved closer to the midterm elections.[43] Dealing with the Congress in an open and honest way regarding Usama Bin Laden would be one way of pro-

viding some insulation for the party against future partisan attacks on
this foreign policy issue.

The Afghan and Sudan bombings also won popular appeal. A poll
taken by *Newsweek* found that 73 percent of the public approved of the
strikes, while a *CBS–New York Times* poll similarly found 70 percent
approval ratings for the strike.[44] Thus, criticizing the president on the
strikes went directly against public opinion. Furthermore, Clinton had
authorized the use of force against targets in two countries with which
the United States had extremely poor diplomatic relations. At the time
of the bombings, Afghanistan was controlled by the Taliban, an extremist Muslim group that sought strict adherence to Islamic law as public
policy. And for over a decade Sudan had been engulfed in a civil war
in which the United States has generally supported the rebel resistance
factions.[45]

The president too made a strong and convincing case for the attack, which was supported by congressional leaders of both parties.
Any member of Congress who might have been motivated to take on
the president would be fighting not only public opinion but his or her
own party leaders in Congress as well. Moreover, American domestic
pressure groups representing Muslim interests in the United States have
traditionally been considered weak and poorly funded.[46] A few Muslim groups rose to challenge the president's decision, but these voices
were few and far between.[47]

In the immediate aftermath of the strikes, most Arab states were
also slow to condemn the United States. By Monday, August 24, four
days after the strikes, Sudan had garnered the support of the Arab
League's twenty-two members and asked the United Nations Security
Council to condemn the United States for its attacks. Yet the Arab
League's condemnation did not completely reflect the Arab world's real
political mood. While all twenty-two states voted uniformly against the
United States, individually many of these states were much more reserved. For example, Egypt initially withheld public judgement on the
strikes. Later, without openly criticizing the United States, the government announced through its state-controlled television station that terrorism must be fought and indicated that the matter of the bombings
should be investigated by the United Nations. Syria condemned the
United States for the strikes but also denounced those who struck the
American embassies. Saudi Arabia and Jordan likewise were notice-

ably restrained in their response to Clinton's actions.[48] At the United Nations, Sudan called for an international investigation of the bombing of the Sudanese pharmaceutical company, Al-Shifa. However, other than tentative backing from the Arab world, it received only limited support in the UN General Assembly. In the UN Security Council, Bahrain, the only Middle Eastern state that held a seat, proved hesitant to push forward with such an investigation.[49] Russian President Boris Yeltsin indicated his displeasure about being left out of the decision-making process but appeared more concerned with the process than the actual policy of the bombing.[50] China also signaled early support for the Clinton administration but later retracted its statement in the early weeks of September.[51] Thus, only countries with whom the United States had very poor relations were willing to strongly condemn the bombings. Otherwise, the United States received essentially universal backing. Some Middle Eastern states generated a great deal of rhetoric but were unwilling to pursue any actions at the United Nations or in other diplomatic circles. American military strikes on Sudan and Afghanistan presented few political risks for the president in domestic or international political circles and were unlikely to lead to further criticism from members of Congress that Clinton's actions constituted a reckless use of force or an unjust violation of these states' sovereignty.

In sum, even though some important similarities exist between the uses of force against Bin Laden and Qaddafi, Congress's reactions to the strikes on Bin Laden were markedly different from its response to the strikes on Qaddafi in 1986. Some Democrats and many Republicans challenged President Clinton's constitutional authority to use force in other military operations, even though Congress remained deferent when the time came to vote. But Clinton was not challenged in his use of force against Usama Bin Laden. Congress widely backed the president.

CONCLUSION

This case represents a unique example of the White House meeting the WPR's minimal criterion of "consultation" with Congress, even though President Clinton had many constitutional arguments in his favor for a unilateral military response. Clinton's level of consultation with Congress prior to the strikes on Usama Bin Laden was unprecedented. While the president could have made a case that consultation was not required against a known terrorist such as Usama Bin Laden, Clinton still interacted with congressional leaders in a manner that meets the minimal standard of the WPR's consultation requirement. This interplay can largely be explained as a result of the domestic political environment, which created strong incentives for the president to consult with congressional leaders prior to the strikes. Because of the nature of the threat, as well as the public support for the strikes, Congress allowed Clinton much leeway in this military endeavor.

Domestic Politics:
Lewinsky and Congressional Support

Due to the president's admission that he had "misled" the American public, a new dynamic was introduced into the war powers question. The president's self-interest, cabinet members' self-interests, strong public support for the attack, and a relatively uncontroversial target created the conditions for the commander in chief to work with Congress in a manner that met the minimal requirements of the WPR. Clinton consulted with Gingrich and Lott, and shared information with the Republican leadership in a way that was convincing to both leaders. However, it was the political circumstances the Clinton presidency faced at the time that produced this interplay, rather than a renewed interest in constitutionalism or the WPR. In this respect, Clinton's strikes against Bin Laden represent the exception rather than the norm.

Clinton's strikes also were on two ill-reputed states in the world with weak or radical governments. Sudan and Afghanistan had few allies in the world who would protest the United States' actions, and few members of Congress would come to these states' defense. Reagan's attack on Qaddafi was similar in this regard. However, without pressing domestic political problems like Clinton's, and with his natural proclivity for preserving his perceived wide powers as commander in chief, Reagan pursued a different course by notifying Congress of his intent to strike Qaddafi only three hours before the strikes. His administration's choices resulted in substantial opposition from House Democrats. Clinton's personal political predicament was such that he could not afford to make a unilateral strike without some political support from the Congress, which had to be established prior to the strikes.

In terms of constitutional compliance, the president discussed the strikes with Gingrich and Lott and, to a lesser extent, with Daschle and Gephardt's staff. To some degree the principle of checks and balances was observed before the strikes took place. At the same time, only two members of Congress were truly consulted in advance, which probably does not fully capture the founding fathers' intent or the intent of the WPR, even at a time when some degree of secrecy was necessary in U.S. foreign policy making. Yet most members of Congress accepted the very minimal degree of consultation that took place. No member of Congress raised constitutional concerns over this process, which essentially included only two Republican leaders and left other Republican and Democratic foreign policy specialists out of the process. The central problem rests in defining what "consultation" means, which the WPR fails to do. If defined quite loosely, the president can take very small steps to meet the WPR's requirements, as demonstrated in this case.

The domestic political conditions also created incentives for Congress to defer to Clinton's leadership. Bin Laden had issued terrorist threats, the strikes were widely supported by the public, and Clinton included Republican members of Congress, albeit minimally, in the decision-making process. Democrats had also witnessed their Democratic president admit to misleading the public: to attack the president at that time might raise further questions about Clinton's character, which also may have hurt the Democratic Party in the upcoming midterm elections. These conditions were very different from Congress's assertiveness when American casualties were taken in Somalia and strong political incentives existed to check the president. With the strikes on Bin Laden, there were few political risks for either party in supporting the president, and as a result the president had essentially universal backing.

Even though Clinton's efforts to consult with Congress represent an outlier from the norm, his decision to consult with the Republican leadership in this case demonstrates the value of real dialogue between the White House and Congress. The president gained a number of foreign policy benefits by working with the Republican leadership in advance. Valuable time was saved in the aftermath of the attacks, in that constitutional questions did not have to be reevaluated through extensive congressional hearings. Washington was able to send a strong message to Usama Bin Laden and other extremists that America will respond vigorously with force to terrorist challenges. As we know now, these strikes were not effective in deterring future attacks upon the United States, but in 1998, they were widely viewed as an appropriate response. American national security interests were advanced with nonpartisan cooperation on war powers between the executive and legislative branches. The domestic political conditions and the international strategic environment would again create incentives for Clinton to break the norm of presidential unilateralism and work with Congress more closely prior to NATO's use of force in Kosovo in March 1999.

6   Kosovo

The political climate surrounding the United States' use of force in Kosovo in 1999 was substantially different than what the Clinton administration had dealt with in its past military actions. First, the United States' and NATO's military operation in the Federal Republic of Yugoslavia was the most prolonged and intense use of force during the Clinton presidency. For seventy-eight days, under American military leadership, NATO launched air attacks against Yugoslavia in an attempt to prevent Slobodan Milosevic from eliminating Kosovo's ethnic Albanian population. Although the actual numbers are open to debate, it is estimated that approximately six hundred soldiers and five hundred civilians were killed by the NATO strikes.[1] These figures represent the largest number of deaths inflicted on another state in a military operation overseen by President Clinton. In contrast, in 1994 and 1995, NATO had bombed the Bosnian Serbs sporadically. Clinton's strikes on Usama Bin Laden occurred on August 20, 1998, and were over in a few hours. Thus the bombings on Milosevic in 1999 were the most aggressive and sustained use of military force during the Clinton presidency.

Bill Clinton's actions in Kosovo also came soon after his House impeachment proceedings and Senate trial. Only once before had the United States experienced such a test of the Constitution, and never before had a president used force after impeachment. Partisanship reached an unsurpassed level in Washington during impeachment, and many in Congress harbored a deep distrust of the president.[2] Clinton used force only a month after the Senate's acquittal, in a new period for the presidency in American history and for Clinton himself. Institutionally, the presidency was in a weakened state, which presumably provided the conditions for a more assertive Congress.

Moreover, the use of force ostensibly entailed considerable risks for American soldiers. Before NATO initiated air strikes, top analysts from the Pentagon predicted American casualties and noted the significant air defense capabilities of the Serbian military. Others in the Pentagon openly questioned the strategic and military importance of Kosovo for the United States.[3] One of the most prominent critics, former Secretary of State Henry Kissinger, wrote and argued in various forums that intervention was dangerous and imprudent.[4] Thus, in light of the gravity of the contemplated use of force and the doubtful prognostications regarding the potential for success of strikes the prospects for a congressional assertion of war powers again seemed high during the post-impeachment period of the Clinton presidency. Despite these conditions, Congress largely—although not entirely—followed its pattern of deference to the president. However, the domestic political conditions, coupled with the international diplomatic issues in play, created new incentives for the president to dialogue with Congress prior to the use of force.

Kosovo and U.S. Foreign Policy

In 1992 President George Bush gave Yugoslav President Slobodan Milosevic a threat that became known as the "Christmas warning." Bush stated that any Yugoslav military action against the ethnic Albanian majority in Kosovo would result in an American military response.[5] Kosovo had enjoyed its essentially autonomous status during Tito's leadership and throughout most of the 1980s. Ninety percent of its population consisted of ethnic Albanians. The remaining 10 percent were mostly Serbs. In 1989, when Milosevic became president of Yugoslavia, he used the minority status of the Kosovar Serbs as a rallying point for Serb nationalism. He quickly stripped the political autonomy and many civil and educational rights enjoyed by the Kosovars, and he encouraged unemployed Serbs throughout Yugoslavia to move to Kosovo by guaranteeing them jobs in the province. In effect, most government positions held by ethnic Albanians were taken away and given to Serbs. Milosevic also appointed Serbs to the top political and law-enforcement positions in Kosovo and thus quickly gained military superiority over the province.[6]

Perhaps Milosevic was discouraged by the "Christmas warning" or occupied with other political and military issues for the next six years, but Serbian military initiatives did not begin in Kosovo until March

1998, when the Kosovo Liberation Army (KLA) and other ethnic Albanians called for independence. In response to KLA military actions, Milosevic's army moved into its southern province to eliminate the movement. Violence escalated between the two factions for the next three months. Most international observers of the crisis blamed the Serbs for their heavy-handed approach in addressing these issues. At the same time, Milosevic was unreceptive to western demands to cease the violence and continued with his efforts to eliminate the opposition.[7] Milosevic's unwillingness to negotiate over ethnic Albanian's rights and status in Kosovo eventually led to the military response from NATO.

Clinton's Threats

In response to Milosevic's aggression and resistance to western demands to end the violence and repression in Kosovo, on June 11, 1998, Secretary of Defense William Cohen asserted that the United States and NATO had the right to use force to protect the ethnic Albanians from Milosevic and his military. Cohen argued that NATO had the authority to conduct these air strikes without the approval of the United Nations Security Council or Congress.[8] Cohen's comments were echoed by Secretary of State Madeline Albright the following day. Albright argued that under Article 51 of the UN Charter, which allows members the right of self-defense, the United States would be authorized to take military action. She repeated Cohen's claim that a United Nations Security Resolution "may be desirable but is not required."[9] At the time, NATO's North Atlantic Council had not authorized military action, nor had the UN Security Council. Congress also had not given its approval to conduct strikes.

The Clinton administration's remarks produced virtually no reaction from Congress, as it followed the norm of deference to the president. Members of the House and Senate did not engage in discussions of war powers on the chamber floors or with the national media. Congress's lack of reaction is also notable given that the administration's legal authority to act was so precarious, both from a domestic constitutional standpoint and according to international law.

Irrespective of the legislative history of the North Atlantic Treaty in 1949, there was no "constitutional process" involved in the decision to threaten force. No vote occurred in either chamber of Congress on the potential strikes. Moreover, no evidence suggests that members of Congress were consulted prior to the threat to use force as required by the WPR. From a constitutional perspective Clinton also was not acting in accordance with James Madison's principle that the president could only act unilaterally to "repel a sudden attack." Several members had called for the use of force at the time and even earlier. Congress's Commission on Security and Cooperation in Europe held hearings on Kosovo as early as March 18, 1998. Members of the commission, including Congressman Steny Hoyer (D-Md.) and Senator Alfonse D'Amato (R-N.Y.), noted that the administration needed to stand firm against Milosevic and that the United States needed to send a strong message to the Yugoslav president that his actions would no longer be tolerated.[10] However, the majority in Congress remained silent about the constitutional issues at stake. Thus, the "constitutional process" protected by the 1949 treaty and in Senator Vandenburg's resolution in 1948 were essentially neglected by Congress when the Clinton administration made its claims of unilateral authority to use force.[11]

From the perspective of international law, NATO strikes on Yugoslavia also entailed a number of new and controversial legal questions. According to the United Nations Charter, "regional arrangements or agencies" may address issues of international peace and security by their own initiative, as long as these activities are in accordance with the United Nations' "Purposes and Principles."[12] Legal analysts agree that at the time of the charter's creation, member states concurred that regional organizations were granted the authority to act without the United Nations approval.[13] However, the proposed attacks were targeting an internationally recognized sovereign state. In contrast, the United Nations Charter is "based on the principle of sovereign equality," and threats or the use of force against another state are prohibited.[14] Moreover, as discussed in Chapter 4, NATO's past uses of force had United Nations Security Council authorization. The Clinton administration's threat in 1998 against Milosevic broke with earlier practice in the Clinton presidency. Thus the international legal issues were complex and in many respects uncharted.

Perhaps even more important, however, as a body NATO had not formally endorsed the air strikes. Prior to Operation Desert Storm in 1991, President Bush gained the United Nations Security Council's endorsement before using force. This support proved to be a crucial and meaningful stamp of multilateral approval for many members of Congress—especially members of the Republican Party.[15] Clinton also gained Security Council approval for an expansion of the mission in Somalia and the deployment to Haiti. However, in this case the absence of a multilateral endorsement from America's NATO allies did not stir members of Congress, even as Clinton officials spoke for NATO without its formal approval. Both congressional chambers deferred to the president, much as the House and Senate had done during the cold war. Congress preferred to let the president take full responsibility for the potential strikes. This strategy allowed Congress to criticize the president later if the mission did not succeed without requiring members of Congress to go on record either in support of or opposition to the policy. Thus this first threat of force against Milosevic elicited Congress's traditional cold war behavior with regard to war powers.

Rambouillet and NATO's Ultimatum

After the Clinton administration's threatened strikes in June, Milosevic curtailed his military initiatives in the short term. Yet some NATO allies were uncomfortable with the United States' assertion of power and NATO's precarious legal authority to conduct the strikes. In June 1998, French Premier Lionel Jospin noted that "in principle" he supported attacks on the Serbs, but he also felt that a United Nations Security Council Resolution authorizing a strike was appropriate.[16] These sentiments were repeated in August 1998, when French President Jacques Chirac noted his preference for Security Council authorization.[17] Newly elected German Chancellor Gerhard Schroeder likewise noted his preference for Security Council approval.[18] To quell these concerns, the United States and Great Britain sponsored Security Council Resolution 1199, which passed with only one abstention, from China. It called for an end to the "excessive and indiscriminate use of force by Serbian security forces and the Yugoslav army," a cessation of all hostilities, and a political agreement to stabilize the situation. This resolution passed under Chapter 7 of the United Nations Charter, which allows member states to use force. However, the resolution did not specifically authorize the use of force.[19] The Security Council decision was followed by NATO's formal activation order on October 13, 1998, allowing air strikes on Yugoslavia if Milosevic failed to cooperate with NATO. In the short term, however, NATO did not act, as Milosevic signaled a willingness to negotiate.

NATO's next major move occurred on January 30, 1999, when it lent its formal support to diplomatic efforts by the Contact Group (Britain, France, Germany, Italy, Russia, and the United States) to resolve the conflict. NATO's decision specifically noted that if an agreement was not reached between the warring factions in Yugoslavia, NATO reserved the right to take whatever steps necessary to avert the "humanitarian catastrophe."[20] The Serbs were essentially given two choices: end the violence in Kosovo and create a political settlement, or take their chances with NATO. The diplomatic meetings that followed took place at Rambouillet, France, where western leaders met with the Kosovars and Yugoslav representatives. The talks were crucial in determining whether NATO would respond with force.

As the United States and NATO moved closer to a military response in the fall of 1998, Congressman Thomas Campbell (R-Calif.) had expressed his concerns to President Clinton about the use of force without congressional authorization. On October 1, 1998, Campbell and Congressman David Skaggs (D-Colo.) issued a letter to all members of Congress reminding their colleagues that "No provision of the United Nations Charter or the North Atlantic Treaty can override this requirement of United States domestic law as set forth in the Constitution."[21] These efforts resulted in a letter from Campbell and forty-two other members of Congress to President Clinton. The letter reiterated that the president was required to gain Congress's authorization prior to any use of American military forces. Other than these efforts, however, Congress remained generally silent on war powers as it watched the United States move closer to using force.

As the attacks on the Kosovars continued and the administration's diplomatic threats heightened, so too did Campbell's challenge to the president. In response to a request from Congressman Campbell on January 15, 1999, National Security Advisor Samuel Berger stated the administration's view on the Constitution and war powers in a letter stating that there was "ample constitutional precedent" for the president to act without congressional authorization. He stated that "the President has broad authority, as Commander in Chief and under his authority to conduct foreign relations, to authorize the use of force in the national interest." He also argued that the United States' military threats were not "offensive," thereby implying a constitutional right to defensive actions in foreign states.[22] These claims are particularly broad in their assertions of power, essentially stating that Congress has no authority to check the president in military matters. Berger's claims do not square with the Constitution and completely disregard the legislative history of the North Atlantic Treaty.

In the immediate weeks to follow, the administration remained consistent in its claims of unilateral authority for commander in chief, but these claims were not without reaction from some members of Congress. At a meeting of the House International Relations Committee on February 10, 1999, under the scrutiny of Doug Bereuter (R-Nebr.) and Tom Campbell, Undersecretary of State for Political Affairs Thomas Pickering echoed Berger's words in his own testimony. In response to a direct question from Campbell regarding when Congress does have the power to declare war, Pickering maintained that there had been no case since December 7, 1941, when it was necessary for Congress to exercise its constitutional right to declare war.[23] In other words, Congress's constitutional war powers did not extend to American military actions in Korea, Vietnam, and the many other uses of force since World War II. Pickering's criteria implied that nothing short of an attack upon the United States justifies the exercise of Congress's war powers. In short, Pickering saw Congress's constitutional power to declare war as irrelevant. At the Constitutional Convention, Pickering would have been viewed as a monarchist, whose ideas were feared and grossly out of synch with the framers' intent.

After the committee hearing, Congressman Campbell sent another letter to the president, which this time had the support of thirty-eight other members of Congress. The letter noted that the proposed attacks were not "defensive" in nature, and that "Congress conditioned U.S. participation in both the UN and NATO on the requirement that Congress retain its constitutional prerogatives."[24] Campbell's letter represents an accurate reading of the debates and agreements made in 1945 and 1949. Further pressure on the president came from Congresswoman Tilly Fowler (R-Fla.) and fifty-two other members who introduced a resolution stating that Congress did not approve of sending American ground troops to Kosovo and that U.S. national security interests were not at stake in the region. Newly elected Speaker of the House Dennis Hastert (R-Ill.) also received considerable pressure from other House

GOP members at a House Republican Conference meeting to take up the issue of Kosovo.[25] In response to these pressures, Hastert agreed to allow floor debate on the issue. Hastert's decision represented a new direction in leadership on war powers. In the Somalian, Haitian, and Bosnian operations, congressional leaders during the Clinton administration had generally avoided voting on war powers questions prior to operations, or prevented such votes from coming to the Senate or House floor. In this sense, Hastert's move was unlike his predecessors. However, the GOP leadership's interest asserting its constitutional powers is much more dubious than it seems prima facie.

When the debate over Kosovo came to the House floor on March 11, 1999, many members stated their concern over Congress's war powers. President Clinton suggested that House actions were "premature," and Secretary of State Madeline Albright strongly encouraged the Congress not to vote on these issues during diplomatic negotiations. However, Hastert went ahead, and Congress approved of American participation in a four-thousand-person peacekeeping force, by a vote of 219–191.[26] Prior to the vote, the Speaker indicated that he would not stand in the administration's way and that he supported the House resolution. Hastert endorsed the president before the debate even began. Hastert's resolution was also offered by House International Relations Chairman, Benjamin Gilman (R-N.Y.),[27] which provides another indication that senior GOP leaders were backing the president, and thus had not intended to stand in the president's way. By bringing the measure to the floor, Hastert kept the rank and file content and averted GOP criticism of his leadership had he not moved forward with the issue.

In contrast, the Democrats, who have traditionally been stronger supporters of congressional war powers and the WPR than the GOP, fought to prevent this resolution from coming to the floor. House Minority Whip David Bonior (D-Mich.), ranking minority member of the House International Relations Committee Sam Gejdenson (D-Conn.), and other senior Democrats argued that this was not the time to discuss Clinton's policy toward Milosevic, as negotiations at Rambouillet were still in progress.[28] Once again the Democrats tried to protect their president from GOP efforts and attempted to push aside Congress's constitutional powers in the process.

Another telling vote on the House's position came with Congresswoman Fowler's resolution, which required congressional authorization before the deployment of any NATO ground troops. Her resolution was defeated, and the "no" vote granted great discretion to the president. Fowler's resolution failed in part because of the GOP leadership's opposition. Congressman Gilman and House Judiciary Chair Henry Hyde (R-Ill.) both argued that it was best not to place any limitations on NATO or the president in this operation.[29]

In sum, as the United States moved closer to using force against Milosevic, the House granted extraordinary military discretion to the president. The House avoided the question of whether the president had authority to use force. The Clinton administration made perfectly clear that force would be used against Milosevic if he did not comply with the Rambouillet agreement, yet the House chose not to deal with this issue. Hastert's leadership represented some change in congressional norms in that the House clearly signaled its support for a peace-keeping force in Kosovo. However, Hastert also chose to endorse the president and distanced the House from use-of-force questions. Hastert or Gilman could have brought the war powers question forward and undoubtedly would have received support from the small coalition of House members that Congressman Campbell had built. Campbell and others would have risen on the House floor to support the Speaker had he chosen this course of action. However, Campbell's coalition was small and consisted mostly of junior members of the House. A specific vote on war powers would have placed members on record either for or against military action and established shared responsibility. Hastert and the GOP leadership determined that such a vote was not in the GOP's best interest. Congress, with the support of its senior leadership, again dodged the more profound questions on Congress's war powers and the president's authority to use force in a NATO military action.

Domestic Politics and Strategic Diplomacy: Striking Milosevic

In his previous uses of force, Clinton generally did not reach out to Congress for its support and never for its formal authorization. One notable exception already examined is Clinton's consultation with GOP leaders prior to the strikes against Usama Bin Laden. Clinton never admitted that he needed congressional authorization to strike Bin Laden, but he did deal with GOP leaders in a noticeably different manner, partly because of his domestic political crisis. In Somalia, Haiti, and Bosnia, Clinton followed the presidential practice established since World War II and did not ask for Congress's advance approval. In contrast, in 1999, after Clinton's impeachment proceedings ended, the president reached out to members of Congress. Constitutionally, the president's position remained consistent with that of other recent presidents: congressional authorization was not necessary. Clinton Press Secretary Joe Lockhart stated that a vote was not "constitutionally necessary" in order for Clinton to use force.[30] However, the events that followed suggest that Clinton also recognized that the political mood of Congress after the impeachment activities demanded a new level of dialogue. Thus the president met with congressional leaders and lobbied individual members before the strikes took place.

Only one month before the strikes in Kosovo, Clinton had survived the most important political test of his life. The Senate acquitted him of two impeachment charges brought forth by the House of Representatives. Although Clinton weathered the political storm and the Senate's judgement, Congress, especially many GOP members, harbored a deep distrust of the president. As is demonstrated in the following chapter, when Clinton used force against Saddam Hussein in Operation Desert Fox during the first days of the House floor impeachment proceedings in December 1998, some Congressmen questioned the legitimacy and necessity of using force. Some of the president's critics, including GOP congressional leaders, were quite personal in their challenges to the president.[31] Another bombing campaign only a month after the impeachment proceedings—without some degree of congressional consultation—probably would have introduced considerable political risks for the president, particularly since the use of force would be against a sovereign state that ostensibly had considerable air defenses. Due to these dynamics, the president had strong domestic political incentives to work with Congress prior to the strikes.

In terms of U.S. foreign policy and the diplomatic issues at stake, Clinton and NATO had threatened Slobodan Milosevic with the use of force on many occasions in the past. As demonstrated throughout the Clinton presidency, U.S. foreign policy usually included a series of diplomatic threats before an actual use of force. This pattern was witnessed prior to the American military intervention in Haiti and before NATO's air strikes in Bosnia in 1994 and early 1995. When Clinton used force, he did so with much initial hesitance. Prior to the strikes in Kosovo, it is conceivable that Clinton saw Congress as another diplomatic tool to use against Milosevic before resorting to force. If the president could gain some degree of Congressional support for the strikes, it would provide another demonstration of the United States' resolve and would send another signal to Milosevic to rethink his opposition to the Rambouillet demands.

Beginning on March 19, six days before the attacks began, Clinton began meeting with small groups of members of Congress in order to make his case for the use of force. Upon the president's invitation a number of members met with the president to discuss the likelihood of NATO's forthcoming air strikes. These meetings continued through March 24, only hours before NATO Secretary General Javier Solana announced publicly that NATO bombings on Milosevic were about to begin.[32] This is not to say that Clinton truly "consulted" with Congress in such a way that Congress felt it had the opportunity to change Clinton's mind and force a policy reversal. However, Clinton did notify Congress days in advance of his intent to use force. If Congress wanted to prevent the operation from going forward, it had plenty of time to react. While Congress's meetings with the White House may not have been perceived as open consultations in which all policy options were available, the timing of the meetings certainly provided Congress an opportunity to raise constitutional concerns well in advance of the air strikes. Clinton's effort to dialogue with Congress seems wise when one considers the very partisan mood in Congress at the time.

Because of Clinton's domestic political circumstances and the diplomatic advantages that Congress's backing might provide, Clinton requested Congress's support in advance. Clinton stated in a letter to congressional leaders that "without regard to our differing views on the Constitution about the use of force, I ask for your legislative support as we address the crisis in Kosovo."[33] Thus, while not relinquishing his own perceived powers as commander in chief, Clinton still asked Congress for its support.

To some degree, Clinton's strategy involved fewer risks than might be expected, especially when one considers the Senate's political demeanor at the time. As a body the Senate had shown much less interest in asserting its constitutional powers than the House. War powers advocates such as Senator Joe Biden (D-Del.) also had not raised constitutional queries with the president over the use of force in Kosovo. In fact, Biden had been actively calling for military strikes for a number of months. Biden also had the support of a number of moderate and well-respected Republican senators, including Senators John Warner (R-Va.), Chuck Hagel (R-Nebr.), Richard Lugar (R-Ind.), and John McCain (R-Ariz.).[34] During the impeachment hearings, the Senate was also more restrained and less vehement in its judgement of the president. Five GOP senators voted against impeachment, and five others in the GOP split their votes on the House's two articles of impeachment.[35] Thus the Senate represented a more politically moderate body than the House and was more willing to support air strikes and less likely to challenge the president's perceived authority as commander in chief. Moreover, if Clinton gained formal approval from at least one congressional chamber, he could make the *political* (though not constitutional) claim that he had Congress's approval.

Clinton's efforts to dialogue with Congress proved successful. On March 23, in a bipartisan resolution cosponsored by Biden and Warner, Clinton gained the Senate's support in a 58–41 vote on a resolution stating "That the President of the United States is authorized to conduct military operations and missile strikes against the Federal Republic of Yugoslavia."[36] Forty-two Democrats joined with sixteen Republicans to give Clinton the authorization he sought.

Clinton's victory placed the House in a difficult situation: if it voted against the president, it also would be voting against the Senate and a number of senior GOP senators. The GOP House leadership was now in a precarious position. Even though the presidency was in a weakened state after impeachment, the House was as well. In the 1998 Congressional midterms, the House Republicans lost five seats to the Democrats, which was largely attributed to the Republicans' vehemence in their pursuit of Clinton's impeachment in the House. If Speaker Hastert had opened the House floor to a constitutional debate over Clinton's authority to use force in a NATO action, he incurred the real possibility that Congressman Campbell and his colleagues could garner enough votes to create a constitutional crisis in which the president and the Senate both supported a use of force that the House opposed. Such a vote would risk making the House appear to be an angry and vengeful body, still vindictive over its inability to remove the president from office. Thus, rather than deliberating on the constitutional issues at stake, the House responded on March 24 by passing a nonbinding resolution that was supportive of the troops that would be engaged in the air strikes to come but took no constitutional position on Clinton's authority to act. Deference remained the norm for the House, but the partisan advantages in *not* voting help to explain the war powers interplay in this instance.

When Clinton addressed the nation on the air strikes on March 24, he made no mention of his constitutional powers to use force.[37] His constitutional justification came in a March 26, 1999, letter to Congress's leaders: "I have taken these actions pursuant to my constitutional authority to conduct U.S. foreign relations and as Commander in Chief and Chief Executive." In an appeal to international law, Clinton also noted that Yugoslavia had violated UN Security Council Resolutions and the United Nations Charter.[38] However, regardless of whether Yugoslavia had broken international law, no UN Security Council Resolution existed that specifically authorized a military enforcement action. Nonetheless, throughout the air strikes Clinton's legal justification remained the same, as was later echoed in additional letters to Congress.[39]

The war powers interplay in late March 1999 demonstrates that domestic political conditions and foreign policy strategies can lead a president to turn to Congress for its support. The acerbic nature of Congress after the impeachment acquittal presented real political incentives for Clinton to seek congressional support before the strikes. This political environment, however, also created additional incentives for the House *not* to vote on Clinton's request for authorization. Moreover, Clinton's diplomatic approach and general hesitance to use force made it a politically useful strategy to gain at least the Senate's approval. Thus the war powers interplay in this case entailed a complex interplay of many variables, involving both domestic and international political strategies and pressures.

Campbell's Invocation
of the War Powers Resolution

As the bombings proceeded, most members of Congress expressed their positions on the strikes. As the strikes continued, some House members again expressed their concerns about the constitutionality of the strikes and the relevance of the WPR. Approximately three weeks into the bombing campaign, on April, 12, 1999, Congressman Campbell introduced two resolutions. The first called for the president to withdraw all troops from the conflict. The second asked for a declaration of war. Campbell hoped that both of these resolutions would fail, which would then, in his view, force the president to gain congressional authorization for further military action in Kosovo. Campbell maintained that without a declaration of war the president was subject to the WPR's requirement that he gain congressional approval within sixty days of the deployment. Campbell viewed these efforts as a means to exhaust all legislative opportunities to challenge the president. In *Dellums v. Bush*, a case involving thirty-eight members of Congress in 1991 who felt that George Bush violated the Constitution during Operation Desert Storm, a district court ruled that the case was not "ripe," because all legislative options involving war powers had not been exercised. In 1990 and 1991, Congress never voted on a declaration of war with Iraq, and thus the court ruled that Congress still had legislative tools to use. Campbell's efforts were intended in part to address this point in any later judicial test that might arise dealing with Kosovo.[40] His resolutions were sent to the House International Relations Committee for consideration.[41]

On April 21, 1999, at the first meeting of the House International Relations Committee since Campbell's resolutions were offered, issues of war powers were openly debated. Appearing on behalf of the administration, Secretary of State Madeleine Albright provided much insight into the administration's position when she noted that the United States was "not at war with Yugoslavia or its people."[42] Despite the daily air strikes on Yugoslavia, an admission by Albright that the United States was at war would have placed the administration in violation of the Constitution, and at minimum, would have triggered the WPR. Congressman Jim Leach (R-Iowa) followed by stating that the administration must consider the constitutionality of its policy and the requirements of the WPR. In response, Albright noted specifically that the

White House had complied with Section 3 of the WPR and had "consulted" with Congress. Referring specifically to Section 4 of the WPR, the reporting clause, she also maintained that the administration was in full compliance.

One of the most interesting exchanges at the hearing came when Congressman Campbell, who chose his words carefully, asked Albright if the United States was experiencing "hostilities" in Yugoslavia. Albright answered by arguing that the administration had consulted with Congress and had no intention of taking Congress out of the decision-making process. However, she stated, "We do not believe in a war powers resolution," but she admitted, "there is a conflict going on." She refused to deal specifically with Campbell's question. In her view, "The President has, we believe, the constitutional authority to do what he is doing."[43] In other words, Albright saw Congress's authority as limited and the president's actions as beyond Congress's legislative control. At the same time, Albright was well versed on all aspects of the WPR's requirements, demonstrating that she was prepared to deal with such questions, and could provide her own broad translation of the resolution.

In the aftermath of the hearings, Campbell's resolution had still not been addressed in either committee or on the House floor. In a clear example of Congress's abdication of its war powers, House leaders from both parties worked to avoid a vote on Campbell's resolutions.[44] House International Relations Committee Chairman Benjamin Gilman pushed backed consideration of Campbell's resolutions in Committee from April 22 to April 27. House Minority Leader Richard Gephardt (D-Mo.) also viewed Campbell's efforts as inappropriate for consideration: "I'm not ready to make a judgement and I don't think Congress should make a judgement. . . . We don't have a plan, we don't have a recommendation, we don't have the thinking behind a plan. It's all premature."[45] This argument echoes the partisan protection of the president that the Democrats had consistently advanced during the Clinton presidency. The Democrats appeared to feel that nearly *any*time—except in the wake of the American casualties in Somalia—was the wrong time to deal with war powers questions.

When Campbell's resolutions made it to the House floor on April 28, 1999, the House leadership again moved to stifle debate. On the eve of the floor debate, the House Rules Committee implemented a rule on Campbell's resolutions, preventing any member of Congress from invoking the WPR again during the 106th Congress.[46] This rule would have defeated the intent of the WPR, which empowers any member of Congress to check the president during times of war. Campbell and other members of both parties had addressed this rule in their opening floor remarks. Many noted its undemocratic nature and their strong opposition to the rule.[47] In response, this rule was withdrawn by House Rules Committee Chair David Dreier (R-Calif.), who argued that the rule had only been implemented because of Democratic pressure in the committee.[48] Whatever the reasons for the rule, the GOP initially allowed it to go forward, demonstrating their ultimate interest in limiting further discussions of war powers. Although he quickly bowed to the bipartisan pressure by recognizing the undemocratic nature of the rule, Dreier was reflective of the House leadership, who preferred not to deal with the WPR, or at least not to allow it to come to the House floor again during the 106th Congress. A chairman committed to protecting Congress's war powers could have prevented this rule from ever coming to the House floor.

Besides the two resolutions offered by Campbell, the House also included resolutions proposed by Tilly Fowler and William Goodling (R-Pa.) and from the ranking minority member of the House International Relations Committee, Sam Gejdenson (D-Conn.). The Fowler-Goodling resolution stated that before the president deployed ground forces in Yugoslavia, congressional authorization would be required in advance. This resolution was the only one of these four that passed. Gejdenson's resolution was introduced only after it was clear that the other resolutions were going to make it to the House floor, and thus the Democrats wanted to put forward one proposal of their own calling for congressional endorsement of the bombings. This vote resulted in a tie, and thus its defeat. Likewise, both of Campbell's resolutions failed. The House refused to vote for a cessation of the bombings but also refused to declare war or to endorse the bombings. Thus the House sought no formal linkage through legislative means to Clinton's bombings in Kosovo.

What is first notable in examining the floor debates of these resolutions is the large number of House Democrats who felt it inappropriate to be considering such resolutions that dealt with congressional war powers. As a caucus, the Democrats and their leadership were only in favor of Congressman Gejdenson's resolution to authorize air strikes. Otherwise, many Democrats expressed their concerns about limiting the powers of the commander in chief. For example, House Minority Whip, David Bonior (D-Mich.) noted, "There are some in Congress who seek to entangle us in legalisms, to micro manage military strategy, and to force us into false choices . . . this amendment ties the hands of our military commanders."[49] Ken Bentsen (D-Tex.) asserted, "The Campbell resolutions . . . are premature and misguided."[50] Eliot Engel (D-N.Y.) asked, "Why would we want to make it difficult for the President to be Commander in Chief? Why would we want to tie the hands of the President?"[51] House Minority Leader Richard Gephardt also felt that Campbell's votes would send the wrong message to Slobodan Milosevic.[52] In short, the Democrats felt that Congress should not even have been voting on the measures.

A few Republicans expressed similar thoughts, advocating a nearly imperial president. Perhaps the most impressive display of modern-day monarchism came from Congressman Peter King (R-N.Y.), who asserted, "The position of the Republican Party has been to support the constitutional right of the Commander in Chief to deploy ground troops. That is why the overwhelming majority of Republicans oppose the War Powers Act."[53] These misunderstandings or denials of Congress's own legitimate war powers are rather astounding, but not surprising considering Congress's historic deference. The House did not want to entangle itself in constitutional questions, and many members, for either partisan or other reasons, did not want the president to be checked by the Congress as the founding fathers intended. For the House, it was easier to let the president assume all responsibility for the military operation. GOP leaders were key in defeating the "constitutionally assertive" measures brought forth by Congressman Campbell. The House did take a stand on NATO ground troops but again avoided the question of whether Clinton and NATO had the authority to bomb Kosovo.

CONCLUSION

Although the political foundation for an assertion of congressional war powers seemed to exist before the bombings in Yugoslavia, in the end Congress again deferred to the White House. However, the congressional-executive interplay over Kosovo was shaped considerably by the many domestic political variables present at the time. These political conditions provided incentives for Clinton to consult with Congress in a manner that was uncharacteristic of presidential practices in the past.

Congress's Deference

As witnessed in earlier chapters, the political dynamics in the House and Senate provide different explanations for each chambers' behavior. From an institutional perspective, Congress deferred to the president during the summer of 1998 with few members raising constitutional concerns about the Clinton administration's assertion of American military power. Again in October 1998, Congress raised few constitutional questions when NATO authorized the use of force. Yet when political conditions changed for the president in 1999, the House and Senate approached Kosovo differently.

In the House, key decisions made by the GOP leadership help explain the politics of war powers. Speaker of the House Dennis Hastert provided a minor check on the president by allowing the House to vote on a NATO peacekeeping operation but avoided the more crucial issue of whether NATO had authority to conduct air strikes on Yugoslavia. American history is clear on the point that Congress protected its war powers upon joining NATO, yet this history meant little to the sitting House leadership. Had the Speaker allowed a real war powers vote, he ran the risk of it passing. Since the House had already taken a political beating in the 1998 elections for pursuing Clinton's impeachment so vigorously, another vote against the president during a foreign policy crisis (and likely genocide in the Balkans) risked the appearance that the House was a highly partisan, even vindictive body. The House Rules Committee and its chairman allowed proposals to go forward that sought to prevent the future invocation of the War Powers Resolution during the 106th Congress. House International Relations Chairman Benjamin Gilman (R-N.Y.) also averted the influence and relevance of Congressman Thomas Campbell's efforts to exercise Congress's constitutional powers both in committee and on the House floor. Gilman acted similarly when Campbell sought to test the WPR in 1998 over the American deployment in Bosnia. Had Congressman Campbell's war powers assertions been supported by House leaders, a constitutional battle over war powers quite likely would have ensued, yet House leaders never let Campbell's efforts go that far.

As in Somalia, Haiti, and Bosnia, the presence of strong partisanship is again witnessed in this war powers interplay. House Democrats fought to prevent any constitutional question of war powers at every stage of the crisis with Milosevic. According to the Democrats, the "timing" was never right for such questions, as they protected the Democrat in the White House at every stage of the conflict.

In the Senate, the presence of a number of moderate Republicans with strong foreign policy credentials, coupled with Democrats who wanted to use force, made this body more openly receptive to Clinton's military endeavors through NATO. The willingness of sixteen Republicans to use force explains why a resolution was able to pass the Senate. However, the resolution supported the use of air power in Yugoslavia, and Clinton was careful at this stage in arguing that ground troops were not an option. Had ground troops been openly considered in Clinton's plans, Congress would probably have taken a stronger stand against the president. It will never be known how Congress would have acted with the policy option of ground troops, but considering its past behavior during the Clinton presidency, especially with regard to Haiti and Bosnia, it also seems possible that Congress would have again deferred to Clinton.

In sum, an institutional analysis of Congress alone, absent an understanding of the domestic political dynamics, misses key aspects of the war powers interplay. An examination of Congress's leaders and the domestic political conditions surrounding the war powers interplay provides a more comprehensive understanding of why the House deferred and why the Senate voted to support NATO air strikes. At the same time, this episode demonstrated that many members of Congress misunderstand, avoid, or do not recognize their constitutional role of checking the president. Most members seem to have little awareness of or interest in the agreements made in negotiating the North Atlantic Treaty or the "constitutional process" that was promised by Secretary of State Dean Acheson at that time. With the exception of Congressman Campbell and his small faction of war powers advocates, Acheson's promises had almost no bearing on the debates surrounding NATO's use of force. To hear some members of Congress argue that Congress should not get in the president's way demonstrates how far the pendulum has swung toward the president. Some members of Congress honestly appear to feel that it is not their place to challenge the president in military decisions, in spite of the unmistakable history surrounding the Constitution and America's entry into NATO in 1949.

Clinton's Domestic and Strategic Considerations

As members of Congress failed to exercise their constitutional powers, the Clinton administration made sweeping claims of the president's constitutional military authority. Secretary of State Madeline Albright and Undersecretary of State Thomas Pickering were especially assertive in their constitutional claims, leaving virtually no room for Congress's legislative authority to prevent the president from acting militarily. These attitudes, both in Congress and the White House, reflect a profound disregard for the notion of checks and balances that was such a central principle in the creation of the Constitution.

Although the formal position taken by the Clinton administration does not square with constitutional history, in practice, the level of consultation between Clinton and Congress in the days preceding NATO's bombings was greater than in some past uses of force during the Clinton presidency. Clinton saw diplomatic reasons and personal incentives for reaching out to Congress in advance for its support. The strategic value of increasing the threat against Milosevic by garnering Congress's support created another incentive for gaining congressional authorization.

Although Clinton formally made unconstitutional claims as commander in chief, he did consult with Congress in advance. In this regard, the president complied with the consultation requirement of the WPR. One can only speculate what the president would have done had the House or Senate chosen not to support him. Regarding other aspects of the WPR, the administration fought any legislative attempts to limit its perceived military authority in Kosovo after the bombings began. Secretary of State Albright was especially well briefed on the WPR's language, as illustrated by her unwillingness to acknowledge whether the United States was engaged in "hostilities." Since Clinton never gained Congress's formal approval after the sixty-day time limit, the administration also was in violation of the WPR's approval requirements. Moreover, Clinton was also not "repelling a sudden attack" upon the United States, and in this sense, was in violation of the Constitution for not gaining Congress's authorization in advance.

At the same time, Clinton's policy toward Milosevic was clear from June 1998. NATO authorized the use of force in October 1998 and again in January 1999. Clinton also met with members of Congress days before the strikes, and specifically requested Congress's support before the strikes commenced. Congress had ample time to assert its war powers before the United States initiated military action. The House in particular did not exercise its congressional war powers through its own fault.

Clinton's willingness to consult with Congress is unlikely to serve as a model for future consultation. As in the case with Usama Bin Laden, the domestic political dynamics that characterized this interplay—a weakened postimpeachment president with strong diplomatic incentives to use Congress as a diplomatic tool against Milosevic—are unlikely to be repeated. Different domestic political circumstances resulted in a much different war powers interplay in Clinton's military strikes on Iraq.

7 Iraq

An ongoing security concern during President Clinton's two terms in office was Iraqi leader Saddam Hussein. Clinton inherited a strategic challenge in Iraq that in many respects plagued his administration for eight years. For various reasons, the United States used military force against Hussein in 1993, 1996, 1998, 1999, and 2000. In his many strikes against Saddam Hussein, Clinton appealed to United Nations Security Council Resolutions or "UN norms" to justify his military conduct. Unlike the Somalian, Haitian, and Bosnian operations, for which there was no doubt that Chapter 7 authorization existed, the strikes on Iraq were carried out by the Clinton administration with questionable international legal authority. The international legal issues at stake in this chapter are significantly different from those in the preceding cases examined.

The war powers interplay between the Clinton administration and Congress regarding Iraq covers a broader time period than the cases discussed previously, and events cannot easily be discussed in simple chronological order. Yet even though these strikes occurred over both of Clinton's terms and at different stages of the Clinton presidency, the pattern of congressional deference and presidential unilateralism with regard to Iraq, and the reasons for that pattern, are similar at all stages. As was the case with Usama Bin Laden, the public's widespread belief that Saddam Hussein represented a national security threat to the United States allowed the president great leeway when employing military force against Iraq.

U.S. Foreign Policy and Iraq

For the past fifty years, the United States' relationship with Iraq has wavered considerably. In the 1950s, the United States had excellent relations with Iraqi leader King Faisal II. Under Faisal II, Iraq was a founding member of the Arab League, which enjoyed strong support from the United States. Analysts contend that during this time, Iraq was "one of the closest allies the United States had in the Arab world."[1] However, this diplomatic cordiality ended in 1958, when the king was ousted in a coup d'etat and killed during an attempted escape. The United States immediately expressed its disapproval. Tensions escalated when the United States supported Great Britain in granting Kuwait its independence in 1961. Iraq opposed the move, viewing Kuwait as part of its own territory. In response, the new Iraqi leader, Abd al-Karim Qassim, moved troops toward the Kuwaiti border. Clashes were avoided when the forces were recalled—perhaps because of Great Britain's ground troop deployment and the Arab League's opposition to Iraq's move. Tensions heightened again in 1967 when the United States supported Israel in its war with Egypt. This time, Iraq formally cut diplomatic ties with the United States. For the next four American presidents, relations only worsened as Iraq capitalized on cold war politics by turning to the Soviet Union for diplomatic and military support.

The eventual policy reversal in American-Iraqi relations that came in 1982 can largely be explained by the United States' relationship with Iran. With assistance from the American Central Intelligence Agency, Shah Mohammed Reza Pahlevi came to power in Iran in 1953. Iran's good relations with the United States remained until the Shah was ousted by the Islamic revolutionary leader Ayatollah Khomeini and his student supporters. In the process, Khomeini took 57 Americans captive and held them hostage for 444 days in the U.S. embassy in Tehran. During his rule, Khomeini referred to the United States as the "Great Satan," and he continued with his vehement denunciations of the United States until his death in 1989. Because of the damaged relations with Iran and the remaining threat to regional stability posed by Khomeini, the Reagan administration reached out to Iraq. Iran and Iraq had gone to war in 1980, soon after Khomeini assumed power. The war provided the United States a new opportunity to place further pressure on Iran and potentially destabilize Khomeini's rule. Thus, on February 26, 1982, one year into the Reagan presidency, Iraq was removed from the United States' list of states who sponsored terrorism, and the United States began to cultivate a new relationship with Iraqi president Saddam Hussein.[2]

Saddam Hussein began his foray into politics began as a twenty-two-year-old "hit man" for the Baath Party in Iraq. The Baathists were essentially power hungry Arab nationalists who also espoused a moderate form of socialism. In 1959, Hussein and other Baathists orchestrated an assassination attempt on President Qassim. The attempt failed, forcing Hussein into exile in Syria and then Egypt. Hussein returned in 1963 after his Baath colleagues succeeded in overthrowing the government. Hussein, who skillfully forged political allies during his exile, rose to prominence upon his return to Iraq when he became the deputy chairman of the Revolutionary Command Council and Iraq's head of internal security in 1968, only one step below the presidency. Hussein retained this position until 1979, when his cousin, Iraqi president Ahmed Hassan al-Bakr, anointed Hussein as his replacement, but not without some controversy. One of Hussein's first steps as president was to purge all those who expressed any opposition to Bakr's decision.[3]

As Iraq's new leader, Hussein spoke of a new pan-Arabism and expressed his strong opposition to the Israeli occupation of Palestinian lands. He also supported Islamic fundamentalist and terrorist groups. However, because the United States so desperately sought a different regime in Iran, the Reagan administration looked past Hussein's diplomatic affronts. The Reagan administration courted Iraq by guaranteeing Hussein $400 million in trade credits from the U.S. Agriculture Department Commodity Credit Corporation. These credits increased to $513 million the following year. By 1984, when the United States restored full diplomatic relations with Iraq, the Reagan administration allowed the sale of commercial trucks and military helicopters to Iraq and supported the transfer of "dual use" technology, which directly impacted Iraq's missile capabilities. Other evidence indicates that as Iraq's war with Iran progressed, the United States waged a quiet diplomatic effort among its closest allies, including France and Italy, to encourage direct arms shipments to Iraq. The Reagan administration also provided Iraq with military intelligence from American satellites to assist them in their war efforts.[4]

While the military cooperation between Hussein and the Reagan administration grew, problems developed that threatened these good relations. U.S. intelligence indicated that Hussein had used chemical weapons against Iran. Hussein also continued to espouse anti-Western rhetoric, which often was directed at the United States for its support

of Israel. Although some differences existed within the Reagan administration over the most appropriate policy toward Iraq, Hussein's of-
fenses were not egregious enough to force a fundamental policy shift
throughout the rest of Reagan's presidency.[5]

When George Bush became president, initially there were similar
efforts to befriend Hussein. Under National Security Directive (NSD)
26, the Bush administration's goal was to "normalize relations with
Iraq." NSD 26 viewed Iraq as a source of regional stability against the
Soviet Union, and the United States also saw economic opportunities
with Iraq. In short, the Bush administration wanted to provide Iraq financial and diplomatic incentives to move closer toward the United
States. Secretary of State James Baker was one of the most vocal advocates of this plan, which included $1 billion in economic assistance. NSD
26, however, became sidetracked when evidence surfaced indicating
that Iraq was involved in a major banking scandal in which past American credits were allegedly being used to purchase military hardware
and materials needed for the development of weapons of mass destruction. The State Department's annual report on human rights also criticized Iraq for its considerable human rights violations. Moreover, intelligence indicated that Iraqi missile capabilities were being tested and
improved. A partial payment of the economic assistance plan went
to Iraq; however, these events, coupled with additional inflamma-
tory rhetoric aimed at the United States and Israel, raised further
doubts in Congress and Bush administration officials about the wisdom of NSD 26.[6]

Diplomatic tensions culminated on August 2, 1990, when Hussein,
making claims of historical injustices regarding territorial border dis-
putes, invaded Kuwait. At the time, Kuwait was also exceeding its
OPEC export quotas by 100 percent, and was very weak militarily, making it an attractive economic and military target for Hussein. In response, President Bush and a coalition of member states from the United
Nations began a military buildup in the region, eventually reaching
approximately 540,000 troops. Operation Desert Storm, which was authorized by United Nations Security Council Resolution 678, ensued
on January 17, 1991. Prior to the use of force, Congress held extensive
debates over constitutional war powers. This debate can partially be
explained by partisan politics; most Democrats supported the continued implementation of economic sanctions that were imposed on Iraq

after the invasion, while Republicans fell solidly in line behind President Bush and the United Nations. On January 12, 1991, Congress voted to endorse United Nations Security Council Resolution 678, which authorized the use of force against Iraq in order to enforce demands for its evacuation from Kuwait. Congress did not, however, vote to declare war.[7] The international coalition assembled through President Bush's efforts resulted in a victory for the United States and its allies. The policy choices made in the war's aftermath established an important foundation for the Clinton administration in the war powers interplay that later ensued.

INHERITING SADDAM HUSSEIN

Upon leaving the White House, President Bush left Bill Clinton with a damaged yet contained Iraqi leader. During his presidential campaign, Clinton, like George Bush, was critical of Hussein for his numerous human rights violations. At one point, Clinton escalated his criticism against Bush's Iraq policy by stating that the Bush administration had "appeased" Hussein prior to the war and that "democratic principles" were not being upheld through Bush's policy after the war.[8] American fighters were also involved in a series of quick strikes on Iraq in the days immediately prior to Clinton's inauguration. Consequently, when the new president entered the Oval Office in 1993, American-Iraqi relations were far from amiable. However, besides inheriting the problem of Hussein, Clinton was bequeathed a set of policies designed to limit Hussein's influence in the region. These policies are crucial to understanding the more recent war powers interplay.

The Legal Foundations

It is first worth recalling that George Bush argued prior to the Persian Gulf War that he did not need Congressional authorization to use force against Saddam Hussein. Bush argued that authority had already been granted to him by United Nations Security Council Resolution 678, which allowed member states of the United Nations to use "all necessary means" to expel Hussein from Kuwait.[9] Many members of Congress did not accept Bush's constitutional claims and, in the days immediately prior to the use of force, Congress engaged in a constitutional debate on the president's authority to use force against Hussein. In the end, Congress passed Public Law 102-1, which granted the president the authority to use force on Iraq as specified in UN Security Council Resolution 678.[10] At the time, ostensibly, the understanding accepted by most members of Congress was that Resolution 678 granted the president the power to remove Hussein from Kuwait. Bush responded to Congress's efforts by arguing that while he welcomed its support, he still asserted the broad authority to use force without congressional approval.[11]

Once the war ended, the UN Security Council negotiated Resolution 687 with Iraq, which gave the UN Special Commission (UNSCOM) complete access in Iraq to search for weapons of mass destruction. The UN Security Council also passed Resolution 688, which condemned Iraq's actions against its Kurdish population and authorized relief organizations to enter the country to provide humanitarian aid. Coupled with this authorization, the United States conducted Operation Provide Comfort, which provided military support and humanitarian aid to the Kurds who were under attack from Hussein's Republican guards.[12] Moreover, the United States and other allies also established a no-fly zone over northern Iraq, which prohibited Iraqi air flights in these protected regions. Before Bush left office, an additional no-fly zone from the 33rd parallel to Iraq's southern border was created. Both no-fly zones were implemented without specific UN Security Council resolutions. Thus, Clinton inherited a host of decisions and policies imposed on Hussein.

1993: George Bush's Visit

It did not take long for newly inaugurated President Bill Clinton to clash with Hussein. After the election, former President Bush visited Kuwait in April 1993. Prior to his visit, an assassination plot against Bush in Kuwait had been uncovered. In the months that followed the attack, the CIA and FBI reported that Saddam Hussein's regime was to blame.[13] Once these intelligence reports had been deemed conclusive evidence of an Iraqi plot to kill Bush, Clinton responded on June 26, 1993, with a nighttime air raid of twenty-three precision guided missiles on Iraqi military posts. In his letter to Congress explaining his actions, Clinton justified the bombings by referring to Article 51 of the

UN Charter, which recognizes the right of self defense. He also made reference to his "constitutional authority with respect to the conduct of foreign relations and as commander in chief."[14] In a national address, Clinton spoke about U.S. national security interests at risk. He argued that Iraq had violated U.S. sovereignty and that the intent of the U.S. response was to send a clear message to Hussein and other terrorists that similar actions against the United States would not be tolerated.[15]

Congress said little about the attack. Congressman Ron Dellums (D-Calif.), who had previously failed to restrict American participation in Operation Desert Storm through legal means,[16] noted his concern with Clinton's decision: "This unilateral U.S. military action was initiated by the executive alone, and is further evidence of the absolute imperative to reestablish the proper balance between the Executive and Congress."[17] However, the vast majority in Congress supported Clinton's action. No one in either the Senate or House protested the bombings, nor were hearings held on the attacks. On the day of the strikes White House operators ostensibly tried to contact Dellums, yet no other evidence suggests that Clinton sought out other members to consult before the strikes.[18]

Why did Congress say nothing about the strikes? In part, the silence is attributable to the public's support for Clinton. Three days after the bombing, opinion polls found that 61 percent of the American public approved of Clinton's actions, and the president received an 11 point boost in his approval rating.[19] This attack, launched from two naval ships stationed in the Red Sea and the Arabian Gulf, also entailed minimal risks for American soldiers. Had the attack been on a more controversial target with greater risks to American soldiers, perhaps less leeway would have been given.

The leeway allowed to Clinton can also be explained through the nature of his target. In many ways, the congressional response mirrors the accepted practice of deference during the cold war. Like the perceived communist threats of the cold war, in Saddam Hussein the Clinton administration had a clearly defined enemy, widely accepted as such by the American public. Few members of Congress were willing to place constitutional process issues over perceived national security interests threats from such a clearly perceived enemy, especially since the Bush administration had warred with Hussein only two years earlier. Congress's political incentives for questioning the commander in chief about an operation with limited risk against Saddam Hussein were minimal, and such questioning could even be harmful to one's political career because of the popularity of the attacks. However, from a constitutional standpoint, the legality of the decision-making process raises serious concern.

Neither the Constitution nor the WPR speaks to the issue of a planned attack on a *former* U.S. president in a foreign country. The legal specifics for such situations are not well articulated. However, had an attack actually occurred and had it been immediately confirmed that Saddam Hussein was responsible, it seems reasonable to conclude that Clinton would have been authorized to respond militarily without congressional approval. Even though George Bush was the former president, as the previous chief executive he still represented an important symbol of the United States. Former President Bush was certainly divorced from official U.S. policy, but by virtue of his former position as the only nationally elected official of the United States, a former president still in many respects embodies and represents the United States. Thus if an attack occurred on a former American president, a military response from the current president seems justified by the Constitution. Yet the *planned* attack on Bush in 1993 never occurred, and no immediate threat to the United States existed. While a military response may have been appropriate to protect national security interests, such an action still demands congressional input. In retrospect, it was clear that members of Congress would have supported the president had they known of the attack in advance. However, constitutional process is different from questions of national security. Even when President Truman deployed American troops to Korea in 1950, Senator Robert Taft (R-Ohio) raised constitutional concerns over the president's actions, even though he was solidly behind the president's effort to combat communism in Asia.[20] In contrast, constitutional questions were completely avoided by Congress in 1993. Like Truman in 1950, President Clinton also assumed unilateral powers as commander in chief.

Other legal problems surround the absence of consultation prior to Clinton's attacks. The Clinton administration clearly had time to consult much more closely with members of Congress. The official meeting among top Clinton administration officials concerning the military response was held Friday, June 23, two days before the attacks. To enhance secrecy, Clinton officials entered through the White House residence rather than through a more visible entry in order to avoid detection by the press. However, this meeting included no members of Congress. The decision to use force was kept secret from Congress for the next forty-eight hours. During the June 23 meeting, some members of Congress tried to reach the president by phone to discuss the president's budget but were not allowed to speak with Clinton.[21] Clearly, Congress was not kept informed about this decision, even though there was ample time to consult with at least a few leading members of Congress. Clinton's unsuccessful effort to reach Congressman Dellums on the day of the strikes seems to have been more of an attempt at "notification" than an instance of "consultation." Even if Clinton had reached Dellums, it seems improbable that the president would have called off the strike had Dellums objected.

From an international legal viewpoint, Clinton's invocation of Article 51 and self-defense is also questionable. In the International Court of Justice's hearing of *Nicaragua v. United States* (1984), the United States claimed that by defending El Salvador from Nicaraguan attacks, the United States was acting in El Salvador's defense as well as its own "collective self-defense." The court ruled that the Reagan administration's self-defense claim did not apply. In the court's view, Nicaragua's actions did not constitute an "armed attack" on the United States, nor had Nicaragua's activities reached a level equivalent to an armed attack. The court also determined that since the United States had not informed the Security Council that it had been "attacked" by Nicaragua, Article 51 did not apply.[22] Whether a planned attack on a former president traveling in a foreign country justifies a state's claim of self-defense under international law is not clear. Yet a strict interpretation of Article 51 using the criteria set forth in *Nicaragua v. United States* raises considerable doubts about the Clinton administration's international legal claims. Nonetheless, this issue prompted no inquiry from Congress.

In sum, Clinton's actions in Iraq in 1993 were those of an imperial presidency, in which the chief executive unilaterally defined the United States' national security interests and justified his actions through a broad definition of presidential powers and international legal appeals. Even if members of Congress agree with an attack ordered by the president, they are not exempt from their war powers responsibilities. Congress could have raised constitutional questions over the lack of consultation, the unilateral decision, the questionable applicability of Article 51, and the lack of compliance with the War Powers Resolution. But the risk to U.S. troops was low, no American casualties were suffered, and the public widely agreed that the attacks were appropriate. Under these conditions Congress sought no functional war powers role.

1996: Protecting the Kurds

For the next three years relations between the United States and Iraq remained generally calm. One exception occurred in 1994, when Iraq moved troops toward the Kuwaiti border, provoking an immediate response and deployment from the United States.[23] This short-term crisis was quickly resolved after Hussein withdrew his troops, and relations seemed to remain stable until September 1996.

Throughout his first term, Clinton provided assistance to a number of Kurdish resistance groups. In doing so, the United States was supporting an internal challenge to the Iraqi regime and sought to build a deterrent to a potential Iranian military intervention into northern Iraq. However, the Kurds do not represent a single entity and historically have not been politically well organized. During its first term, the Clinton administration intervened diplomatically a number of times to negotiate differences between the often uncooperative factions. Tensions peaked in 1996 when one faction, the Patriotic Union of Kurdistan (PUK) accepted arms from Iran. In response, the Kurdistan Democratic Party appealed to Hussein for military support and protection. Hussein then moved toward the PUK's headquarters in the northern Iraqi city of Irbil and waged a fierce battle to crush the opposition.[24] Clinton responded on September 3 and 4, 1996, by firing forty-four cruise missiles on military outposts in southern Iraq. He justified his missile strikes by noting, "When you abuse your own people or threaten your neighbors, you must pay a price."[25] In another address, he stated that Hussein's actions had "threatened the stability of the entire region for some years now."[26] On September 4, Clinton added that Hussein had stepped "over the line that the United Nations resolutions imposed."[27]

Congress strongly backed the attacks. One of Clinton's strongest supporters, Senate Minority Leader Tom Daschle (D-S.D.) argued that UN Security Council Resolution 688 authorized Clinton to conduct the strikes and that President Clinton had sent a powerful message to

Hussein that he could not use his military to violate widely recognized human rights.[28] There was some hesitance to explicitly commend the President for his actions, but in a 96–1 vote the Senate passed a resolution "commending the U.S. armed forces for their successful attack."[29] The House took no formal action, but there, too, support for striking Iraq was high. However, constitutional responsibilities were neglected again by both the Congress and the president with regard to these strikes.

One of the first legal questions regarding these attacks concerns Clinton's appeal to United Nations' authorization. Presumably, Clinton, like Senator Biden, was referring to 1991 UN Security Council Resolution 688, which authorized member states to use all necessary means to protect the Kurds in 1991.[30] However, the United States stood alone with Great Britain in appealing to United Nations authorization. Other permanent members of the Security Council, including China, France, Russia, argued that diplomacy would have been the better approach and that there was no authorization for the United States to act.[31] Moreover, Resolution 688 had been passed five years earlier, prior to the United States' support for opposition rebel groups, and when relations between Iraq and the United States were fundamentally different. Resolution 688 did not authorize the United States to use force whenever its national security interests were challenged by Hussein.

Clinton also used force without consulting or even notifying members of Congress prior to the attack, just as he did in his 1993 air strikes on Hussein. In this case, neither Republicans, Democrats, nor senior ranking members in Congress were notified prior to the strikes.[32] Senate Majority Leader Trent Lott (R-Miss.) expressed concern over this violation of the WPR,[33] as did Senators John McCain (R-Ariz.) and John Kyl (R-Ariz.).[34] Yet in the aftermath of the strikes, neither Lott nor other leaders pursued this constitutional question. Members quickly expressed their constitutional concerns and moved on to other issues. As was the case for the 1993 air strikes, Congress's deference to the president in this instance can be explained in part by public opinion. Less than a week after the strikes, a national public opinion poll found that 58 percent of Americans approved of the way Clinton was handling Iraq, while only 31 percent disapproved. Among those that were more likely to vote—persons with higher levels of formal education— the support was even higher for the president.[35] For members of Congress, with an election only two months away, it made political sense to show patriotic support for the president and please the public by supporting the strikes.

The Republicans in particular had political incentives to abandon the constitutional issues. Clinton's strikes came only two months before the presidential elections. In the days preceding the attack, GOP nominee Bob Dole had criticized Clinton for being weak toward Hussein. However, once the strikes occurred, Dole quickly rallied behind the president. In fact, Dole's spokesman noted, "Bob Dole, among all men in public life today, has certainly demonstrated that he was willing to stand with the President."[36] With Dole and Clinton holding essentially identical positions on the strikes, the GOP decided to back the president and in effect rallied around candidate Dole as well. Had they criticized Clinton, they would also have been opposing the GOP presidential nominee.

At the same time, many in Congress felt the necessity of taking strong action against Hussein and thus supported the strikes. In this respect, Congress's deference signaled support for the president. Members of Congress could justify their silence as one way of sending a message to Hussein that they would not challenge Clinton's authority. However, Congress cannot abdicate its war powers responsibilities to the president by allowing the commander in chief to be the sole military decision maker for the United States.

Thus, again in 1996, the president used force without consulting members of Congress and put forward dubious legal claims to establish his authority to act. The consultation requirement of the WPR was completely neglected. No direct attack against the United States had been made, and no United Nations resolutions existed authorizing the United States' conduct. Yet the use of force against a popular enemy of the United States only two months before a presidential election created incentives for Congress to abdicate its war powers.

UNSCOM and U.S. Threats

After the 1996 bombings, the next major crisis with Iraq began on January 13, 1998, when Saddam Hussein refused to allow United Nations weapons inspection teams to search certain sites within Iraq under the provisions of United Nations Security Council Resolution 687. This was not the first time Hussein had been uncooperative with UNSCOM, but diplomacy had not been this tense and near conflict in previous instances of Iraqi belligerence. Hussein's resistence to UNSCOM was attributed to the United States' involvement. He argued that U.S. representatives of UNSCOM were agents of U.S. covert intelligence-gathering operations, working under the guise of UN weapons inspectors and refused to allow further inspections.[37]

As the crisis progressed into February, Iraq continued to bar UNSCOM from doing its work. The Clinton administration unequivocally maintained that diplomacy was the preferred option for addressing these differences but the use of force was also a possibility if Iraq did not comply.[38] Implicit in these statements was the argument that the use of force was constitutional. The administration's view was stated most bluntly by Secretary of State Albright. On the issue of conducting "substantial strikes" against Iraq, she remarked: "Let no one miscalculate. We have authority to do this, the responsibility to do this, the means and the will."[39] The administration's position was clear.

When the 1998 crisis developed, the Senate quickly drafted a resolution of support for the president. The resolution urged "the President to take all necessary and appropriate actions to respond to the threat posed by Iraq's refusal to end its weapons of mass destruction program."[40] This resolution generated a good deal of debate but not over the president's authority to use force. Rather, the Senate's attention focused on whether bombing was the best *policy* option for the United States. When constitutional issues were raised, they were even discarded by some members. Senator Kyl urged, "Let's not focus on legalism here. We know what needs to be done—get a good plan and sell it to the American people."[41] In contrast, Senator Max Cleland (D-Ga.) expressed concern with the resolution's language, noting that it was open-ended, unclear, and dangerously similar to the Gulf of Tonkin Resolution, which gave President Johnson unlimited authority to initiate the bombing of North Vietnam.[42] Yet most debate centered on the utility of bombing and its long-term strategic objectives.

After nearly two weeks of debate, the Senate was unable to agree on any resolution. Before the Senate's ten-day recess during the midst of the crisis, Senator Lott and Minority Leader Daschle appeared together on the Senate floor to state that in no way did the Senate's indecision reflect any faltering in its opposition to Hussein's lack of compliance. Yet the Senators chose to leave for their ten day recess without any resolution passed, while the crisis was at its apex and the administration threatening force. In a rare discussion of the legalities surrounding the Clinton's administration's claims for authority to use force, Senator Joe Biden stated that the administration's authority was "legally tenable" but that it would be "wise" for the president to gain formal congressional approval.[43] Senator Arlen Specter (R-Pa.) also sent a letter to President Clinton stating that before any strike on Iraq, congressional approval would be required.[44] Otherwise, senators' remarks generally condemned Hussein for his actions and tacitly granted the president authority to do whatever he felt necessary as commander in chief. Senator Joseph Lieberman (D-Conn.) seemed resigned that diplomacy would not work and force was the only likely option. In deferring to the president's judgement he said, "Mr. President, if you, as commander in chief, act in this circumstance, in this crisis, you and the troops who serve under you will have broad bipartisan support in the U.S. Senate."[45] In short, the overwhelming majority in the Senate remained unwilling to place any constitutional restrictions on the president and preferred to debate policy than to raise constitutional issues.

The Senate's courage soared after its recess, when the crisis had subsided. UN Secretary General Kofi Annan convinced Hussein on February 22, 1998 to allow UNSCOM to resume its work. Once the Senate returned, a resolution offered by Senator Specter passed unanimously. It labeled Saddam Hussein a war criminal and encouraged the formation of a special international court to adjudicate his crimes.[46]

In the House, even less was said on the possibility of using force. One exception was Representative Ron Paul (R-Tex.), who maintained that no UN Security Council resolution provided an adequate legal basis for the bombing.[47] Otherwise, the House acted very much like the Senate. Some concerns were voiced again on *policy*, but virtually no attention was devoted to questions of legal authority. In the strongest show of legal assertiveness offered in Congress, Representative David Skaggs (D-Colo.) maintained that the president did not have authority to use force without congressional consent. Skaggs cited a Congressional Research Services' report that examined the president's authority under UN Security Council Resolution 687 to use force and concluded, as Skaggs argued, that a Security Council resolution did not provide sufficient constitutional authority for conducting "substantial air strikes."[48]

In another example of ostensible assertiveness, on February 26, 1998, Representative Roscoe Bartlett (R-Md.) and seventy-five cosponsors introduced a resolution stating that any military action taken against Iraq must be "authorized by law."[49] However, both of these efforts came after Kofi Annan had negotiated a diplomatic solution to the crisis. Thus, like the Senate, the House gave little attention to the legal implications of a strike, and the principle constitutional challenges came only after Congress's recess and Annan's successful diplomacy.

Regarding Iraq's belligerence toward UNSCOM, Congress showed some policy assertiveness by asking questions on the utility of bombing. Just as with American participation in IFOR in 1995, Congress was certainly not disinterested in Clinton's actions and openly debated the best direction for U.S. foreign policy toward Iraq. In the end, constitutional issues were avoided again and Congress granted the president unilateral authority to use force. With congressional elections only two months away and still nearly universal condemnation of Saddam Hussein in the United States, Congress was unwilling to restrict Clinton's perceived legal authority to strike Iraq.

It is also notable that Congress's limited legal assertiveness only came after Annan's diplomatic success and its own recess. Members became more confidant after their recess trips and once the crisis subsided. Once the crisis was at least temporarily dormant, Congress could not be accused of being unpatriotic or obstructionist by displaying more assertiveness against the president. Moreover, Congressman Bartlett's resolution cannot be construed as firm "legal assertiveness." The resolution only required the president to act "within the law." Yet, Clinton already felt that he had constitutional authority to act, and the resolution does not specify what "the law" is. Most of the assertiveness Congress showed came from junior members of the House and Senate. In the House, the GOP's constitutional protagonists were recently elected members: Congressmen Roscoe Bartlett (1992) and Ron Paul (1996)— both of whom did not have long leadership records in U.S. foreign affairs. Democrat David Skaggs had been in the House longer (since 1986), but he had lost war powers battles in his own party before.[50] In the Senate, Max Cleland had been elected only recently (in 1996) and did not yet have Senate leadership credentials in foreign policy. Senator Specter has also been regarded as a maverick throughout his entire Senate career, and although he served as chair of the Senate Intelligence

Committee, he is not regarded as one who can easily generate followers in the Senate.[51] Thus the principal opposition to the administration did not come from Congress's foreign policy elites, and this also helps to explain why constitutional issues never moved to the top agenda in either chamber.

After Annan negotiated the agreement with Hussein, the Clinton administration sponsored a successful resolution in the United Nations Security Council stating that if Iraq did not comply with past resolutions, it would face the "severest consequences."[52] Yet Resolution 1154 authorized nothing, unlike past resolutions on Somalia, Haiti, and Bosnia. Other actions taken by the Council employ language that specifically authorizes member states to use "all necessary means," or language to that effect, in order to accomplish the mandate. Yet in the days following the passage of 1154, the Clinton administration openly stated that the Security Council's decision authorized the use of force if Iraq opposed further inspections. These statements were made in the face of opposition from then current Security Council members, who notably did not allow more specific use-of-force resolutions to pass.[53] After the vote, the Brazilian representative on the Security Council stated explicitly that further authorization was required before military action could be taken against Iraq.[54] It is also noteworthy that the Clinton administration felt compelled to return to the UN Security Council for additional multilateral endorsement. These actions suggest an implicit recognition that prior resolutions, such as Resolution 687 (as Senator Biden noted), no longer applied under the current conditions. Had past Security Council resolutions allowed for military action against Hussein in 1998, there would be no need to gain further authorization.

In the aftermath of the Security Council's decision, Congress again raised no questions on this resolution or the Clinton administration's interpretations. Congress's constitutional authority under Article 43 of the UN Charter and the UN Participation Act was forgotten historical parchment in light of the national consensus against Saddam Hussein. With the exception of the strikes on Bin Laden, earlier uses of force and deployments by the Clinton administration at least generated some opposition and a few constitutional questions from Congress. In contrast, Congress strongly backed Clinton's policy toward Iraq, despite its dubious international legal status. Had it not been for Clinton's domestic political troubles with Monica Lewinsky that were to come, Congress would likely have continued its near total deference to the president during Operation Desert Fox.

Operation Desert Fox

On November 15, 1998, after a series of diplomatic clashes between the United States and Iraq over UNSCOM, at Clinton's request the Department of Defense began planning for a military strike on Iraq if Hussein rejected UNSCOM's authority again. One month later, when Iraq spurned UNSCOM once more, the United States and Britain responded with four days of military strikes. In an address to the nation, Clinton noted that Hussein was given numerous chances to comply with UNSCOM, and in an apparent reference to UN Security Council Resolution 1154, Clinton added that Iraq must now face the "consequences of defying the UN."[55] In a letter to Congressional leaders two days later, Clinton cited past Security Council Resolutions 678 and 687, which authorized UN member states to use force against Iraq in 1991. He also referred to the power granted to the president under Public Law 102-1, which authorized President Bush to use force in Iraq.[56]

The actual decision to use force in 1998 was made without any consultation with members of Congress. By the president's own acknowledgment, his national security team alone produced the unanimous decision.[57] On the eve before the strikes, while Clinton was traveling home from the Middle East on Air Force One, he spoke with Secretary of State Albright, Secretary of Defense Cohen, National Security Advisor Sandy Berger, Chairman of the Joint Chiefs of Staff Henry Shelton, Central Intelligence Agency Director George Tenet, and Vice President Gore on a secure conference call. During this phone call, the decision to use force was made. Upon arriving at the White House, Clinton held further meetings with Berger and White House Chief of Staff John Podesta to review the decision. No evidence exists that any member of Congress was among the inner group of key decision makers.[58] Berger stressed that the decision had to be made quickly in order for the strikes to occur before Ramadan, the Muslim holy month, which began on December 19. Eight B-52 bombers had also just arrived in the Middle East to replace seven aircraft and pilots who were due to return to the United States. The additional aircraft provided another incentive to act, as the force strength was high. Moreover, according to Berger, an international coalition had not been assembled due to fear that the media would publicize the effort and in effect give Hussein time to hide his valuable military hardware.[59] A few members of Congress were notified in advance, mostly through discussions with Secretary Cohen, but were not involved in the actual decision to use force.[60]

Initial reactions from Congress were mixed, as some members expressed strong reservations and distrust of the president's motives. On the day of the attack, the House was scheduled to begin voting on the president's impeachment for his inaccurate testimony regarding his extramarital relationship with White House intern Monica Lewinsky. Before the president had even addressed the nation about the attack, Senator Lott stated that "both the timing and the policy are subject to question." House Majority Leader Dick Armey (R-Tex.) also questioned the president's motives, and House Rules Chairman Gerald Solomon (R-N.Y.) added: "Never underestimate a desperate president."[61] Solomon was more critical in an interview with CNN when he noted that the White House was "doing everything they can to postpone impeachment. . . . This president ought to know better. We should not be handling impeachment while bombing is going on, and that's exactly why he is doing it."[62] Other members expressed concern about the lack of consultation and the need for better communication with Congress. In a rare occurrence over the eight years of the Clinton administration, at least three members raised the WPR and questioned Clinton's legal authority to conduct the strikes. In one of the most articulate challenges to the president, Congressman Bernie Sanders (I-Vt.) noted: "[T]his action took place with no real discussion in the United States Congress despite the fact that the Constitution makes it very clear that it is the body which declares war. I am concerned that while we are ostensibly supporting a United Nations resolution, the UN did not vote for this attack, does not support this attack, and that country after country throughout the world are condemning this attack."[63] There was also "no real discussion" between Congress and the White House. Moreover, of the five permanent members of the UN Security Council, only Great Britain publicly supported and participated in the operation.[64]

As it had done in response to Clinton's previous strikes on Iraq, the majority in Congress again rallied behind the president. The supporters included GOP leaders Senator Jesse Helms (R-N.C.), Senator Richard Lugar (R-Ind.), and Congressman Benjamin Gilman (R-N.Y.).

The Democrats provided essentially universal support, and like most Republicans, maintained that Clinton had authority to carry out the attacks. This position closely reflected public opinion. A Gallup poll found that 74 percent of Americans supported the air strikes.[65] A Time/ CNN poll also found that 67 percent of the public felt that the Republicans' efforts to link the president's motives for the attacks to his impending impeachment were inappropriate.[66] Thus, despite the complete absence of consultation, only cursory notification, and deficient authorization from the UN Security Council, Congress supported the bombings. Clinton's most vocal critics questioned him not on his constitutional authority to use force but on his domestic political motives. GOP leaders Lott, Armey, and Solomon raised no concerns with respect to the UN Participation Act or the specifics of the WPR but focused mostly on the possibility that Clinton was using the strikes to distract the public from his domestic political troubles. With the overwhelming majority in the United States supporting the strikes, Congress had few incentives to raise constitutional concerns.

Policing the No-Fly Zones

After Operation Desert Fox, the Clinton administration became much more vigorous in its enforcement of the southern and northern no-fly zones established over Iraq: Operation Northern Watch (ONW) and Operation Southern Watch (OSW).[67] Unlike the Bosnian no-fly zones established by the UN Security Council, the no-fly zones in Iraq were created without the Security Council's explicit approval.[68] Clinton also unilaterally extended the southern zone after the 1996 air strikes. During the Clinton administration, ONW was monitored by the United States, the United Kingdom, and Turkey, where the operation is based. The Turkish parliament determined semiannually whether to renew the agreement. OSW was established initially by France, the United States, the United Kingdom, and Saudi Arabia, where the operation is located. In 2000, ONW aircraft struck Iraqi military installations, aircraft and other military targets on at least forty-eight different occasions. In 1999, ONW used force at least 106 times. OSW used force on military sites on at least twenty days in 1999.

After Operation Desert Fox, Congress exhibited no interest in war powers or Clinton's authority to use force in the no-fly zones, despite protests from other Security Council members. This is not to say that Clinton was free from congressional criticism. Congressional committees examined other aspects of Clinton's policy toward Iraq, including American participation in the UN-imposed economic embargo, the strategy of supporting Iraqi opposition groups, and the effort to reimpose a weapon's inspection team.[69] However, as commander in chief the president enjoyed unilateral power concerning the use of force, free of congressional interference. With a foundation established by President George Bush in 1990 and 1991 that Saddam Hussein was the moral equivalent of Adolf Hitler,[70] the American public and Congress granted President Clinton essentially unlimited authority to use force on Iraq. The exercise of congressional war powers has been noticeably absent from American uses of force against Iraq for the last eight years.

CONCLUSION: SADDAM HUSSEIN AS ENEMY NUMBER ONE

Of all the cases examined in this book, Bill Clinton's uses of force against Iraq represent the greatest degree of congressional deference and abdication of war powers to the president. In other deployments and uses of force, occasional questions of Clinton's authority to use force arose. American military actions in Somalia, Haiti, Bosnia, and Kosovo generated some controversy among members of Congress over Clinton's constitutional authority to use force. In this case, however the domestic political conditions were so favorable to the use of force against Iraq that Congress essentially gave Clinton a green light to use force at will, especially after Operation Desert Fox. Congress's only noteworthy opposition came in 1998, when the president used force at the onset of the House's impeachment votes, when the mood in Congress was highly partisan. When members of Congress questioned the president on Operation Desert Fox, public opinion polls showed that a wide majority of Americans viewed the GOP challenges as "inappropriate." Opposition party presidential candidate Bob Dole understood these dynamics in 1996 and chose to support Clinton's military strikes. Thus the public's strong support for aggressive action against Iraq created strong political incentives not to oppose the president.

Undoubtedly some members of Congress also stayed silent because they too supported military action against Hussein. In this sense, Congress's behavior cannot be described completely as "deference," in that Congress generally supported the president, just as it did when Clinton struck Usama Bin Laden. However, the Constitution and the WPR do not allow Congress to abdicate its responsibilities. Even if every member of Congress believed American military strikes in Iraq served U.S. national security interests, Congress still had constitutional obligations that, again, were abdicated to the commander in chief.

In his uses of force in Iraq, Clinton relied extensively upon precarious international legal authority for his actions. Very broad interpretations of past United Nations Security Council Resolutions were central to his claims that international law granted him authority to act in 1993, 1996, and 1998 and in policing no-fly zones. Since Congress seemed to accept these arguments, Clinton's appeals to past United Nations Security Council resolutions served him extremely well. However, considering that only two of the five permanent members of the Security Council supported the use of force in Iraq, it is difficult if not impossible to conclude that Clinton had UN authorization to act. Unlike the military actions in Somalia, Haiti, and Bosnia, for which international legal issues were not in question, Clinton's bombings of Iraq did not have explicit approval of the UN Security Council. This became especially evident when the Clinton administration sought additional Security Council authorization in March 1998 in an unsuccessful effort to broaden its military mandate.

Clinton also appealed to Public Law 102-1 to justify his military authority to act. Such appeals were made through 2000 when Clinton continued to use force to police the no-fly zones.[71] However, it is difficult to conclude that in 1991 Congress intended that all commanders in chief to follow President Bush would have unlimited authority and discretion to use force against Iraq anytime they desired.

As in the deployment to Haiti, Clinton also gave scant attention to the requirements of the WPR. When Clinton bombed Bin Laden, and later when NATO attacked Yugoslavia, Clinton reached out to Congress much more aggressively. In the strikes on Iraq, Clinton barely went through the motions of including members of Congress in even superficial talks prior to the strikes.

Clinton's ability to assert wide military powers and Congress's willingness to defer to the commander in chief with regard to Iraq is best explained by overwhelmingly unfavorable public opinion toward Iraq.

When the public widely accepts a foreign actor as "the enemy"—as it had Saddam Hussein during the Clinton years—and if the United States experiences no casualties in its military conduct, virtually no political incentive exists for Congress to introduce legal and constitutional qualms with the president. Even if one grants that Clinton's international legal claims were legitimate, Congress still could have raised objections to the president based on Article 43 of the United Nations Charter, or the UN Participation Act of 1945. However, had a member of Congress raised constitutional or other international legal concerns, especially a member of the House of Representatives who faces reelection every two years, the member ran the risk of being viewed as "weak" toward Hussein. Just as with communism during the cold war, members had political incentives to talk and act tough against Hussein and to push constitutional questions aside.

However, when a country [the United States] openly calls for a new government in a foreign country, as the United States has called for in Iraq, provides funding for rebel groups within that foreign state, conducts air strikes against that state without specific UN approval, and brands the country's head of state a "war criminal," it seems reasonable to conclude that a "war" is in progress. Yet, Congress refused to declare war or give statutory authorization to Clinton for his military strikes in Iraq.

During Operation Desert Fox, Senator Connie Mack (R-Fla.) noted, "I have always—from Reagan to Bush to President Clinton—felt that under the authority as commander in chief, the president has the ability to take action."[72] Viewpoints such as these contrast sharply with those of James Madison and other founding fathers at the Constitutional Convention and represent a complete surrender of Congress's endowed war powers.

8   The Politics and Future of War Powers

In the aftermath of the Persian Gulf War and as George Bush spoke of a "new world order," the prospects for international peace and security seemed considerably better for the post–cold war world. Yet through the eight years of the Clinton presidency, ethnic conflicts, civil wars, and even incidents of genocide continued in disturbingly high numbers. In response to violations of human rights, as part of peace-building operations, and in the enforcement of UN Security Council resolutions, the United States became engaged in a number of conflicts under Clinton's leadership. After the September 11, 2001, terrorist attacks and with the American military response initiated on October 7, 2001, the United States is now involved in a new "war on terrorism" that which will target those responsible for the attacks on America as well as those states or organizations that harbor such terrorists. The use of force in American foreign policy thus remains a key component of U.S. national security policy in an uncertain world.

For centuries, international jurists, and constitutional scholars have debated the question of when a government may legitimately use force abroad.[1] In the United States, James Madison's notes from the Constitutional Convention in 1787 offer Americans a historical record of how the founding fathers answered this question. Under the principle of checks and balances, Congress was given the power to "declare war." The president, as commander in chief, can use force without congressional approval to "repel sudden attacks." Otherwise, congressional authorization is needed before military action can be taken. Congress protected these powers when the United States joined the United Nations and NATO. During the cold war, however, presidents claimed unilateral powers as commander in chief when fighting communism, and Congress largely abdicated its constitutional responsibilities to the president. Congress attempted to reassert its war powers in 1973 under the War Powers Resolution, but law has been ineffective in restoring a balance of power. With the widely perceived threat of communism accepted by most Americans, Congress pushed aside constitutional questions and responsibilities. However, with the Soviet Union's collapse, less consensus in defining the nation's security threats, and the election of Bill Clinton to the presidency, the prospects for a congressional reassertion of its war powers seemed strong, particularly considering the newly elected president's inexperience in foreign policy and military affairs.[2] These prospects ostensibly heightened when the GOP gained majority status in Congress in the 1994 midterm elections and later with the president in a weakened state during the impeachment proceedings. Yet despite these developments, the pattern of congressional deference largely remained the norm. This deference is best explained as resulting from the influence of various factors: the domestic political environment on the occasions when force was used, the roles of key congressional leaders in each instance, and the partisan political choices that shaped the war powers interplay. The evidence presented for these six cases suggests that congressional deference and presidential unilateralism in war powers involved many political variables that were specific to the time and conditions when force was used, which cannot be captured by viewing Congress's deference simply as an institutional norm.

The President

As commander in chief, President Clinton's constitutional arguments were very similar to those of other presidents in recent history. Clinton claimed essentially unilateral powers as commander in chief, as he and other top ranking officials in the executive branch consistently argued that Congress had no formal authority to restrict the president in any of his military deployments or uses of force. However, consideration of certain nuances of Clinton's political strategies with Congress yield different insights and conclusions about the war powers interplay during his administration.

With regard to the War Powers Resolution, when the domestic political conditions demanded, the Clinton administration clearly employed the *rhetoric* of "consultation" to appease members of Congress. This was especially true prior to IFOR, when Clinton was buying time to negotiate a peace agreement with Bosnian diplomats at Dayton, and because of the presence of an ostensibly assertive Republican majority that might reign in his exercise of perceived broad war powers. Very astutely, the president reached out to Congress in recognizing his responsibilities under the WPR. However, once the Dayton negotiations were concluded, it was clear that Clinton would deploy troops with or without congressional support. The WPR shaped the way in which Clinton interacted politically with Congress but made little real difference in how Clinton utilized his powers as commander in chief.

On two occasions, Bill Clinton also reached out to Congress in a manner that was uncharacteristic of recent presidents. Prior to bombing the alleged military headquarters of Usama Bin Laden, Clinton consulted with congressional GOP leaders. Before NATO's actions in Kosovo, Clinton again reached out to Congress to build domestic support. Clinton's strategy with Congress developed in part because of the political dynamics created by the Monica Lewinsky scandal and the ensuing impeachment. With Kosovo, Clinton's dialogue with and eventual support from the Senate served another useful purpose by placing further diplomatic pressure on Slobodan Milosevic. In neither case did Clinton recognize Congress's formal authority, but he did bring Congress more closely into the decision-making process prior to the use of force. The strategy Clinton employed before the implementation of IFOR and before the strikes on Bin Laden and Milosevic in 1999 suggests that Clinton understood his own political limitations and risks in acting without some discussions with Congress when support from the public was less than certain. Clinton did not always turn to Congress when the public was likely to question his use of force, as it did his deployment of troops to Haiti, but the events surrounding the war in Kosovo and the strikes against Bin Laden demonstrate that domestic political conditions influenced the president's level of consultation with Congress.

In other respects the president acted very much like past administrations in dealing with Congress with regard to the WPR. The Clinton administration's broad and liberal interpretations of the WPR are not new to congressional-executive interplay. Assistant Secretary of State Wendy Sherman, Secretary Albright, Undersecretary Thomas Pickering, and Clinton's legal counsel Walter Dellinger demonstrated great fluency and rhetorical skills in dealing with the WPR to justify essentially unilateral military powers for the president. The differences in interpretation between Congress and the administration appeared most acute when Clinton officials were questioned over the definitions of "consultation," "hostilities," and "war." In all cases Clinton representatives argued that the WPR did not apply. In this regard, Clinton officials acted very similar to other administrations.

Multilateral endorsement of the use of force proved to be another important component of Clinton's dialogue with Congress. In order to keep Congress subordinate to the president, Clinton and other administration officials justified uses of force by noting that a variety of international organizations approved of military action. These endorsements, whether from CARICOM, NATO, or the United Nations, were used to weaken congressional assertions of war powers. This practice is also not new to the war powers interplay. The Reagan administration justified its use of force in Grenada in part by gaining the support of the Organization of Eastern Caribbean States, an organization that had no legal powers to authorize military action.[3] George Bush also explicitly asserted that UN authorization was all he needed to use force in Kuwait and Iraq in 1991, with no reference to Section 6 of the UN Participation Act.[4] International support, however, is not constitutional authorization to use force, which was made clear in 1945 when the United States joined the United Nations and in 1949 when the United States entered NATO. Nonetheless, Clinton justified his military actions in Somalia, Haiti, Bosnia, and especially Iraq by appealing to international endorsements. Clinton's most precarious international legal appeal came with the Operation Desert Fox campaign and the subsequent enforcement of no-fly zones in Iraq in 1999 and 2000, when the United States had no specific approval from the UN Security Council to conduct attacks. Appeals to international endorsements, however, often worked well in quelling Congress's infrequent assertions of its war powers.

During the bombings in Kosovo, Undersecretary Pickering remarked that Congress had no authority to restrict the president's use of force in Kosovo and added that Congress has had no authority to exercise its war powers since the beginning of World War II.[5] Such statements illustrate how expansively the White House viewed its powers and how grossly it distorted Congress's constitutional powers. Institutionally and constitutionally, Clinton left office as a commander in chief who was nearly omnipotent in military affairs.

The Congress

Institutionally, during the Clinton administration, Congress acted much as it had in the cold war. Members of Congress, both Democrats and Republicans, often deferred to Bill Clinton and let the president assume the full political risks for the potential failure or success of each military mission. These findings contrast with recent literature on Congress and foreign policy after the cold war. In many foreign policy areas, such as the environment, defense spending, foreign trade, and foreign aid programs, Congress has been an assertive actor against the president. Clinton was forced to bargain and negotiate with Congress across a broad spectrum of issues in order to achieve his foreign policy goals.[6] However, Clinton's actions as commander in chief did not require this level of negotiation. Congress essentially deferred its war powers to the president with little resistance.

Choices made by individual members of Congress are crucial in the war powers interplay. Senate Majority Leader George Mitchell (D-Maine) was instrumental in preventing the Republicans from registering a meaningful vote on war powers in 1994 over the deployment to Haiti. Quite possibly, such a vote would have gained support from nearly all Republicans and many Democrats. Mitchell protected his Democratic colleague in the White House from meaningful war powers challenges early in his presidency. Speaker of the House Newt Gingrich (R-Ga.) was instrumental in setting Congress's priorities in 1995 as the president moved toward deployment of twenty thousand troops to Bosnia. Even after pressure from the Republican conference and the efforts of the GOP rank and file to restore Congress's war powers as provided in the UN Participation Act, Gingrich crafted a House resolution that allowed members to vote for the troops and not the policy. In choosing to fight the president over budgetary politics rather than war powers, Gingrich was central to Congress's abdication of its war powers.

House International Relations Chairman Benjamin Gilman (R-N.Y.) too was integral in limiting the efforts of Congressman Thomas Campbell (R-Calif.) to restore some degree of balance to war powers. Gilman opposed his Republican colleague's efforts to bring meaningful votes before Congress involving its authority in the deployment to Bosnia and with regard to the NATO bombings in Kosovo. Gilman openly opposed and postponed committee votes on such constitutional questions, even when Campbell argued at great length that his proposals were about the constitution and the WPR, not the policy itself. Gilman's efforts were supported by other ranking GOP leaders in the House. By keeping all military responsibility with the president, the Republicans could not be blamed for a failed operation. The unwillingness of senator and presidential candidate Bob Dole (R-Kans.) to criticize Clinton on his uses of force in Bosnia and later in Iraq were also important in muting other GOP leaders' concerns about Clinton's foreign policy choices. The roles played by congressional leaders in these cases provide a more complete understanding of the war powers interplay. Congress continues to defer to the president, but the reasons for this deference often vary according to the choices made by congressional leaders in each case.

The choices made by congressional leaders were frequently influenced by the domestic political conditions at the time when force was used. Gingrich's deference to the president over Bosnia occurred at the same time the Republicans were positioning themselves for a budget battle with the president. The decision of Speaker of the House Dennis Hastert (R-Ill.) not to schedule a meaningful vote on war powers prior to the strikes on Kosovo took place soon after the Senate's impeachment acquittal of the president, when House Republicans had incentives not to look vindictive against the president by voting against NATO's plans in the Balkans. The popularity of the strikes on Usama Bin Laden and Clinton's many assaults on Saddam Hussein also provided Congress few political incentives to assert constitutional war powers. When the public strongly backs the president, it is much easier for Congress to abandon its constitutional obligations and defer to the commander in chief. Even if Congress agrees in principle with the strikes and finds that the military actions fit national security objectives, it is not relieved of its war powers responsibilities.

Another domestic political condition that encouraged presidential leadership was the aggressiveness and effectiveness of the Congressional Black Caucus in advocating military intervention in Haiti. The caucus had become a well-organized and vocal body that gained the attention of both the president and other members of Congress. House Democrats had incentives to avoid criticism of Clinton's intervention in Haiti, which could have resulted in a battle with the Black Caucus as well. Clinton's strikes on Iraq in 1996 also came only two months before the November elections, and Clinton's attack on Bin Laden came only three months before the congressional midterms in 1998. Members of Congress do not want to appear weak on foreign policy toward widely accepted enemies of the United States only a few weeks before their elections. The reasons for Congress's deference again vary in each case depending on the domestic political circumstances.

Partisan politics, as part of the domestic political environment, also played a role in Congress's deference to the president. Democrats fell in line behind their leaders in protecting Clinton during much of the deployment to Somalia and prior to the deployment in Haiti. House Democrats also appeared especially partisan prior to and during NATO's operation in Kosovo. In contrast, House Republicans battled with Clinton during all stages of the deployment in Somalia.

While Congress most often abdicated its constitutional responsibilities to the president, the findings presented here also suggest that deference does not completely capture the full congressional-executive interplay of the Clinton presidency. Congress challenged the president most aggressively on Somalia. This case was markedly different from the others in that the United States experienced casualties that were widely broadcast by the major news networks. Congress's strong reaction was surely instrumental in forcing Clinton to set a departure date for the operation and may have discouraged Clinton from intervening in other African conflicts and humanitarian crises, such as those in Rwanda, Sudan, and Zaire. The GOP's threats in 1995 over a possible deployment prior to the Dayton Peace Accords probably influenced the president at least to employ the rhetoric of "consulting" with Congress over Bosnia. The new Republican majority shifted the American political environment by discussing war powers vis-à-vis American participation in United Nations operations, which the Clinton administration recognized. Congress also expressed concerns over the deployment of NATO ground troops to Kosovo and perhaps limited Clinton's military options in this regard.

However, at other times Congress simply took no constitutional stand, which appeared to be the preference of most members, Democrats and Republicans alike. After the military deployment to Haiti both chambers of Congress stood on the sidelines, uninterested in accepting any constitutional responsibility. The House was unwilling to register a vote on war powers during the seventy-eight days of bombing in

Kosovo. Congress placed no restrictions on the president in his many uses of force against Iraq. These choices violate the principle of checks and balances in a constitutional government, dishonor the spirit of the treaties the United States entered into when joining the United Nations and NATO, and clearly break with the purpose of the War Powers Resolution. At best, members of Congress appear to misunderstand their well-articulated war powers. At worst, members conveniently avoid their constitutional responsibilities in order to serve political interests. With the notable exception of Congressman Tom Campbell (R-Calif.), Senator Russ Feingold (D-Wis.), Congressman Ron Paul (R-Tex.), Congressman Peter DeFazio (D-Oreg.), and a few others, most members of Congress avoid legal references to their war powers responsibilities. This imbalance of power and failure to apply Congress's war powers demands attention and policy reforms.

Policy Reforms

Many arguments can be made against a Congress that is overly assertive in foreign affairs. Ample evidence suggests that Congress is often parochial in its outlook, partisan in its policy preferences, and focused on the short-term rather than the long-term interests of the country. Congress has also been criticized for being a cumbersome and deliberative body, prone to gridlock and inaction.[7] In many respects, these criticisms are accurate. Congress has 535 different personalities, egos, and interests. At the same time, there is no reason to place the president on an institutional pedestal. Presidents too can be parochial, partisan, and myopic in defining national interests. Moreover, recent presidents have been far from perfect. Clinton "misled the public;" Nixon orchestrated a robbery of the Democratic National Committee headquarters; Reagan's National Security Council appears to have conducted American foreign policy with minimal presidential oversight in Iran and Nicaragua.

From a constitutional perspective, it is worth recalling that the founders fully intended for it to be difficult for one person, the chief executive, to use force without congressional approval. The founders wanted no kings in the White House. Our constitutional government demands a balance between the president and the Congress. It is easy to imagine a situation in which a president has engaged troops in a military deployment that experiences casualties; Congress responds by calling for the troops' removal. Such a crisis over the proper direction for U.S. foreign policy in the Clinton administration was averted when Clinton agreed to withdraw troops from Somalia after Congress invoked its war powers authority. Clinton, a president with little experience in foreign policy who would also be seeking a second term, understood the wisdom in cutting his political losses and responded to congressional pressure. However, it is just as easy to envision a president who does not want to bring the troops home after Congress says otherwise. The Vietnam War is one such example.

The current practice of presidential unilateralism places the United States at great risk. A foreign adversary could capitalize on the American public's very low tolerance for casualties and Congress's initial deference to a presidential deployment to force a constitutional battle between the branches. By taking a clearer stand prior to a deployment, the United States avoids this risk, and in effect strengthens U.S. foreign policy.

Moreover, the president has strong incentives to consult with members of Congress during times of national crisis. By working with Congress and gaining its support, the president can overcome partisanship and distrust and send a strong signal to foreign adversaries. In one example of cooperation during the Clinton administration, the president consulted and worked with congressional leaders prior to the strikes on Usama Bin Laden. Similarly, the Senate's vote prior to the Kosovo deployment sent Slobodan Milosevic a strong signal that there was congressional support for a major bombing campaign if the Yugoslav tyrant did not change course. Proper presidential consultation with Congress could also help prevent tragic mistakes. President Carter wrote in his memoir that he regretted not consulting more closely with Senator Byrd on the evening before the failed hostage rescue attempt in 1980, which cost the lives of eight Americans.[8] Had the president more openly discussed these plans, perhaps that result could have been averted.

Some critics of congressional war power argue that including Congress in use-of-force decisions is a logistical nightmare, and the president should not be hampered by such cumbersome obstacles as commander in chief. Members of Congress can be difficult to contact, particularly if they are on recess or if the president is traveling abroad. However, in an age of technological advances, with secured telephone lines, teleconferencing, and computer video-imaging, this argument is increasingly weak. With an array of technological tools and options, even during times of crisis the president can at minimum consult with the congressional leadership in both parties and Congress's key foreign policy committee chairs. An advanced technological age brings many opportunities to enhance democratic institutions, allowing for greater checks and balances.

One of the first steps that should be taken is to repeal the WPR. With its imprecise definitions, especially surrounding the word *consult,* the resolution does more harm than good. Its purpose of bringing Congress more closely into the decision-making process has not been achieved. This was best demonstrated in the Clinton years with the president's uses of force in Iraq, where the WPR's consultation requirement had virtually no relevance. Congress was also not consulted over the Haitian deployment, and when Clinton spoke with only two GOP leaders prior to using force on Bin Laden, the level of dialogue probably did not fully comply with the intentions of the authors of the WPR, even though some level of secrecy may have been necessary.

One recently introduced reform of war powers is Senator Joe Biden's Use of Force Act. The act would allow the president to use force without congressional approval to "repel an armed attack" against the United States; when the president must protect the supreme national interests in emergency conditions; and when U.S. citizens abroad are experiencing a "direct and imminent threat to their lives." Biden suggests the formation of a Congressional Leadership Group that would consist of eighteen congressional leaders from both parties, representing key foreign policy committees. This group would have to be consulted before any use of force that does not have emergency status or involve the supreme national interests. The president and his advisors would also be required to meet with the leadership group approximately once every two months to discuss any possible uses of force that may be forthcoming.[9] Biden offers a good start toward addressing the imbalance of war powers. However, his proposal has problems, in that like the WPR, semantical controversies again seem likely. It is not clear what "supreme national interests" are, nor is it clear when a "direct and imminent threat" to Americans' lives abroad exists. One can easily imagine a presidential interpretation that is much different from Congress's under both of these conditions.

Others reformers suggest that war powers responsibilities should follow the founders' intent as closely possible; that is, the president is allowed to use force unilaterally only to "repel sudden attacks" or "defend" the United States. Any offensive use of force must be approved by Congress.[10] This proposal too is prone to exploitation by the president and inaction by the Congress. Clinton invoked the "self-defense" clause of Article 51 of the UN Charter when he used force in Iraq, and Congress accepted this justification despite its legally questionable validity. The administration also appealed to Article 51 to justify NATO's threatened use of force against Milosevic in 1998. Using the criteria of "defensive" and "offensive" uses of force would do little to change presidential unilateralism and congressional deference.

What is needed is a statutory requirement, similar to Biden's, that explicitly requires congressional approval for the use of force. An official panel of congressional military advisors could be designated to advise the president on uses of force, consisting of the Speaker of the House, House and Senate majority and minority leaders, and the chairs and minority ranking members of the House International Relations Committee, the Senate Foreign Relations Committee, the House Permanent Select Committee on Intelligence, and the Senate Select Committee on Intelligence. In the event that all members could not be assembled, the second ranking member below the absent individual would fill the position, so that there would always be thirteen members to register votes. In conditions when national security requires some secrecy, the president would have to consult with this group and gain its specific approval. The Speaker of the House would record the individual votes. In cases when the president acted unilaterally to "repel a sudden attack," the president would be required to notify Congress in writing within forty-eight hours to explain why the steps were taken and, if applicable, why the panel of congressional military advisors was not consulted. When national security interests do not demand secrecy, the advisors would have to be consulted and would be required to vote as a committee. Their decision would then have to be considered and voted upon by both congressional chambers before the president could take action.

At minimum, this proposal would produce greater deliberation between the two branches. It would require that the president consult with Congress and that at least some members of Congress consider and vote on the use of force prior to the military action; it would also protect national security interests when secrecy may be necessary. This proposal also avoids the issue of defining *war*. Some members of Congress and presidents mistakenly feel that in situations "short of war," the president should have authority and discretion on whether to use force. This was not the founding fathers' intent, nor was unlimited military discretion for the president approved with the passage of the WPR. This proposal would include Congress in all the United States' military decisions as the founders intended. It would not allow a president to make arbitrary distinctions about when the United States is truly engaged in "war." The Clinton administration argued that the United States and NATO were not at war in 1999 despite seventy-eight straight days of bombing sorties on Yugoslavia. Similar claims were made with regard to Iraq despite the many strikes conducted by the Clinton administration on Saddam Hussein since 1998. It seems safe to conclude that by most standards, Clinton's policies toward Iraq and Yugoslavia qualified as "war" and thus demanded specific congressional approval. This proposal would force members of Congress to vote on the president's military actions in such circumstances.

Like other proposals, however, this recommendation would be open to abuse by the president. As under Biden's Use of Force Act, under this proposal the president could claim that in an emergency and to repel a sudden attack, it had been impossible to consult with the congressional military advisors in a timely way. Even if the punitive measures against the president for violating the law were to include impeachment, it still seems unlikely that it would deter a determined White House from acting unilaterally. However, if this proposal were enforced in its infancy by committed members of Congress, a precedent could be established that would be increasingly difficult for the president to violate.

It is also necessary to educate the American public better on war powers and the need for and wisdom of checks and balances.[11] The American public appears to like a strong commander in chief, who will not bow to the likes of Saddam Hussein, Slobodan Milosevic, or Usama Bin Laden. Certainly the United States must face its enemies aggressively, but it must do so in a way that meets the most basic constitutional and democratic criteria. After the September 11 terrorist attacks, Congress accepted President Bush's invitation to grant him wide powers as commander in chief to fight terrorism. In this instance, Congress and the president acted in a constitutional manner: Congress discussed, albeit briefly, the merits of using force, and then granted the president military authority to act. While Congress sent its own strong signal to terrorists, it also empowered President Bush in a way that is strikingly similar to the Tonkin Gulf Resolution in 1964, granting him very wide, almost unlimited military powers. Following the onset of the American military strikes in October 2001, one hopes that Bush will use his military powers judiciously and with much discretion. Given Congress's past behavior and presidents' tendencies to interpret their military powers broadly, however, it will be extremely difficult to control Bush in whatever military direction he chooses. Congress sent a strong message to terrorists in SJR 23, but in practical political terms, that resolution empowered the president in a way that will make it nearly impossible to force the administration to change course if disagreements surface as the war on terrorism evolves and expands. It is noteworthy that in the first days of the bombings in Afghanistan, President Bush became angry over leaks to the media by members of Congress from confidential security briefings with the executive branch. Bush threatened to limit all future briefings to only a small group of congressional leaders. In bipartisan fashion, Congress agreed to respect the confidentiality of sensitive intelligence briefings more fully but also noted that its constitutional rights cannot be ignored by the president. Bush later compromised on his threats, but early signals of a perceived presidential omnipotence surfaced quickly in America's war against terrorism.[12] An imperial presidency does not serve the national interests, as many discovered during the Vietnam War.[13]

Statutory reforms such as Biden's and others seem unlikely, especially in the aftermath of the September 11 strikes. With American patriotism in its current heightened state and the new war on terrorism taking shape, members of Congress will not raise war powers reforms for fear of being perceived as un-American. Although members of Congress occasionally lament the imbalance of power, most members appear content with the current arrangement. If a military mission abroad goes badly, members of Congress can tell their constituents that it is not their fault. During the Clinton administration, Congress did not formally approve or disapprove of all military missions. Granting the president such wide powers works to Congress members' political advantage. In voting for vacuous resolutions that show "support for the troops," members also protect themselves from criticisms that they are partisan or obstructionist in times of crisis. Whether they are Democrat or Republican, party leaders are also likely to rally around their president to protect him from partisan challenges. Only after the casualties in Somalia did senior Democrats wage a war powers battle with Clinton over that deployment. Otherwise the Democrats, who were largely responsible for the passage of the WPR, insulated President Clinton from GOP challenges when possible.

One cannot expect reforms of this nature from the chief executive. Clinton, like all presidents since World War II, made wide assertions of power as commander in chief. Even though he and members of his administration initially expressed some interest in restoring a balance of war powers, the political reality was that Clinton preferred the well-entrenched practice of congressional deference and presidential unilateralism. When Clinton did consult with Congress, actions were attributable more to his own precarious political circumstances than to a genuine commitment to respect Congress's war powers. Like Clinton, future presidents will continue to seek autonomy in U.S. foreign policy making and avoid bringing Congress into the loop unless the domestic political conditions dictate. It might have been expected that if there was any time that Congress would reassert its war powers, it would have occurred with the Republican revolution after the 1994 midterm elections, when the presidency was in a weakened state. As demonstrated, however, such assertiveness did not take place. Leading members of Congress chose to pursue other political priorities rather than their constitutional war powers responsibilities. In fact, substantive reform seems possible only in the event that a constitutional crisis occurs. It took 58,000 American deaths in the Vietnam War for Congress to seek a restoration of its war powers via the War Powers Resolution of 1973. It will probably take more American casualties in what the public sees as a questionable use of force abroad before Congress seeks to restore the war powers granted to it by the founding fathers.

Appendix

Joint Resolution Concerning the War Powers of Congress and the President.

Resolved by the Senate and the House of Representatives of the United States of America in Congress assembled,

SHORT TITLE

SECTION 1. This joint resolution may be cited as the "War Powers Resolution."

PURPOSE AND POLICY

SEC. 2. (a) It is the purpose of this joint resolution to fulfill the intent of the framers of the Constitution of the United States and insure that the collective judgement of both the Congress and the President will apply to the introduction of United States Armed Forces into hostilities, or into situations where imminent involvement in hostilities is clearly indicated by the circumstances, and to the continued use of such forces in hostilities or in such situations.

(b) Under article I, section 8, of the Constitution, it is specifically provided that the Congress shall have the power to make all laws necessary and proper for carrying into execution, not only its own powers but also all other powers vested by the Constitution in the Government of the United States, or in any department or officer thereof.

(c) The constitutional powers of the President as Commander-in-Chief to introduce United States Armed Forces into hostilities, or into situations where imminent involvement in hostilities is clearly indicated by the circumstances, are exercised only pursuant to (1) a declaration of war, (2) specific statutory authorization, or (3) a national emergency created by attack upon the United States, its territories or possessions, or its armed forces.

CONSULTATION

SEC. 3. The President in every possible instance shall consult with Congress before introducing United States Armed Forces into hostilities or into situation where imminent involvement in hostilities is clearly indicated by the circumstances, and after every such introduction shall consult regularly with the Congress until United States Armed Forces are no longer engaged in hostilities or have been removed from such situations.

REPORTING

SEC. 4. (a) In the absence of a declaration of war, in any case in which United States Armed Forces are introduced—

(1) into hostilities or into situations where imminent involvement in hostilities is clearly indicated by the circumstances;

(2) into the territory, airspace or waters of a foreign nation, while equipped for combat, except for deployments which relate solely to supply, replacement, repair, or training of such forces; or

(3) in numbers which substantially enlarge United States Armed Forces equipped for combat already located in a foreign nation; the president shall submit within 48 hours to the Speaker of the House of Representatives and to the President pro tempore of the Senate a report, in writing, setting forth—

(A) the circumstances necessitating the introduction of United States Armed Forces;

(B) the constitutional and legislative authority under which such introduction took place; and

(C) the estimated scope and duration of the hostilities or involvement.

(b) The President shall provide such other information as the Congress may request in the fulfillment of its constitutional responsibilities with respect to committing the Nation to war and to the use of United States Armed Forces abroad

(c) Whenever United States Armed Forces are introduced into hostilities or into any situation described in subsection (a) of this section, the President shall, so long as such armed forces continue to be engaged in such hostilities or situation, report to the Congress periodically on the status of such hostilities or situation as well as on the scope and duration of such hostilities or situation, but in no event shall he report to the Congress less often than once every six months.

CONGRESSIONAL ACTION

SEC. 5. (a) Each report submitted pursuant to section 4(a)(1) shall be transmitted to the Speaker of the House of Representatives and to the President pro tempore of the Senate on the same calendar day. Each report so transmitted shall be referred to the Committee on Foreign Affairs of the House of Representatives and to the Committee on Foreign Relations of the Senate for appropriate action. If, when the report is transmitted, the Congress has adjourned sine die or has adjourned for any period in excess of three calendar days, the Speaker of the House of Representatives and the President pro tempore of the Senate, if they deem it advisable (or if petitioned by at least 30 percent of the membership of their respective Houses) shall jointly request the President to convene Congress in order that it may consider the report and take appropriate action pursuant to this section.

(b) Within sixty calendar days after a report is submitted or is required to be submitted pursuant to section 4(a)(1), whichever is earlier, the President shall terminate any use of United States Armed Forces with respect to which such report was submitted (or required to be submitted), unless the Congress (1) has declared war or has enacted a specific authorization for such use of United States Armed Forces, (2) has extended by law such sixty-day period, or (3) is physically unable to meet as a result of an armed attack upon the United States. Such sixty-day period shall be extended for not more than an additional thirty days if the President determines and certifies to the Congress in writing that unavoidable military necessity respecting the safety of United States Armed Forces requires the continued use of such armed forces in the course of bringing about a prompt removal of such forces.

(c) Notwithstanding subsection (b), at any time that United States Armed Forces are engaged in hostilities outside the territory of the United States, its possessions and territories without a declaration of war or specific statutory authorization, such forces shall be removed by the President if the Congress so directs by concurrent resolution.

CONGRESSIONAL PRIORITY PROCEDURES
FOR JOINT RESOLUTION OR BILL

SEC. 6. (a) Any joint resolution or bill introduced pursuant to section 5(b) at least thirty calendar days before the expiration of the sixty-day period specified in such section shall be referred to the Committee on Foreign Affairs of the House of Representatives or the Committee on Foreign Relations of the Senate, as the case may be, and such committee shall report one such joint resolution or bill, together with its recommendations, not later than twenty-four calendar days before the expiration of the sixty-day period specified in such section, unless such House shall otherwise determine by the yeas and nays.

(b) Any joint resolution or bill so reported shall become the pending business of the House in question (in the case of the Senate the time for debate shall be equally divided between the proponents and the opponents), and shall be voted on within three calendar days thereafter, unless such House shall otherwise determine by yeas and nays.

(c) Such a joint resolution or bill passed by one House shall be referred to the committee of the other House named in subsection (a) and shall be reported out not later than fourteen calendar days before the expiration of the sixty-day period specified in section 5(b). The joint resolution or bill so reported shall become the pending business of the House in question and shall be voted on within three calendar days after it has been reported, unless such House shall otherwise determine by yeas and nays.

(d) In the case of any disagreement between the two Houses of Congress with respect to a joint resolution or bill passed by both Houses, conferees shall be promptly appointed and the committee of conference shall make and file a report with respect to such resolution or bill not later than four calendar days before the expiration of the sixty-day period specified in section 5(b). In the event the conferees are unable to agree within 48 hours, they shall report back to their respective Houses in disagreement. Notwithstanding any rule in either House concerning the printing of conference reports in the Record or concerning any delay in the consideration of such reports, such report shall be acted on by both Houses not later than the expiration of such sixty-day period.

CONGRESSIONAL PRIORITY PROCEDURES
FOR CONCURRENT RESOLUTION

SEC. 7. (a) Any concurrent resolution introduced pursuant to section 5(b) at least thirty calendar days before the expiration of the sixty-day period specified in such section shall be referred to the Committee on Foreign Affairs of the House of Representatives or the Committee on Foreign Relations of the Senate, as the case may be, and one such concurrent resolution shall be reported out by such committee together with its recommendations within fifteen calendar days, unless such House shall otherwise determine by the yeas and nays.

(b) Any concurrent resolution so reported shall become the pending business of the House in question (in the case of the Senate the time for debate shall be equally divided between the proponents and the opponents), and shall be voted on within three calendar days thereafter, unless such House shall otherwise determine by yeas and nays.

(c) Such a concurrent resolution passed by one House shall be referred to the committee of the other House named in subsection (a) and shall be reported out by such committee together with its recommendations within fifteen calendar days and shall thereupon become the pending business of such House and shall be voted on within three calendar days after it has been reported, unless such House shall otherwise determine by yeas and nays.

(d) In the case of any disagreement between the two Houses of Congress with respect to a concurrent resolution passed by both Houses, conferees shall be promptly appointed and the committee of conference shall make and file a report with respect to such concurrent resolution within six calendar days after the legislation is referred to the committee of conference. Notwithstanding any rule in either House concerning the printing of conference reports in the Record or concerning any delay in the consideration of such reports, such report shall be acted on by both Houses not later than six calendar days after the conference report is filed. In the event the conferees are unable to agree within 48 hours, they shall report back to their respective Houses in disagreement.

INTERPRETATION OF JOINT RESOLUTION

SEC. 8. (a) Authority to introduce United States Armed Forces into hostilities or into situations wherein involvement in hostilities is clearly indicated by the circumstances shall not be inferred—

(1) from any provision of law (whether or not in effect before the date of the enactment of this joint resolution), including any provision contained in any appropriation Act, unless such provision specifically authorizes the introduction of United States Armed Forces into hostilities or into such situations and

stating that it is intended to constitute specific statutory authorization within the meaning of this joint resolution; or

(2) from any treaty heretofore or hereafter ratified unless such treaty is implemented by legislation specifically authorizing the introduction of United States Armed Forces into hostilities or into such situations and stating that it is intended to constitute specific statutory authorization within the meaning of this joint resolution.

(b) Nothing in this joint resolution shall be construed to require any further specific statutory authorization to permit members of United States Armed Forces to participate jointly with members of the armed forces of one or more foreign countries in the headquarters operations of high-level military commands which were established prior to the date of enactment of this joint resolution and pursuant to the United Nations Charter or any treaty ratified by the United States prior to such date.

(c) For purposes of this joint resolution, the term "introduction of United States Armed Forces" includes the assignment of member of such armed forces to command, coordinate, participate in the movement of, or accompany the regular or irregular military forces of any foreign country or government when such military forces are engaged, or there exists an imminent threat that such forces will become engaged, in hostilities.

(d) Nothing in this joint resolution—

(1) is intended to alter the constitutional authority of the Congress or of the President, or the provision of existing treaties; or

(2) shall be construed as granting any authority to the President with respect to the introduction of United States Armed Forces into hostilities or into situations wherein involvement in hostilities is clearly indicated by the circumstances which authority he would not have had in the absence of this joint resolution.

SEPARABILITY CLAUSE

SEC. 9. If any provision of this joint resolution or the application thereof to any person or circumstance is held invalid, the remainder of the joint resolution and the application of such provision to any other person or circumstance shall not be affected thereby.

EFFECTIVE DATE

SEC. 10. This joint resolution shall take effect on the date of its enactment.

CARL ALBERT
Speaker of the House of Representatives.

JAMES O. EASTLAND
President of the Senate pro tempore.

IN THE HOUSE OF REPRESENTATIVES, U.S.,
November 7, 1973.

The House of Representatives having proceeded to reconsider the resolution (H. J. Res 542) entitled "Joint resolution concerning the war powers of Congress and the President", returned by the President of the United States with his objections, to the House of Representatives, in which it originated, it was

Resolved, That the said resolution pass, two-thirds of the House of Representatives agreeing to pass the same.
Attest:
W. PAT JENNINGS
Clerk.

I certify that this Joint Resolution originated in the House of Representatives.
W. PAT JENNINGS
Clerk.

IN THE SENATE OF THE UNITED STATES
November 7, 1973

The Senate having proceeded to reconsider the joint resolution (H. J. Res. 542) entitled "Joint resolution concerning the war powers of Congress and the President", returned by the President of the United States with his objections to the House of Representatives, in which it originate, it was

Resolved, That the said joint resolution pass, two-thirds of the Senators present having voted in the affirmative.

Notes

Introduction

1. Senate Joint Resolution (SJR) 23 Congressional Record (September 14, 2001): H5683.

2. Quoted in Francis D. Wormuth and Edwin B. Firmage, *To Chain the Dog of War: The War Power of Congress in History and Law,* 2d ed. (Dallas: Southern Methodist University Press, 1986; reprint, Urbana: University of Illinois Press: 1989), 58.

3. *Congressional Record* (March 23, 1999): S 3067.

4. *Congressional Record* (April 28, 1999): H 2423.

5. Edward Keynes, *Undeclared War: Twilight Zone of Constitutional Power* (University Park: Pennsylvania State University Press, 1982); Steven J. Young, "Comment: A Bicentennial View of the Role of Congress, the President, and the Judiciary in Regard to the Power Over War," *Pace Law Review* 7 (1987): 695–758; Michael Ratner and David Cole, "The Force of Law: Judicial Enforcement of the War Powers Resolution," *Loyola of Los Angeles Law Review* 17 (1984): 715–66.

6. Louis Fisher, *Presidential War Power* (Lawrence: University Press of Kansas, 1995); Wormuth and Firmage, *To Chain the Dog of War*. On the nineteenth century, see Abraham D. Sofaer, *War, Foreign Affairs, and Constitutional Power* (Cambridge, Mass.: Ballinger, 1976). For broader studies of Congress and foreign policy that do not focus exclusively on war powers but give this issue substantive treatment see Gordon Silverstein, *Imbalance of Powers: Constitutional Interpretation and the Making of American Foreign Policy* (New York: Oxford University Press, 1997), and Michael Glennon, *Constitutional Diplomacy* (Princeton: Princeton University Press, 1990).

7. Public Law 93-148 (November 7, 1973).

8. David Gray Adler and Louis Fisher, "The War Powers Resolution: Time to Say Goodbye," *Political Science Quarterly* 113, no. 1 (1998): 1–20; Michael J. Glennon, "Too Far Apart: The War Powers Resolution," *University of Miami Law Review* 50, no. 17 (1995): 17–31; John Hart Ely, *War and Responsibility: Constitutional Lessons of Vietnam and Its Aftermath* (Princeton: Princeton University

Press, 1993); Edward Keynes, "The War Powers Resolution: A Bad Idea Whose Time Has Come and Gone," *University of Toledo Law Review* 23 (1992): 343–62; Eileen Burgin, "Congress, the War Powers Resolution, and the Invasion of Panama," *Polity* 25 (1992): 217–42; Robert Turner, *Repealing the War Powers Resolution: Restoring the Rule of Law in U.S. Foreign Policy* (Washington: Brassey's, 1991); Mark L. Krotski, "Essential Elements of Reform of the War Powers Resolution," *Santa Clara Law Review* 29 (1989): 607–752; Matthew D. Berger, "Implementing a United Nations Security Council Resolution: The President's Power to Use Force without Authorization of Congress," *Hastings International and Comparative Law Review* 15 (1991): 83–109; Michael Rubner, "The Reagan Administration, the 1973 War Powers Resolution, and the Invasion of Grenada," *Political Science Quarterly* 100 (1985–86), 627–47; Michael Glennon, "The War Powers Resolution Ten Years Later: More Politics Than Law," *American Journal of International Law* 78 (1984), 574–75; James A. Nathan, "The Mayaguez, Presidential War, and Congressional Senescence," *Intellect* 104 (1976), 360–62; Robert Zutz, "The Recapture of the S.S. Mayaguez: Failure of the Consultation Clause of the War Powers Resolution," *International Law and Politics* 8 (1976): 457–78.

9. For a few exceptions, see Donald L. Westerfield, *War Powers: The President, the Congress, and the Question of War* (Westport, Conn.: Praeger, 1996); Walter Dellinger, "After the Cold War: Presidential Power and the Use of Military Force," *University of Miami Law Review* 50 (1995), 107–18; David Locke Hall, *The Reagan Wars: A Constitutional Perspective on War Powers and the Presidency* (Boulder, Colo.: Westview, 1991).

10. For treatment of Congressional assertiveness during the Clinton administration, see Ralph G. Carter, ed., *Contemporary Cases in U.S. Foreign Policy: From Terrorism to Trade* (Washington, D.C.: Congressional Quarterly Press, 2001); James M. Scott, ed., *After the End: Making U.S. Foreign Policy in the Post–Cold War World* (Durham, N.C.: Duke University Press, 1998); James M. Lindsay, *Congress and the Politics of U.S. Foreign Policy* (Baltimore: Johns Hopkins University, 1994); Randall B. Ripley and James M. Lindsay, eds., *Congress Resurgent: Foreign and Defense Policy on Capitol Hill* (Ann Arbor: University of Michigan Press, 1993).

11. Clyde Wilcox, *The Latest American Revolution?: The 1994 Elections and Their Implications for Governance* (New York: St. Martins, 1995).

12. The Federal Bureau of Investigation uses the spelling "Usama Bin Laden" rather than "Osama," which is more frequently used by the mass media. This book follows the FBI's spelling.

13. The rescue missions conducted by the Clinton administration are not examined in this book. Little controversy between the president and Congress exists on the commander in chief's power to rescue Americans abroad. For a listing of these cases, see James M. Smith, "War Powers, Peace Powers: Presi-

dential Prerogative and Military Operations Other than War," *National Security Studies Quarterly* 6, no. 3 (2000): 1–24.

14. While recognizing the limits of case studies, I seek to follow Alexander L. George's criteria for "structured, focused comparisons." Each case includes examinations of the constitutional and legal claims provided by Congress and President Clinton when force was used. See Alexander L. George, "Case Studies and Theory Development: The Method of Structured, Focused, Comparison," in *Diplomacy: New Approaches in History, Theory, and Policy*, ed. Paul Gordon Lauren (New York: Free Press, 1979).

Chapter 1

1. See Francis D. Wormuth and Edwin B. Firmage, *To Chain the Dog of War: The War Powers of Congress in History and Law*, 2nd ed. (Urbana: University of Illinois Press, 1989), 29. See also John Yoo, "The Continuation of Politics by Other Means: The Original Understanding of War Powers," *California Law Review* 84 (1996), for an extended interpretation of the founding fathers' intent that generally corresponds with Goldwater's view.

2. John Tower, "Congress versus the President: The Formulation and Implementation of American Foreign Policy," *Foreign Affairs* (Winter 1981–82): 229–46.

3. Robert Bork, "Erosion of the President's Power in Foreign Affairs," *Washington University Law Quarterly* 68 (1990): 694–701.

4. See for example Joseph Avella, "Whose Decision to Use Force," *Presidential Studies Quarterly* 26, no. 2 (1996): 485–95.

5. 299 U.S. 304. See also David P. Forsythe and Ryan C. Hendrickson, "U.S. Use of Force Abroad: What Law for the President?" *Presidential Studies Quarterly* 26, no. 4 (1996): 951.

6. 389 U.S. 934.

7. 400 U.S. 886.

8. "Authority of the President to Repel the Attack in Korea," *Department of State Bulletin* (July 31, 1950): 173.

9. Quoted in Jean Edward Smith, *George Bush's War* (New York: Henry Holt and Co., 1992), 227. Cheney's figure of two hundred strikes does not include the numerous strikes on Iraq during the Clinton administration.

10. George Bush, "Statement on Signing the Resolution Authorizing the Use of Military Force against Iraq," *Public Papers of the Presidents of the United States* (January 14, 1991).

11. George Bush, "Remarks at the Texas State Republican Convention in Dallas, Texas," *Public Papers of the Presidents* (June 20, 1992): 995.

12. *Congressional Record* (June 20, 1950): 9450.

13. See Senators Eugene Miliken (R-Colo.) and Ralph Flanders' (R-Vt.) remarks in *Congressional Record* (June 20, 1950): 9541. See also Senator Paul Douglas (D-Ill.) for the widest interpretation of the president's powers as commander in chief, *Congressional Record* (July 5, 1950): 9647. Some senators argued that the Constitution had been violated, but these voices were in the minority. See for example, Senator Robert Taft (R-Ohio), *Congressional Record* (June 28, 1950): 9320, and Senator Kenneth Wherry (R-Nebr.), *Congressional Record* (June 30, 1950): 9538.

14. Thomas M. Franck and Faiza Patel, "UN Police Action in Lieu of War: 'The Old Order Changeth,'" *American Journal of International Law* 85 (1991): 63–74.

15. James Madison, *Notes of Debates in the Federal Convention of 1787* (1966; reprint New York: W. W. Norton, 1987), 476.

16. Ibid.

17. U.S. Constitution, Article I, Section 8.

18. See also John Hart Ely, *War and Responsibility: Constitutional Lessons of Vietnam and Its Aftermath* (Princeton: Princeton University Press, 1993).

19. See also Michael J. Glennon, *Constitutional Diplomacy* (Princeton: Princeton University Press, 1990).

20. David Gray Adler, "The Constitution and Presidential Warmaking: The Enduring Debate," *Political Science Quarterly* 103, no. 1 (1988): 1–36. Many of the arguments that follow are, in part, drawn from Adler's research on the conventions. See also Charles A. Lofgren, "War-Making under the Constitution: The Original Understanding," *Yale Law Journal* 81 (1972): 672–702.

21. Quoted in Charles Lofgren, "War-Making under the Constitution," 683.

22. See Adler, "The Constitution and Presidential Warmaking," 5.

23. Quoted in Wormuth and Firmage, *To Chain the Dog of War*, 61.

24. Adler, "The Constitution and Presidential Warmaking," 7.

25. The research of two scholars has been especially helpful in uncovering Congress's legislative intent at this time. Much of this section relies upon their research on the U.S. entry into the United Nations and NATO. See Louis Fisher, "Congressional Abdication: War and Spending Powers," *Saint Louis University Law Journal* 43, no. 3 (1999): 931–1012; Michael J. Glennon, "The Constitution and Chapter VII of the United Nations Charter," *American Journal of International Law* 85 (1991): 74–88. See also Matthew D. Berger, "Implementing a United Nations Security Council Resolution: The President's Power to Use Force with the Authorization of Congress," *Hastings International and Comparative Law Review* 15 (1991): 83–109.

26. *Congressional Record* (November 5, 1943): 9187, 9222.

27. *Congressional Record* (July 28, 1945): 8135.

28. Emphasis added. See UN Charter, Chapter 7, Article 43.

29. For additional analysis of these meetings, see Louis Fisher, "The Ko-

rean War: On What Legal Basis Did Truman Act?" *American Journal of International Law* 89 (1995): 26–27.

30. Public Law 79-264 (June 26, 1945), Chapter 583.

31. U.S. House of Representatives, Committee on Foreign Affairs, "Participation by the United States in United Nations Organization" (1945).

32. See Sean Kay, *NATO and the Future of European Security* (Lanham, Md.: Rowman and Littlefield, 1998), especially Chapter 2.

33. North Atlantic Treaty, Article 5.

34. U.S. House of Representatives, Committee on Foreign Affairs, "North Atlantic Treaty" (1949), 11. See also Michael J. Glennon, "United States Mutual Security Treaties: The Commitment Myth," *Columbia Journal of Transnational Law* 24 (1986): 530–32.

35. Ibid., 18, 25.

36. Ibid., 80.

37. Ibid., 261. See also pp. 262 and 263, where Lovett expounds upon Congress's role in declaring war and NATO military operations.

38. Emphasis added. I am indebted to Cecil V. Crabb Jr., *American Foreign Policy in the Nuclear Age*, 2d ed. (New York: Harper and Row, 1965), 210, for his research on this point.

39. *The Private Papers of Senator Vandenberg*, ed. Arthur H. Vandenberg Jr. (Boston: Houghton Mifflin, 1952), 418.

40. Michael J. Glennon, "United States Mutual Security Treaties: The Commitment Myth," *Columbia Journal of Trasnational Law* 24 (1986): 535. See also *Congressional Record* (July 21, 1949): 9915–16.

41. For more on the alleged attacks by the North Vietnamese and the faulty claims made by the Johnson administration about these events, see Robert S. McNamara, James G. Blight, and Robert K. Brigham, *Argument without End: In Search of Answers to the Vietnam Tragedy* (New York: Public Affairs, 1999), 167. See also Richard M. Pious, *The American Presidency* (New York: Basic Books, 1979), 386–87.

42. *Congressional Record* (August 7, 1964): 18471.

43. For the full legal claims, including an appeal to international law to justify the Johnson administration's position, see Leonard Meeker, "The Legality of United States Participation in the Defense of Vietnam," *Department of State Bulletin* (March 4, 1966), 484–85.

44. For the early opposition to President Johnson, see William Conrad Gibbons, *The U.S. Government and the Vietnam War*, Part 4, *July 1965–January 1968* (Princeton: Princeton University Press, 1995), especially Chapter 6. In contrast, see John Hart Ely, who argues in *War and Responsibility: Constitutional Lessons of Vietnam and Its Aftermath* (Princeton: Princeton University Press, 1993) that Congress consistently avoided its responsibility to check the president during the Vietnam War and preferred to voice its opposition to American military

involvement but at the same time did not want to be seen as "unpatriotic" or as "obstructionists" to the president. See also Arthur M. Schlesinger Jr., *The Imperial Presidency* (Boston: Houghton Mifflin, 1973).

45. *Congressional Record* (October 22, 1965): 28372. See also Fulbright's remarks in his *Arrogance of Power* (New York: Random House, 1966), especially 82–105.

46. *Congressional Record* (July 31, 1967): 20702.

47. For more analysis of these events, see Duane Tananbaum, "Not For the First Time: Antecedents and Origins of the War Powers Resolution, 1945–1970," in *Congress and United States Foreign Policy: Controlling the Use of Force in the Nuclear Age,* ed. Michael Barnhart (Albany: State University of New York Press, 1987), 39–54.

48. *Congressional Record* (June 15, 1970): 19656–58. For his early efforts on the resolution, see Senator Jacob K. Javits with Rafael Steinberg, *Javits: The Autobiography of a Public Man* (Boston: Houghton Mifflin, 1981).

49. See Pat M. Holt, *The War Powers Resolution: The Role of Congress in U.S. Armed Intervention* (Washington, D.C.: American Enterprise Institute for Public Policy Research, 1978): 1–9. For earlier attempts to assert congressional war powers during the cold war see Tananbaum, "Not for the First Time," 39–54.

50. Public Law 93-148 (November 7, 1973), Sec. 2(a).

51. Ibid., Sec. 2(c).

52. Ibid., Sec. 4(a)(2).

53. *Congressional Record* (November 7, 1973): 36206.

54. Public Law 93–148, Sec. 3, Sec. 5(a), and Sec. 5(b).

55. One notable exception is President Jimmy Carter, whose administration argued that the WPR was an understandable effort to check the president to prevent another Vietnam War and agreed that the United States' entry into war should be a collective judgement. See the remarks of Carter administration official Herbert Hansell, State Department legal advisor in U.S. Senate, Committee on Foreign Relations, "A Review of the Operation and Effectiveness of the War Powers Resolution" (1977), 188–90. See also Joseph R. Biden and John B. Ritch III, "The War Power at a Constitutional Impasse," *Georgetown Law Journal* 77 (1988): 392. However, in practice Carter avoided the requirement to "consult" with Congress during the American hostage rescue attempt in Iran.

56. *Congressional Record* (November 7, 1973): 36202, 36208, 36209, 36214.

57. Jacob K. Javits, "The Debate over the War Powers Resolution," in *Barnhart, Congress and United States Foreign Policy*, 55–59.

58. The opposition to the WPR has been well chronicled by Louis Fisher and David Gray Adler in "The War Powers Resolution: Time to Say Goodbye," *Political Science Quarterly* 113, no. 1 (1998): 1–20.

59. Robert A. Katzman, "War Powers: Toward a New Accommodation," in

A Question of Balance: The President, the Congress, and Foreign Policy, ed. Thomas E. Mann (Washington, D.C.: Brookings Institution, 1990), 35–69. The critiques of the WPR that follow can all be found in Katzman's essay.

60. This recollection is provided by Carter himself in *Keeping Faith: Memoirs of a President* (New York: Bantam Books, 1982): 513–14. Carter later regretted not consulting with Byrd in advance.

61. George P. Shultz, *Turmoil and Triumph: My Years as Secretary of State* (New York: Charles Scribner's Sons, 1993), 334–35.

62. Michael Rubner, "The Reagan Administration, the 1973 War Powers Resolution, and the Invasion of Grenada," *Political Science Quarterly* 100 (1985–86): 627–47. This violation of the WPR prompted eleven members of Congress to file suit against the Reagan administration. See *Conyers v. Reagan*, 578 F. Supp. 323 (D.D.C. 1984).

63. Eileen Burgin, "Congress, the War Powers Resolution, and the Invasion of Panama," *Polity* 25 (1992): 217–42.

64. Katzman, "War Powers," 60.

65. *Congressional Record* (September 14, 1983): 24036; John Lehman, *Making War: The 200-Year-Old Battle between the President and Congress over How America Goes to War* (New York: Charles Scribner's Sons, 1992), 101–9.

66. Ronald Reagan, *Public Papers of the Presidents,* "Statement on Signing the Multinational Force in Lebanon Resolution" (October 12, 1983): 1444.

67. Michael Rubner, "Reagan Administration."

68. Eileen Burgin, "Congress, the War Powers Resolution."

69. Judicial observers also point to the Supreme Court's decision in *Immigration and Naturalization Service v. Chadha,* 462 U.S. 919 (1983), in which the Court ruled that the legislative veto was unconstitutional. This decision potentially has relevance to the WPR and its language that allows Congress to force the president to bring deployed troops back to the United States. The WPR language has never been tested by the Supreme Court, but the *Chadha* decision represents another potential weakness of the WPR in the event that Congress should choose to enforce it strictly. See Katzman, "War Powers," 47.

Chapter 2

1. UN Security Council Resolution 794, paragraph 10.

2. Richard H. Shultz Jr., "State Disintegration and Ethnic Conflict: A Framework for Analysis," in *Annals* (September 1995): 75–88; and I. M. Lewis, *Somali Culture, History, and Social Institutions* (London: London School of Economics and Political Science, 1981).

3. Peter J. Schraeder, "From Ally to Orphan: Understanding U.S. Foreign Policy toward Somalia after the Cold War," in *After the End: Making U.S. Foreign Policy in the Post–Cold War World,* ed. James M. Scott (Durham, N.C.: Duke

University Press, 1998), 331; Anna Simons, *Networks of Dissolution: Somalia Undone* (Boulder, Colo.: Westview Press, 1995); Jonathan Stevenson, *Losing Mogadishu: Testing U.S. Policy in Somalia* (Annapolis: Naval Institute Press, 1995); Jeffrey Clarke, "Debacle in Somalia: Failure of the Collective Response," in *Enforcing Restraint: Collective Intervention in Internal Conflicts,* ed. Lori Fisler Damrosch (New York: Council of Foreign Relations Press, 1993).

4. See R. Shultz, "State Disintegration and Ethnic Conflict," 87, for his analysis of Barre. For congressional opinions of Barre, see statements of Sam Gejdenson (D-Conn.) in *Congressional Record* (September 8, 1988): E 2849; Paul Simon (D-Ill.), *Congressional Record* (September 20, 1988): S 12984; and Hamilton Fish (R-N.Y.), *Congressional Record* (November 10, 1987): E 4434.

5. U.S. House of Representatives, Committee on Foreign Affairs, *Consideration of Miscellaneous Bills and Resolutions,* Vol. 2 (February 19, 1992): 120.

6. Jane Perlez, "U.S. and Italy Evacuating Foreigners in Somalia" *New York Times* (January 6, 1991): A3.

7. Jennifer Parmelee, "Waltzing with Warlords," *New York Times* (June 20, 1993): C1.

8. See U.S. House of Representatives, Select Committee on Hunger, "Somalia: Case for Action," (July 22, 1992); U.S. House of Representatives, Committee on Foreign Affairs, Subcommittee on Africa, "A Review of U.S. Policy and Current Events in Kenya, Malawi, and Somalia," (June 23, 1992); and U.S. Senate, Committee on Foreign Relations, Subcommittee on African Affairs, "UN Peacekeeping in Africa: The Western Sahara and Somalia," (October 1, 1992); Senators Paul Simon (D-Ill.) and Howard Metzenbaum (D-Ohio), "Visit to Somalia, Kenya, Pakistan, India, Singapore, and the Philippines," Report to the Senate Committee on Foreign Relations (November 1992).

9. U.S. House of Representatives, Select Committee on Hunger, "Somalia: Case for Action," 85–87.

10. Mark R. Amstutz, *International Ethics: Concepts, Theories, and Cases in Global Politics* (Lanham, Md.: Rowman and Littlefield, 1999), 138–40; Mohamed Sahnoun, *Somalia: The Missed Opportunities* (Washington, D.C.: United States Institute of Peace Press, 1994).

11. George Bush, "Humanitarian Mission to Somalia," *Department of State Dispatch* (December 4, 1992).

12. Richard Benedetto, "Presidential Approval," *USA Today* (December 10, 1992): 6A; Richard Morin, "Poll Finds Public Is Optimistic about Economy and Clinton," *Washington Post* (December 16, 1992): A16; Bill Schneider, "CNN Pollster Finds Americans Approve of Somalia Mission," *CNN: Inside Politics*, Lexis-Nexis, all news file.

13. E. J. Dionne, "Clinton Turns Sights to Foreign Policy," *Washington Post* (July 29, 1992): A1; John M. Goshko, "U.N. Orders U.S.-Led Military Force in Somalia," *Washington Post* (December 4, 1992): A1.

14. UN Security Council Resolution 794.

15. *Congressional Record* (February 4, 1993): S 1363.

16. Ibid.

17. Stephen R. Weissman, *A Culture of Deference: Congress's Failure of Leadership in Foreign Policy* (New York: Basic Books, 1995).

18. U.S. Senate, Armed Services Committee, "Current Military Operations in Somalia (March 25, 1993): 20.

19. U.S. Senate, Armed Services Committee, "Current Military Operations in Somalia," 21, 28–29.

20. *Congressional Record* (May 8, 1986): 9968–71.

21. Clifford Krauss, "Mission to Somalia," *New York Times* (December 7, 1992): A13.

22. U.S. House of Representatives, Committee on Foreign Affairs, Subcommittee on Africa, "Recent Developments in Somalia" (February 17, 1993): 10.

23. Ibid., 17.

24. U.S. House of Representatives, Committee on Foreign Affairs, Subcommittee on International Security, International Organizations, and Human Rights, "Authorizing the Use of United States Armed Forces in Somalia," (April 27, 1993): 20.

25. Bill Clinton, "Letter to Congressional Leaders on the Situation in Somalia," *Public Papers of the Presidents* (June 10, 1993): 836–37.

26. *Congressional Record* (May 20, 1993): H 2614.

27. *Congressional Record* (May 25, 1993): H 2612.

28. *Congressional Record* (May 20, 1993): H 2608.

29. Ibid., H 2617.

30. *Congressional Record* (May 28, 1993): E 1401.

31. Michael Barone and Grant Ujifusa, comp. *The Almanac of American Politics 1994*, (Washington, D.C.: National Journal, 1994): 911.

32. *Congressional Record* (October 1, 1990): H 8441.

33. *Congressional Record* (January 10, 1991): H 175.

34. Quoted in Robert W. Gregg, *About Face? The United States and the United Nations* (Boulder, Colo.: Lynne Rienner, 1993), 117.

35. Quoted in Gregory J. Bowens, "House Backs Measure Allowing U.S. Role in UN Operation," *Congressional Quarterly Weekly* (May 29, 1993): 1373.

36. *Congressional Record* (May 20, 1993): H 2608.

37. Ibid., H 2612.

38. Ibid., H 2614.

39. *Congressional Quarterly Almanac* (1993): 485.

40. John M. Broder and Doyle McManus, "Clinton's Bosnia Plan Expected on Saturday," *Los Angeles Times* (April 30, 1993): A1.

41. *Congressional Record* (April 19, 1993): H 1899.

42. See Gary M. Stern and Morton H. Halperin, eds., *The U.S. Constitution*

and the Power to Go to War: Historical and Current Perspectives (Westport: Conn.: Greenwood, 1994), 168.

43. Past presidents have used the phrase "consistent with the War Powers Resolution" to show that they remain opposed to the resolution but are willing to report on their deployments within the forty-eight-hour time limit.

44. Bill Clinton, "Letter to Congressional Leaders on the Situation in Somalia," *Public Papers of the Presidents* (June 10, 1993): 836–37.

45. George Bush, "Statement on Signing the Resolution Authorizing the Use of Military Force Against Iraq," *Public Papers of the Presidents* (January 14, 1991): 40.

46. *Congressional Record* (August 4, 1993): E 1984–85.

47. Ibid., E 1985.

48. *Congressional Record* (September 14, 1983): 24036. See also John Lehman, *Making War: The 200-Year-Old Battle between the President and Congress over How America Goes to War* (New York: Scribner's, 1992), 101–9, for a good discussion of the legal semantics surrounding the U.S. deployment to Lebanon.

49. Donatella Lorch, "UN Troops Begin an Effort to Take Over Somali Streets," *New York Times* (July 11, 1993): Sec. 1, p. 14.

50. Carroll J. Doherty, "Byrd's Caution a Vietnam Legacy," *Congressional Quarterly Weekly* (October 16, 1993): 2824.

51. Quoted in Elizabeth A. Palmer, "Senate Demands Voice in Policy but Shies from Confrontation," *Congressional Quarterly Weekly* (September 11, 1993): 2399.

52. Palmer, "Senate Demands Voice," 2399.

53. Donatella Lorch, "Hunted Somalia General Lashes Out," *New York Times* (September 26, 1993): Sec. 1, p. 22.

54. Carroll J. Doherty, "Contrary Paths to Peacekeeping Converge in Wake of Violence," *Congressional Quarterly Weekly* (October 2, 1993): 2656.

55. Reid G. Miller, "American Body Paraded through Mogadishu," AP Worldstream (October 4, 1993). Reuters reported that a Time/CNN poll found that 60 percent of Americans felt that an immediate withdrawal would not undermine U.S. prestige in the world, and 37 percent favored an immediate withdrawal. "Most Americans Oppose Somalia Mission," Reuters Library Report, (October 9, 1993).

56. *Congressional Record* (October 5, 1993): S 13081.

57. *Congressional Record* (October 7, 1993): H 7550.

58. *Congressional Record* (October 6, 1993): S 13145–47.

59. Ibid., H 7460.

60. Carroll J. Doherty, "Clinton Calms Rebellion on Hill by Retooling Somalia Mission," *Congressional Quarterly Weekly* (October 9, 1993): 2751.

61. *Congressional Record* (October 6, 1993): S 13125. For Helms' feelings on the UN see Jesse Helms, "Saving the UN," *Foreign Affairs* 75 (September–Octo-

ber 1996): 2–8; Gregg, *About Face?*; and David P. Forsythe, *The Politics of International Law: U.S. Foreign Policy Reconsidered* (Boulder, Colo.: Lynne Rienner, 1990): 121.

62. Walter Clarke and Jeffrey Herbst, "Somalia and the Future of Humanitarian Intervention," *Foreign Affairs* 75 (March–April 1996): 73.

63. Bill Clinton, "The President's News Conference," *Public Papers of the Presidents* (October 14, 1993), 1746.

64. Doherty, "Clinton Calms Rebellion," 2750.

65. *Congressional Record* (October 14, 1993): H 7833.

66. *Congressional Record* (October 19, 1993): S 13927. See also Pat Towell, "Behind Solid Vote on Somalia: A Hollow Victory for Clinton," *Congressional Quarterly Weekly* (October 16, 1993): 2823.

67. U.S. Senate, Committee on Foreign Relations, "U.S. Participation in Somalia Peacekeeping," (October 19, 1993):15, 29, 43.

68. Ibid., 69–70.

69. *Congressional Record* (October 21, 1993): S 14157.

70. U.S. House of Representatives, Committee on Foreign Affairs, "Withdrawal of U.S. Forces from Somalia" (November 3, 1993): 33.

71. Carroll Doherty, "A Close Vote on War Powers," *Congressional Quarterly Weekly* (November 6, 1993): 3060.

72. Ibid., 3060.

Chapter 3

1. Paul Gordon Lauren, *Power and Prejudice: The Politics and Diplomacy of Racial Discrimination* (Boulder, Colo.: Westview, 1988), 24; Brian Weinstein and Aaron Segal, *Haiti: The Failure of Politics* (New York: Praeger, 1992), 22; Patrick Bellegarde-Smith, *Haiti: The Breached Citadel* (Boulder, Colo.: Westview, 1990), 45–48.

2. David Nicholls, *From Dessalines to Duvalier: Race, Colour, and National Independence in Haiti* (Cambridge: Cambridge University Press, 1979), 146; Weinstein and Segal, *Haiti*, 28; Julius W. Pratt, *A History of United States Foreign Policy*, 2nd. ed. (Englewood Cliffs: Prentice Hall, 1965), 232. See also Michael H. Hunt, *Ideology in U.S. Foreign Policy* (New Haven: Yale University Press, 1987), 100, and Lauren, *Power and Prejudice*, 24, for interpretations of American motives that are based more explicitly on racism.

3. See Bellegarde-Smith, *Haiti*, 95. Robert Lawless, *Haiti's Bad Press* (Rochester: Schenkman Books, 1992), 59, challenges the notion that the elections were corrupt but does note that some "minor irregularities" occurred. However, the evidence seems to be much stronger that serious corruption occurred.

4. Weinstein and Segal, *Haiti*, 38. Other historians have reached different

conclusions about the amount of U.S. support given to Duvalier. See Bellegarde-Smith, *Haiti*, 95.

5. Nicholls, *Dessalines to Duvalier*, 221.

6. Bellegarde-Smith, *Haiti*, 105. See also Domingo E. Acevedo, "The Haitian Crisis and the OAS Response: A Test of Effectiveness in Protecting Democracy," in *Enforcing Restraint: Collective Intervention in Internal Conflicts*, ed. Lori Fisler Damrosch (New York: Council on Foreign Relations, 1993), 126.

7. George Bush, "The President's News Conference," *Public Papers of the Presidents* (October 4, 1991): 1263.

8. See Assistant Secretary of State for Inter-American Affairs Bernard Aronson's comments in U.S. House of Representatives, Committee on Foreign Affairs, Subcommittee on Western Hemisphere Affairs, "Update on the Situation in Haiti" (October 31, 1991).

9. *Congressional Record* (October 2, 1991): H 7250, S 14201.

10. Quoted in Thomas Friedman, "Haitians Returned under New Policy," *New York Times* (May 27, 1992): A1.

11. Some members had also called for Bush to be more assertive earlier in the year by pushing for a wider economic embargo via UN Security Council Resolution. Other members felt that the OAS sanctions had little impact on Haiti. U.S. House of Representatives, Committee on Foreign Affairs, Subcommittee on Human Rights and International Organizations, "The Situation in Haiti and U.S. Policy," (February 19, 1992). See also U.S. House of Representatives, Subcommittee on Western Hemisphere Affairs, "U.S. Policy towards Haitian Refugees," (June 11 and 17, 1992).

12. Howard W. French, "Haitians' Advocates Admit Some Feelings of Betrayal," *New York Times* (January 15, 1993): A2.

13. Bill Clinton, "Remarks with President Jean-Bertrand Aristide of Haiti and an Exchange with Reporters," *Public Papers of the Presidents* (March 16, 1993): 309–11.

14. Bill Clinton, "The President's News Conference," *Public Papers of the Presidents* (June 17, 1993): 873.

15. Roland I. Perusse, *Haitian Democracy Restored: 1991–1995* (Lanham, Md.: University Press of America, 1995): 55.

16. *Congressional Record* (October 18, 1993): S 13565.

17. Bill Clinton, "Letter to Congressional Leaders on the use of United States Armed Forces in International Operations," *Public Papers of the Presidents* (October 18, 1993): 1770–71.

18. U.S. House of Representatives, Committee on Foreign Affairs, "Roundtable on Haiti—October 1993," (October 20, 1993): 7–8.

19. Howard French, "Aristide Team, with Help, Blocks the Sale of Gasoline," *New York Times* (October 22, 1993): A10.

20. See *Congressional Quarterly Weekly* (1993): 2925.

21. *Congressional Record* (October 27, 1993): H 8543.

22. *Congressional Record* (November 9, 1993): H 9050.

23. Quoted in Gregory J. Bowens, "'Bad Rap' for the CIA?" *Congressional Quarterly Weekly* (November 6, 1993): 3061.

24. Quoted in David Shanks, "Campaign to Discredit Aristide in the Final Phase," *Irish Times* (October 23, 1993): 8.

25. See Bowens, "'Bad Rap' for the CIA?" 3061.

26. Steven A. Holmes, "With Persuasion and Muscle, Black Caucus Reshapes Haiti Policy," *New York Times* (July 14, 1994): A10. See also Susan Webb Hammond, *Congressional Caucuses in National Policy Making* (Baltimore: Johns Hopkins University Press, 1998), 184.

27. *Congressional Record* (November 16, 1993): E 2892.

28. Bill Clinton, "Interview with Timothy Russert and Tom Brokaw on 'Meet the Press,'" *Public Papers of the Presidents* (November 7, 1993): 1926. See also Warren Christopher, "The Strategic Priorities of American Foreign Policy," *Department of State Dispatch* (November 22, 1993).

29. Bill Clinton, "Interview of CNN's Global Forum with President Clinton," *Public Papers of the Presidents* (May 3, 1994): 823–24.

30. Bureau of International Organization Affairs, "The Clinton Administration's Policy on Reforming Multilateral Peace Operations," Department of State (May 1994).

31. Ibid., 14–15.

32. Clinton notified Congress in April that naval forces were still deployed off Haiti's coast. See Bill Clinton, "Letter to Congressional Leaders Reporting on the Embargo on Haiti," *Public Papers of the Presidents* (April 20, 1994): 736–37.

33. See *Congressional Record* (January 26, 1994): E 35. Henry Hyde (R-Ill.) also introduced the Peace Powers Act in the House with Benjamin Gilman (R-N.Y.) as a cosponsor. However, the bill's primary author was Senator Bob Dole (R-Kans.), who introduced the act on the same day in the Senate.

34. See for example the statements of Lincoln Diaz-Balart (D-Fla.) regarding Haiti, *Congressional Record* (August 3, 1994): H 6739. Some members of the Florida delegation, however, were opposed to intervention. See *Congressional Record* (July 19, 1994): H 5870.

35. Steven Greenhouse, "Aristide Condemns U.S. Policy on Haiti," *Houston Chronicle* (April 22, 1994): A1. Other members of Congress who were arrested included some higher-profile Black Caucus leaders, including Ron Dellums (D-Calif.), Kweisi Mfume (D-Md.), and Major Owens (D-N.Y.). Others included Donald Payne (D-N.J.) and Barbara-Rose Collins (D-Mich.).

36. Michael Mandelbaum, "Foreign Policy as Social Work," *Foreign Affairs* 75 (January–February 1996): 16–32; Kevin Merida, "Hill's Black Caucus Faults U.S. Policy on Haiti," *Washington Post* (March 24, 1994): A7.

37. Robinson quoted in Alan Elsner, "Activist Begins Fast for Haiti Migrants," Reuters World Service (April 12, 1994). For more on Aristide's spending and lobbying efforts, see Julia Malone, "$90 Million Fund Was Depleted by Aristide in Exile," *New Orleans Times-Picayune* (September 28, 1994): A15.

38. U.S. House of Representatives, Committee on Foreign Affairs, Subcommittee on International Security, International Organizations, and Human Rights, "The War Powers Resolution," (May 1994).

39. *Congressional Record* (May 24, 1994): H 3933

40. Pat Towell, "On Issue of Using Military Abroad House Marches to a Different Drum," *Congressional Quarterly Weekly* (May 28, 1994): 1402–3.

41. Goss, who spoke on the House floor on the day of the vote, noted that there had been a "tortuous two weeks of arm twisting" after the vote in the Committee of the Whole. *Congressional Record* (June 9, 1994): H 4227. On the same day, Bill Richardson (D-N.M.) noted that because the Clinton administration had changed its refugee policy, the Goss amendment was no longer needed. Ibid., H 4278. This provides a partial explanation for the Democrats' defeat of Goss's amendment. The vote totals are given in *Congressional Quarterly Almanac* (1994): 68-H.

42. U.S. House of Representatives, Committee on Foreign Affairs, "U.S. Policy toward Haiti," (June 8, 1994): 41–42.

43. *Congressional Record* (August 2, 1994): H 6552.

44. U.S. House of Representatives, Committee on Foreign Affairs, Subcommittee on the Western Hemisphere, "Haiti: Views from Congress and Legislative Approaches," (July 27, 1994): 2.

45. *Congressional Record* (August 3, 1994): H 6703.

46. *Congressional Record* (August 12, 1994): H 8044.

47. Ibid.

48. *Congressional Record* (August 1, 1994): H 6545.

49. *Congressional Record* (January 26, 1994): S 181.

50. U.S. Senate, Committee on Foreign Relations, Subcommittee on Western Hemisphere and Peace Corps Affairs (March 8, 1994): 9.

51. *Congressional Record* (April 19, 1994): S 4466. The Democrats who introduced the measure included Christopher Dodd (D-Conn.), Tom Harkin (D-Iowa), Russ Feingold (D-Wis.), John Kerry (D-Mass.), Carol Moseley Braun (D-Ill.), and Paul Wellstone (D-Minn.). See *Congressional Quarterly Almanac* (1994), 449–50, and *Congressional Record* (April 19, 1994): S 4466. Paul Simon (D-Ill.) also added his name to the list of cosponsors. *Congressional Record* (April 21, 1994): S 4751.

52. *Congressional Quarterly Almanac* (1994): 43-S.

53. *Congressional Record* (August 1, 1994): S 10176–79.

54. Ibid., S 10180.

55. *Congressional Record* (August 5, 1994): S 10662.

56. Ibid., S 10665.

57. *Congressional Quarterly Almanac* (1994): 2377.

58. Steven Greenhouse, "A Haiti Invasion Wins Hemisphere Support," *New York Times* (June 13, 1994): A10. See also David P. Forsythe, *The Internationalization of Human Rights* (Lexington, Mass.: Lexington Books, 1991), 93, for more on anti-American sentiments in Latin America.

59. "Mexico 'Deplores' UN Resolution on Force in Haiti," Reuters News Service (July 31, 1994); "Cuba: Strongly Condemns UN Haiti Resolution," Reuters News Service (August 1, 1994).

60. Strobe Talbott, "U.S.-CARICOM Efforts to Support UN Security Council," *Department of State Dispatch* (September 5, 1994).

61. Adrian Dickson, "Brazil: U.S. Delegation to Brief Ministers on Haiti," Reuters News Conference (September 8, 1994).

62. *Congressional Record* (August 1, 1994): S 10178.

63. Talbott, "U.S.-CARICOM Efforts," 62.

64. U.S. House of Representatives, Committee on Foreign Affairs, "U.S. Policy Toward, and Presence in, Haiti," (September 13, 27, and 28, 1994): 2.

65. Ibid., 4.

66. Ibid., 6–7.

67. In the House, Congressmen Chris Cox (R-Calif.) and Gene Taylor (D-Miss.) attempted to introduce legislation calling for prior congressional approval of an intervention. *Congressional Record* (September 13, 1994): H9146. In the Senate, John McCain (R-Ariz.) and cosponsor Bob Dole (R-Kans.) introduced a nonbinding resolution stating that American soldiers' lives should not be risked trying to restore Aristide to power. *Congressional Record* (September 14, 1994): S 12862. See also Carroll J. Doherty, "President, Rebuffing Congress, Prepares to Launch Invasion," *Congressional Quarterly Weekly* (September 17, 1994): 2582.

68. Bill Clinton, "Address to the Nation on Haiti," *Public Papers of the Presidents* (September 15, 1994): 2605.

69. Ibid.

70. Douglas Jehl, "Threats in the Gulf," *New York Times* (October 11, 1994): A1.

71. Bill Clinton, "Letter to Congressional Leaders on Deployment of United States Armed Forces to Haiti," *Public Papers of the Presidents* (September 21, 1994): 1594–95.

72. Michael R. Kagay, "Occupation Lifts Clinton's Standing in Poll," *New York Times* (September 21, 1994): A16.

73. Carroll J. Doherty, "As U.S. Troops Deploy Peacefully, Clinton's Battle Has Just Begun," *Congressional Quarterly Weekly* (September 24, 1994): 2703.

74. See *Congressional Record* (October 6, 1994): S 14302 ff.

75. Quoted in Doherty, "As U.S. Troops Deploy," 2703.

76. *Congressional Record* (October 6, 1994): S 14310.

77. Ibid., S 14319.

78. Ibid., S 14313.

79. See Public Law 103-139, Sec. 17 (November 11, 1993).

80. *Congressional Record* (October 6, 1994): S 14313.

81. Carroll J. Doherty, "Congress, after Sharp Debate, Gives Clinton a Free Hand," *Congressional Quarterly Weekly* (October 8, 1994): 2895–96.

82. Quoted in ibid, 2895.

83. U.S. House of Representatives, Committee on Foreign Affairs, "Limited Authorization for the United States–Led Force in Haiti Resolution," Rept. 103–819 (October 3, 1994): 10.

84. Quoted in Doherty, "Congress, after Sharp Debate," 2896.

85. U.S. House of Representatives, Committee on Foreign Affairs, "U.S. Policy toward, and Presence in, Haiti," (September 13, 27, and 28, 1994): 77.

86. George Will, "And Then What?" *Washington Post* (September 18, 1994): C9; Roger Cohen, "Bosnia Foes Agree to 4-Month Truce, Carter Reports," *New York Times* (December 21, 1994): A1.

Chapter 4

1. Wilson's conception of self-determination was limited, in that only white Europeans were included among those who were allowed to create their own states. See Paul Gordon Lauren, *Power and Prejudice: The Politics and Diplomacy of Racial Discrimination* (Boulder, Colo.: Westview, 1988), 112.

2. Susan L. Woodward, *Balkan Tragedy: Chaos and Dissolution after the Cold War* (Washington, D.C.: Brookings Institute, 1995), 31–39.

3. Ibid.; Misha Glenny, *The Fall of Yugoslavia: The Third Balkan War* (New York: Penguin, 1993), 13.

4. Woodward, *Balkan Tragedy*, 25.

5. For the perspective of the U.S. Ambassador to Yugoslavia, see Warren Zimmermann, *Origins of a Catastrophe: Yugoslavia and Its Destroyers—America's Last Ambassador Tells What Happened and Why* (New York: Random House, 1996), 92.

6. V. P. Gagnon Jr., "Historical Roots of the Yugoslav Conflict," in *International Organizations and Ethnic Conflict*, ed. Milton J. Esman and Shibley Telhami (Ithaca, N.Y.: Cornell University Press, 1995), 188; John R. Lampe, *Yugoslavia as History: Twice There Was a Country* (New York: Cambridge University Press, 1996); James B. Moodie, "International Involvement in the Yugoslavia Conflict," in *Enforcing Restraint: Collective Intervention in Internal Conflicts*, ed. Lori Fisler Damrosch (New York: Council on Foreign Relations, 1993), 31.

7. Michael A. Sells, *The Bridge Betrayed: Religion and Genocide in Bosnia* (Berkeley: University of California Press, 1996); Gale Stokes, *Three Eras of Political*

Change in Eastern Europe (New York: Oxford University Press, 1997); Julie Kim, "Congress and the Conflict in Yugoslavia in 1992," in *Congress and Foreign Policy 1992* (Committee on Foreign Affairs, 1993), 58.

8. James A. Baker III with Thomas M. DeFrank, *The Politics of Diplomacy: Revolution, War, and Peace, 1989–1992* (New York: G. P. Putnam's Sons, 1995), 481. See also Zimmermann, *Origins of a Catastrophe*, 133.

9. Richard Holbrooke, *To End a War* (Random House: New York, 1998), 27.

10. See Baker, *Politics of Diplomacy*, 636.

11. Quoted in Holbrooke, *To End a War*, 27.

12. Zimmermann, *Origins of a Catastrophe*, 219; Baker, *Politics of Diplomacy*, 631. See also Blaine Harden, "Croatia Charges Army Shadows Its Officials," *Washington Post* (January 19, 1991): A10, on CIA predictions in early 1991 that a civil war could erupt in the former Yugoslavia and would entail many casualties.

13. See George Bush, "The President's News Conference in Kennebukport, Maine," *Public Papers of the Presidents* (August 11, 1992): 1326–30, for more on Bush's policy regarding humanitarian assistance.

14. Baker, *Politics of Diplomacy*, 651.

15. See Paul Claesson and Trevor Findlay, "Case Studies in Peacekeeping," in *SIPRI Yearbook 1994* (Oxford: Oxford University Press, 1994) and UN Security Council Resolutions 743 and 749 for more on UNPROFOR in its initial stages.

16. John M. Goshko, "UN Readies Sanctions on Belgrade," *New York Times* (May 29, 1992): A25. The Bosnian-Serbs also held five thousand Bosnian civilians hostage after an attack on Sarajevo in mid-May 1992. Carol J. Williams, "Serb Gunmen Hold 5,000 Muslim Women and Children," *Houston Chronicle* (May 21, 1992): A21.

17. Kim, "Congress and the Conflict in Yugoslavia," 66–67.

18. Kim, "Congress and the Conflict in Yugoslavia," 56; Public Law 102-391 (October 6, 1992).

19. Public Law 102-420 (October 16, 1992). See also Kim, "Congress and the Conflict in Yugoslavia," 77–78.

20. Quoted in Barton Gellman, "U.S. Military Fears Balkan Intervention," *Washington Post* (August 12, 1992): A24. See also Lee Michael Katz, "The New World Poses Same Old Threats," *USA Today* (November 6, 1992): 3A.

21. UN Security Council Resolution 781 and UN Security Council Resolution 786.

22. Frank J. Prial, "UN Tightens Curbs on Belgrade by Authorizing a Naval Blockade," *New York Times* (November 17, 1992): A1.

23. Bill Clinton, "Remarks at a Town Meeting in Detroit," *Public Papers of the Presidents* (February 10, 1993): 79–80.

24. Bill Clinton, "The President's News Conference with President Francois Mitterrand of France," *Public Papers of the Presidents* (March 9, 1993): 259.

25. Warren Christopher, "Capitol Hill Hearing with Defense Department Personnel, Confirmation Hearing for Warren Christopher," Federal Information Systems Corporation (January 13, 1993).

26. Warren Christopher, "New Steps towards Conflict Resolution in the Former Yugoslavia," *Department of State Dispatch* (February, 15, 1993).

27. Bill Clinton, "Statement Announcing Airdrops to Provide Humanitarian Aid to Bosnia-Herzegovina," *Public Papers of the Presidents* (February 25, 1993): 206.

28. The Macedonian peacekeeping force had been authorized by UN Security Council Resolution 795 on December 11, 1992, but U.S. troops did not arrive until July 1993. For more on Macedonian peacekeeping forces, see President Clinton's 1994 letters to Congress: "Letter to Congressional Leaders Reporting on Peacekeeping Operations in the Former Yugoslav Republic of Macedonia," *Public Papers of the Presidents* (January 8, 1994):17–18; and "Letter to Congressional Leaders Reporting on Peacekeeping Operations in the Former Yugoslav Republic of Macedonia," *Public Papers of the Presidents* (April 19, 1994): 728.

29. *Congressional Quarterly Almanac* (1993): 494.

30. See Philip Crane (R-Ill.), *Congressional Record* (June 23, 1993): 1608, and Toby Roth (R-Wis.), *Congressional Record* (June 21, 1993): 3857.

31. See Senator Carl Levine (R-Mich.), *Congressional Record* (June 9, 1993): S 6998.

32. *Congressional Quarterly Almanac* (1993): 495. See also the statements of Dave Durenberger (R-Minn.), *Congressional Record* (March 4, 1993): S2444; John Warner (R-Va.), *Congressional Record* (February 25, 1993): S2085; and Arlen Specter (R-Pa.), *Congressional Record* (February 25, 1993): S2061.

33. See *Congressional Record* (October 6, 1993): S 13102, and *Congressional Record* (October 7, 1993): S 13183. See also Senator Dan Coats' (R-Ind.) reservations about a troop deployment to Yugoslavia, *Congressional Record* (October 7, 1993): S 13214, and *Congressional Record* (October 21, 1993): S 14042. Hearings were also held on September 29, 1993, in the House on the crisis in the former Yugoslavia, but there were no major policy recommendations or calls for extreme caution. See U.S. House of Representatives, Committee on Foreign Affairs, "The Crisis in the Former Yugoslavia and the U.S. Role," (September 29, 1993).

34. Public Law 103-139 (November 11,1993).

35. Bill Clinton, "Letter to Congressional Leaders Reporting on the Conflict in the Former Yugoslavia," *Public Papers of the Presidents* (February 17, 1994): 281–83.

36. Bill Clinton, "Letter to Congressional Leaders Reporting on NATO Ac-

tion in Bosnia," *Public Papers of the Presidents* (March 1, 1994): 354–55; Bill Clinton, "Letter to Congressional Leaders on Protection of United Nations Personnel in Bosnia-Herzegovina," *Public Papers of the Presidents* (April 12, 1994): 679–80.

37. Quoted in *Facts on File*, "NATO Jets Down Suspected Bosnian Serb Warplanes" (April 14, 1994): 253.

38. Bill Clinton, "Letter to Congressional Leaders on Protection of United Nations Personnel," 679–80.

39. See Bill Clinton, "Interview of CNN's Global Forum with President Clinton," *Public Papers of the Presidents* (May 3, 1994): 820, which emphasized the importance of U.S. allies to Clinton's foreign policy justifications.

40. Bill Clinton, "Letter to Congressional Leaders Reporting on Peacekeeping Operations in the Former Yugoslavia Republic of Macedonia," *Public Papers of the Presidents* (April 19, 1994): 728.

41. *Congressional Record* (January 26, 1994): S 180.

42. *Congressional Quarterly Almanac* (1994): 445.

43. House of Representatives Committee of Foreign Affairs, Subcommittee on Europe and the Middle East, "The NATO Summit and the Future of European Security," (February 2, 1994): 42.

44. For Biden's comments, see Senate Committee on Foreign Relations and Senate Committee on Armed Services, "The Future of NATO," (February 1 and February 23, 1994). For more on McCloskey's position, see *Congressional Record* (March 16, 1993): E 639, and *Congressional Record* (April 20, 1994): E 2539. McCloskey was recognized as one of the key leaders in the House calling for a much more active approach to solving the conflict, including the use of force.

45. See Carroll J. Doherty, "U.S. Policy in Use of Force Puzzles Many Lawmakers," *Congressional Quarterly Weekly*, (April 16, 1994): 906; Carroll J. Doherty, "Authorization Bill Urges Clinton to Arm Bosnian Muslims," *Congressional Quarterly Weekly* (April 23, 1994): 1010.

46. *Congressional Record* (April 21, 1994): S 4607.

47. *Congressional Record* (April 19, 1994): H 2496.

48. *Congressional Record* (April 21, 1994): S 4602; *Congressional Record* (April 20, 1994): S 4550.

49. Public Law 103-236 (April 30, 1994).

50. Quoted in Clyde Wilcox, *The Latest American Revolution?* (New York: St. Martin's, 1995), 70.

51. Wilcox, *The Latest American Revolution?* 21; Gary C. Jacobson, *The Politics of Congressional Elections*, 4th ed. (New York: Addison Wesley, 1997), 162.

52. Maureen Dowd, "The Gap: Guess Who's Coming to Diplomacy," *New York Times* (September 25, 1994): A1.

53. Anthony Lake, "American Power and American Diplomacy," *Department of State Dispatch* (November 14, 1994).

54. Robert W. Gregg, *About Face? The United States and the United Nations* (Boulder, Colo.: Lynne Reinner, 1993); David P. Forsythe, *The Politics of International Law* (Boulder, Colo.: Lynne Reinner, 1990).

55. Quoted in Pat Towell, "House Votes Sharply to Reign in U.S. Peacekeeping Expenses," *Congressional Quarterly Weekly* (February 18, 1995): 535.

56. Quoted in Donna Cassata, "As UN marks its 50th Year, Congress Demands Change," *Congressional Quarterly Weekly*, (October 21, 1995): 3214.

57. Larry Combest, "Report National Security Revitalization Act," *House of Representatives International Relations Committee*, Rept. 104–18 (February 6, 1995): 11.

58. Floyd Spence, "Report: National Security Revitalization Act," *House of Representatives, International Relations Committee*, Part 1 (February 6, 1995).

59. Quoted in Towell, "House Votes Sharply to Reign in Peacekeeping Expenses," 535.

60. *Congressional Record* (February 16, 1995): H 1862.

61. *Congressional Quarterly Almanac* (1995): H-40.

62. *Congressional Quarterly Almanac* Ibid., 9-18.

63. Dole had earlier supported another version of his Peace Powers Act in 1994. *Congressional Record* (January 25, 1994): S 180.

64. *Congressional Record* (January 4, 1995): S 101.

65. Ibid.

66. U.S. Senate Committee on Foreign Relations, "The Peace Powers Act (S.5) and the National Security Revitalization Act (H.R. 7)," (March 21, 1995): 63.

67. Ibid., 25.

68. *Congressional Record* (June 7, 1995): H 5655–56, H 5672, H 5673.

69. Carroll J. Doherty, "House Approves Overhaul of Agencies, Policies," *Congressional Quarterly Weekly* (June 10, 1995): 1656.

70. For more on how the Speaker's role has changed in the House, especially under Newt Gingrich, see Douglas B. Harris, "The Rise of the Public Speakership," *Political Science Quarterly* 113, no. 2 (1998): 193–212, who says, "Gingrich was defying the traditional understanding of what a congressional party leader does" (193). See also Steven S. Smith and Eric D. Lawrence, "Party Control of Committees in the Republican Congress," in *Congress Reconsidered*, 6th ed., ed. Lawrence C. Dodd and Bruce I. Oppenheimer (Washington, D.C.: Congressional Quarterly Weekly, 1997).

71. Bill Clinton, "Communication from the President of the United States: H.R. 872," House Document 104–35 (February 14, 1995).

72. Bill Clinton, "Letter to Congressional Leaders on Reform of United Nations Peacekeeping," *Public Papers of the Presidents* (February 13, 1995).

73. Bill Clinton, "Remarks to the Nixon Center for Peace and Freedom Policy Conference," *Public Papers of the Presidents* (March 1, 1995). Similar sentiments

were expressed by Madeleine Albright, as well as Secretary Christopher. See Madeleine K. Albright, "Advancing American Interests through the United Nations," *Department of State Dispatch* (February 20, 1995); Warren Christopher, "Maintaining the Instruments of America's Global Leadership," *Department of State Dispatch* (March 6, 1995).

74. Elaine Sciolino, "Conflict in the Balkans," *New York Times* (June 6, 1995): A12.

75. Quoted on National Public Radio, *Morning Edition*, "Time For UN to Get Out of Bosnia," transcript 1648-10 (July 12, 1995).

76. On the issue of NATO enlargement as connected to NATO's new mission in Europe see James M. Goldgeier, *Not Whether but When: The Decision to Enlarge NATO* (Washington, D.C.: Brookings Institution Press, 1999): 35. See also Gerald B. Solomon, *The NATO Enlargement Debate, 1990–1997* (Westport, CT: Praeger, 1998).

77. U.S. House of Representatives, Committee on International Relations, "Situation in Bosnia," (June 8, 1995): 2, 22.

78. *Congressional Quarterly Almanac* (1995): 10–11.

79. For a full discussion of this policy change, see Ivo H. Daalder, *Getting to Dayton: The Making of America's Bosnia Policy* (Washington, D.C.: Brookings Institution Press, 2000).

80. Rich Atkinson, "With Deliberate Force in Bosnia," *Washington Post Weekly* (November 7, 1995): 6.

81. Bill Clinton, "Letter to Congressional Leaders Reporting on the Deployment of United States Aircraft to Bosnia-Herzegovina," *Public Papers of the Presidents* (September 1, 1995): 1279–80.

82. Congressman Bill Baker (R-Calif.) did oppose the bombings, but most members said very little. *Congressional Record* (September 14, 1995): H 8913.

83. Carroll J. Doherty, "Clinton Vow to Provide Troops Revives War Powers Conflict," *Congressional Quarterly Weekly* (October 14, 1995): 3158.

84. Quoted in Steve Holland, "Christopher Says Congress Must Sign Off on Bosnia," Reuters North American Wire (September 27, 1995).

85. Bill Clinton, "America Must Continue to Bear the Responsibility of World Leadership," *Department of State Dispatch* (October 16, 1995).

86. Pat Towell, "White House Tries to Head Off Hill's Curbs on Peacekeeping," *Congressional Quarterly Weekly* (November 11, 1995): 3467.

87. Pat Towell and Donna Cassata, "House Votes to Block Clinton from Sending Peacekeepers," *Congressional Quarterly Weekly* (November 18, 1995): 3549.

88. Bill Clinton, "Address to the Nation on Implementation of the Peace Agreement in Bosnia-Herzegovina," *Public Papers of the Presidents* (November 27, 1995): 1784–87.

89. Bill Clinton, "Letter to Congressional Leaders on the Deployment of

United States Military Forces for Implementation of the Balkan Peace Process," *Public Papers of the Presidents* (December 6, 1995): 1856–57.

90. Bill Clinton, "Letter to Congressional Leaders on the Deployment of United States Military Forces for Implementation of the Balkan Peace Process," *Public Papers of the Presidents* (December 21, 1995): 1917–18.

91. *Congressional Quarterly Almanac* (1995): H-214.

92. Quoted in Pat Towell, "House Opposes Peacekeeping Role, Delays Vote on Cutoff of Funds," *Congressional Quarterly Weekly* (November 4, 1995): 3390.

93. See Towell, "White House Tries," 3467.

94. Adam Clymer, "Big Risk for the GOP," *New York Times* (November 11, 1995): Sec. 1, p. 10.

95. *Congressional Quarterly Almanac* (1995): H-234.

96. U.S. House of Representatives, Committee on International Relations, "U.S. Policy towards Bosnia," (December 6, 1995): 40.

97. Doug Bereuter, interview with the author, April 25, 1997.

98. Quoted in Pat Towell, "Congress Torn over Response as Deployment Begins," *Congressional Quarterly Weekly* (December 9, 1995): 3750.

99. See for example the comments of Helen Chenoweth (R-Idaho) and Bob Dornan (R-Calif.), *Congressional Record* (December 7, 1995): H 14229–31.

100. *Congressional Record* (December 13, 1995): H 14849.

101. *Congressional Record* (September 26, 1995): S 14271.

102. *Congressional Quarterly Almanac* (1995): S-77.

103. U.S. Senate, Committee on Foreign Relations, "The Peace Process in the Former Yugoslavia," (October 17 and December 1, 1995): 31.

104. Ibid.

105. Jim Exon, interview with the author, March 25, 1997.

106. *Congressional Record* (October 20, 1995): S 15399.

107. See Ralph Hallow, "Bosnia Sharpens Choice for GOP," *Washington Times* (November 29, 1995): A12.

108. *Congressional Quarterly Almanac* (1995): S-99. Feingold opposed U.S. military involvement in Bosnia on constitutional grounds until the very end. See *Congressional Record* (December 13, 1995): S 18552.

109. Richard Benedetto, "Clinton Numbers Looking Up," *USA Today* (July 26, 1995): 5A.

110. *Congressional Record* (March 18, 1998): H 1260.

111. See the remarks of Representatives Jack Metcalf, (R-Wis.), Ron Paul (R-Tex.) and Marshall Sanford (R-S.C.). See especially the remarks of Henry Bonilla (R-Tex.). *Congressional Record* (March 18): H1264–68.

112. *Congressional Record* (March 18, 1998): H1261, H1265.

113. Historically Speakers have not participated in open floor debates. However, given Gingrich's past ability to use the media effectively on the House floor as the Republican Minority Whip, his absence as Speaker is noteworthy.

See David W. Rohde, *Parties and Leaders in the Postreform House* (Chicago: University of Chicago Press, 1991).

114. Gingrich did not register on the vote. *Congressional Record* (March 18, 1998): H 1279.

115. Ibid., H 1276.

116. See especially the remarks of Representatives Steve Buyer (R-Ind.) and Charles Taylor (R-Miss.) in the *Congressional Record* (March 18, 1998): H 1264, H 1268.

117. *Congressional Record* (February 7, 1990): H 324.

118. Carroll J. Doherty, "A Close Vote on War Powers" *Congressional Quarterly Weekly* (November 6, 1993): 3060.

119. *Congressional Record* (March 18, 1998): H 1269.

Chapter 5

1. Public Law 93-148 (November 7, 1993), Sec. 2 (c)(3).

2. Ibid., Section 3.

3. Public Opinion Online, Roper Center (April 3–6, 1997, accession no. 0276690, question no. 055, and September 4–11, 1997, accession no. 0285442, question no. 003) at LexisNexis, polls and surveys.

4. In the Saudi Arabian attack, approximately 250 other Americans were injured, as well as 147 Saudis and 118 Bangladeshis. See Douglas Jehl, "Bombings in Saudi Arabia: The Overview," *New York Times* (June 27, 1996): A1.

5. David Tucker, "Responding to Terrorism," *Washington Quarterly* (1998): 103–17.

6. John Deutch, "Terrorism," *Foreign Policy* (Fall 1997): 10–22; Walter Laqueur, "Postmodern Terrorism," *Foreign Affairs* (September–October, 1996): 24–36. See also Walter Enders and Todd Sandler, "Transnational Terrorism in the Post–Cold War Era," *International Studies Quarterly* 43 (1999): 145, for more on post–Cold War trends and terrorism.

7. See www.state.gov/www/global/terrorism/index.html.

8. U.S. State Department, Office for Counterterrorism, "International Terrorism Conventions," August 17, 1998 (currently available at www.state.gov/www/global/terrorism/980817_terror_conv.html).

9. See Deutch, "Terrorism."

10. Vernon Lobe, "A Global Pan-Islamic Network: Terrorism Entrepreneur Unifies Groups Financially, Politically," *Washington Post* (August 23, 1998): A1; U.S. State Department, "Fact Sheet: Usama bin Laden" (August 21, 1998), released by the Coordinator for Counterterrorism; *Intelligence Newsletter*, "Bin Laden Acts after Treasurer's Defection" (March 19, 1998), LexisNexis, Middle East news file.

11. Lobe, "A Global Pan-Islamic Network." See also Magnus Ranstorp, "Interpreting the Broader Context and Meaning of Bin-Laden's *Fatwa*," *Studies in Conflict and Terrorism* 21 (1998): 321–30, for a reprint of the text and analysis of Bin Laden and Bernard Lewis, "License to Kill: Usama bin Ladin's Declaration of Jihad," *Foreign Affairs* (November–December 1998): 14–19.

12. Lillian Craig Harris, *Libya: Qadhafi's Revolution and the Modern State* (Boulder, Colo.: Westview, 1986); David Blundy and Andrew Lycett, *Qaddafi and the Libyan Revolution* (Boston: Little, Brown, 1987).

13. Don Oberdorfer, "U.S., Libya Near State of Undeclared War," *Washington Post* (April 6, 1986): A35; Associated Press, "U.S., Libya Have Been at Odds Since Khadafy Came to Power," *San Diego Union-Tribune* (March 25, 1986): A8.

14. *Congressional Quarterly Almanac* (1986): 199; Pat Towel, "After Raid on Libya, New Questions on Hill," *Congressional Quarterly Weekly* (April 19, 1986): 838. See also Associated Press, "Qaddafi's Wife Is Angry," *New York Times* (April 22, 1986): A8. For doubts on Qaddafi's claims regarding the death of the adopted daughter, see Bob Woodward, "Libyans Show Bombed Naval School," *Washington Post* (April 21, 1986): A1.

15. "Reagan, Officials' Statements on Libya," *Congressional Quarterly Weekly* (April 19, 1986): 881.

16. Ronald Reagan, "Letter to the Speaker of the House of Representatives and the President Pro Tempore of the Senate of the United States on the United States Air Strike against Libya." *Public Papers of the Presidents* (April 16, 1986): 478.

17. James Reston, "Leave It to the People," *New York Times* (April 20, 1986): Sec. 4, p. 25; Tom Wicker, "After the Raids," *New York Times* (April 18, 1986): A35.

18. Pat Towell, "After Raid on Libya, New Questions on Hill," *Congressional Quarterly Weekly* (April 19, 1986): 839.

19. See John Felton, "In Wake of Libya, Skirmishing over War Powers," *Congressional Quarterly Weekly* (May 10, 1986): 1022–23.

20. *Congressional Record* (April 17, 1986): 7894–97.

21. U.S. House of Representatives, Subcommittee on Arms Control, International Security, and Science, "War Powers, Libya, and State-Sponsored Terrorism" (April 29, May 1 and 15, 1986): 12–32.

22. Madeleine K. Albright and Sandy Berger, "Press Briefing on U.S. Strikes on Sudan and Afghanistan," Office of Press Secretary, U.S. State Department (August 20, 1998), secretary.state.gov/www/statements/1998/980820.html.

23. Bill Clinton, "Remarks on Departure for Washington, D.C., from Martha's Vineyard, Massachusetts," *Weekly Compilation of Presidential Documents* (August 20, 1998): 1642–43. For more detailed presentation to the public, see Bill Clinton, "Address to the Nation on Military Action against Terrorist Sites in Afghanistan and Sudan," *Weekly Compilation of Presidential Documents* (August 20, 1998):

1643. Many of these arguments were repeated in the president's weekly radio address two days later. See Bill Clinton, "The President's Radio Address," *Weekly Compilation of Presidential Documents* (August 22, 1998): 1651–52.

24. Bill Clinton, "Letter to Congressional Leaders Reporting on Military Action against Terrorist Sites in Afghanistan and Sudan," *Weekly Compilation of Presidential Documents* (August 21, 1998): 1650–51.

25. See for example Bill Clinton, "Letter to Congressional Leaders on the Strike on Iraqi Intelligence Headquarters," *Public Papers of the Presidents* (June 28, 1993): 940–41. This strike is treated more extensively in Chapter 7.

26. Mike McCurry, "Remarks in Gaggle," Office of the Press Secretary, the White House (August 20, 1998); Chuck McCutcheon, "Lawmakers Back Missile Strikes Despite a Bit of GOP Skepticism," *Congressional Quarterly Weekly* (August 22, 1998): 2289–90.

27. Albright and Berger, "Press Briefing on U.S. Strikes." For an excellent journalistic chronology, see Doyle McManus and Alan C. Miller, "For Clinton Team, Fortnight Spent Battling on Two Fronts," *Los Angeles Times* (August 21, 1998): A1.

28. McCutcheon, "Lawmakers Back Missile Strikes."

29. Ibid., 2289.

30. Guy Gugliotta and Juliet Eilperin, "Tough Response Appeals to Critics of President," *Washington Post* (August 21, 1998): A17. For more on Galen's relationship with Gingrich see Michael Kranish, "Biggest Battle Could Lie Ahead," *Boston Globe* (August 18, 1998): A1.

31. For Dicks' quote see Wendy Koch and Jessica Lee, "Support on Hill Mostly Solid," *USA Today* (August 21, 1998): 6A. See also Gugliotta and Eilperin, "Tough Response Appeals to Critics of President."

32. James Risen, "Question of Evidence," *New York Times* (October 27, 1999): A1.

33. See Tim Weiner, "U.S. Hard Put to Find Proof Bin Laden Directed Attacks," *New York Times* (April 13, 1999): A1. However, these efforts have drawn minimal attention from Congress. For one exception, see *Congressional Record* (September 23, 1998): H 8508.

34. Douglas Turner, "Credibility of President Is in Crisis, Polls Show," *Buffalo News* (August 19, 1998): A1.

35. Mark Z. Barabak, "The Times Poll," *Los Angeles Times* (August 23, 1998): A1.

36. Biden's interest in war powers is well established. For example, see Joseph R. Biden and John B. Ritch III, "The War Power at a Constitutional Impasse," *Georgetown Law Journal* 77 (1988), and Biden's effort to reassert Congress's war powers in *Congressional Record* (July 30, 1998): S 9444. For Feingold's interest see Russ Feingold, "The Role of Congress in Deploying U.S. Troops Abroad," *Brown Journal of International Affairs* 3 (Winter–Spring 1996).

37. For a similar interpretation of the requirements of "consultation" and terrorists, see the remarks of John F. Seiberling (D-Ohio) in U.S. House of Representatives, Subcommittee on Arms Control, International Security, and Science, "War Powers, Libya, and State-Sponsored Terrorism" (April 29, May 1 and 15, 1986): 288.

38. See Thomas G. Paterson, "Congress, the CIA, and Covert Actions," in *Congress and United States Foreign Policy: Controlling the Use of Force in the Nuclear Age*, ed. Michael Barnhart (Albany: State University of New York Press, 1987): 165.

39. Bill Clinton, "Address to the Nation on Testimony before the Independent Counsel's Grand Jury," *Public Papers of the Presidents* (August 17, 1998): 1638.

40. See Turner, "Credibility of President"; Mark Suzman, "Lewinsky Called Back to Appear before Grand Jury," *Financial News* (August 19, 1998): 1.

41. Clyde Wilcox, *The Latest American Revolution?: The 1994 Elections and Their Implications for Governance* (New York: St. Martins, 1995).

42. Stephen R. Weissman, *A Culture of Deference: Congress's Failure of Leadership in Foreign Policy* (New York: Basic Books, 1995); Joseph S. Nye, "The Domestic Environment of U.S. Policy Making," in *U.S.-Soviet Relations: The Next Phase,* ed. Arnold L. Horelick (Ithaca, N.Y.: Cornell University Press, 1986).

43. See David Maraniss, *First in His Class: The Biography of Bill Clinton* (New York: Simon and Schuster, 1996).

44. Kathy Kiely and Richard Sisk, "Prez Goes After Terror Assets," *New York Daily News* (August 23, 1998): 3. See also Brian McGrory, "U.S. Calls Terrorists' Losses Significant," *Boston Globe* (August 22, 1998): A1.

45. On November 29, 1999, President Clinton signed a bill into law that allowed the United States to direct its foreign assistance to rebel groups in Sudan. See *Houston Chronicle*, "Measure Lets U.S. Give Food to Sudanese Rebels; Critics Say Law Violates Neutrality Principle," (November 30, 1999): A19.

46. Ira Rifkin, "Muslims on Rise, Urged to Flex Political Muscle," *Arizona Republic* (April 25, 1998): R1.

47. Colum Lynch, "Saudi Exile Vows 'War' on U.S.," *Boston Globe* (August 22, 1998): A1.

48. Elizabeth Bryant, "Targeting Terrorism," *Houston Chronicle* (August 22, 1998): A19. See also John Daniszewski and Dexter Filkins, "Attack on Terrorism" *Los Angeles Times* (August 22, 1998): A19.

49. Craig Turner and Doyle McManus, "Sudan Gets Little Support for a UN Probe of U.S. Attack," *Los Angeles Times* (August 25, 1998): A6.

50. Hugh Davies and Tim Butcher, "U.S. Strikes 'First Blow in War of Future': FBI Heightens Security as Millionaire Terrorist Promises to Retaliate," *Ottawa Citizen* (August 22, 1998): A3.

51. Frank Ching, "China Feels Let Down by U.S.," *Far Eastern Economic Review* (September 24, 1998): 38.

Chapter 6

1. Elizabeth Becker, "Rights Group Says NATO Killed 500 Civilians in Kosovo War," *New York Times* (February 7, 2000): A10. By Serbian estimates two thousand civilians were killed by NATO. Kevin Cullen, "Amid Rubble and Death, Few Find Elation in Milosevic's 'Victory,'" *Boston Globe* (June 11, 1999): A22; Michael Binyon and Charles Bremner, "NATO Words 'Matched by Deeds,'" *London Times* (June 22, 1999): LexisNexis world news file, Europe.

2. "Beyond Impeachment," *New York Times* (February 14, 1999): Sec. 4, p. 12; "Clinton, Congress Leaders to Meet," *Boston Globe* (February 22, 1999): A8.

3. Jane Perlez, "Doubts on NATO Air Raids As the Talks on Kosovo End," *New York Times* (March 19, 1999): A1.

4. Henry Kissinger, "U.S. Intervention in Kosovo Is a Mistake," *Boston Globe* (March 1, 1999): A15. See also U.S. House of Representatives, Committee on International Relations, "The United States' Role in Kosovo" (March 10, 1999).

5. John Goshko, "Bush Threatens 'Military Force' If Serbs Attack Ethnic Albanians," *Washington Post* (December 29, 1992): A10.

6. Tim Judah, *Kosovo: War and Revenge* (New Haven: Yale University Press, 2000); Misha Glenny, *The Fall of Yugoslavia: The Third Balkan War* (London: Penguin, 1992), 32; Christopher Bennett, *Yugoslavia's Bloody Collapse: Causes, Course, and Consequences* (New York: New York University Press, 1995), 215.

7. Guy Dinmore and Lionel Barber, "Kosovo Violence 'Spinning out of Control,'" *Financial Times* (April 28, 1998): 2; Tracy Wilkinson, "Kosovo Rallies Mark Passage of Deadline," *Los Angeles Times* (March 20, 1998): A4.

8. William Cohen, "Remarks at NATO Headquarters, Brussels, Belgium," Department of Defense press statement (June 11, 1998). See also Susan M. Schafer, "Cohen: NATO Doesn't Need UN Permission for Kosovo Action," Associated Press (June 13, 1998), LexisNexis, general news file.

9. Madeleine K. Albright, "Press Conference, Lancaster House, Foreign and Commonwealth Office" (June 12, 1998), secretary.state.gov/www/statements/1998/980612a.html.

10. U.S. Congress, Commission on Security and Cooperation in Europe, "Repression and Violence in Kosovo" (March 18, 1998) and "Kosovo—The Humanitarian Perspective" (June 25, 1998).

11. Congressman Thomas Campbell (R-Calif.) and fifteen other members of Congress sent a letter to President Clinton on August 7, 1999, stating that any "hostile military action" by the United States in Yugoslavia would require advance authorization from Congress. However, these efforts received little

publicity and represented less than 10 percent of the House of Representatives. Thomas Campbell, "Letter to White House," *Personal Papers of Thomas Campbell* (August 7, 1998).

12. UN Charter, Chapter 8, Article 52.

13. Jane A. Meyer, "Collective Self-Defense and Regional Security: Necessary Exceptions to a Globalist Doctrine," *Boston University International Law Journal* 11 (1993): 407–8; Thomas K. Plofchan, "Article 51: Limits on Self-Defense," *Michigan Journal of International Law* 13 (Winter 1992): 348–49.

14. UN Charter, Chapter 1, Article 2.

15. Robert W. Gregg, *About Face?: The United States and the United Nations* (Boulder, Colo.: Lynne Reinner, 1993), especially Chapter 5.

16. "France Ready to Back Military Intervention in Kosovo," Xinhua News Agency (June 9, 1998), LexisNexis, European news file.

17. "Military Action in Kosovo Risky, France's Chirac Tells Yeltsin," *Agence France Presse* (August 20, 1998), LexisNexis, European news file.

18. "Incoming German Chancellor Wants UN Mandate for Kosovo Intervention," *Agence France Presse* (September 28, 1998), LexisNexis, European news file; Henriette Lowisch, "Washington, Bonn Agree on NATO Strikes on Kosovo, Economic Concerns," *Agence France Presse* (October 9, 1998), LexisNexis, European news file.

19. UN Security Council Resolution 1199.

20. "Statement by the North Atlantic Council on Kosovo," NATO Press Release (99) 12 (January 30, 1999), www.nato.int/docu/pr/1999/p99-012e.htm; Madeleine K. Albright, "Statement on NATO Final Warning on Kosovo," U.S. Department of State (January 30, 1999).

21. Correspondence from David E. Skaggs and Thomas Campbell to All Members of Congress, "Air Strikes Require Authority from Congress" (October 1, 1998).

22. Samuel Berger, letter to Congressman Thomas Campbell. (January 15, 1999).

23. U.S. House of Representatives, Committee on International Relations, "The U.S. Role in Kosovo," (February 10, 1999): 17.

24. Personal papers of Thomas Campbell, letter to White House, February 19, 1999.

25. See also Miles A. Pomper, "Congress Wants a Bigger Voice on Sending Troops to Kosovo," *Congressional Quarterly Weekly* (February 27, 1999): 499.

26. *Congressional Record* (March 11, 1999): H 1249.

27. Ibid., H 1180.

28. Ibid., H 1182, H1185.

29. Miles A. Pomper, "Kosovo Vote, Though Won by Clinton, May Signal New Level of Hill Involvement," *Congressional Quarterly Weekly* (March 13, 1999): 621–22.

30. Joe Lockhart, "Press Briefing," White House, Office of the Press Secretary (March 23, 1999).

31. Chapter 7 addresses these dynamics in greater detail. See Miles Pomper, Chuck McCutcheon, and Pat Towell, "GOP Leaders Refuse to Close Ranks with Clinton on Bombing of Iraq," *Congressional Quarterly Weekly* (December 22, 1998): 3359.

32. Miles A. Pomper, "Members Rally around Kosovo Mission Despite Misgivings about Strategy," *Congressional Quarterly Weekly* (March 27, 1999): 763; Joe Lockhart, "Press Briefing"; Eric Schmitt, "Conflict in the Balkans," *New York Times* (March 23, 1999): A11.

33. *Congressional Record* (March 23, 1999): S 3101.

34. See Miles A. Pomper, "U.S. Offers a Final Chance for Serbs to Avert Air Strikes, Saying 'Time Is Out,'" *Congressional Quarterly Weekly* (October 10, 1998): 2759.

35. "How Senators Voted," *Congressional Quarterly Weekly* (February 13, 1999): 363.

36. *Congressional Record* (March 23, 1999): S 3110.

37. See Bill Clinton, "Remarks Announcing Airstrikes against Serbian Targets in the Federal Republic of Yugoslavia (Serbia and Montenegro)," *Public Papers of the Presidents* (March 24, 1999): 449, and "Address to the Nation Airstrikes against Serbian Targets in the Federal Republic of Yugoslavia (Serbia and Montenegro)," *Public Papers of the Presidents* (March 24, 1999): 451–53.

38. Bill Clinton, "Letter to Congressional Leaders Reporting on Airstrikes against Serbian Targets in the Federal Republic of Yugoslavia (Serbia and Montenegro)," *Public Papers of the Presidents* (March 26, 1999): 459–60.

39. Bill Clinton, "Letter to Congressional Leaders Reporting on Airstrikes against Serbian Targets in the Federal Republic of Yugoslavia (Serbia and Montenegro)," *Public Papers of the Presidents* (April 7, 1999): 516–17.

40. Joel Starr, legislative aid to Congressman Campbell, interview with the author, January 28, 2000.

41. Another committed critic of President Clinton's broadly perceived powers as commander in chief, Congressman Ron Paul (R-Tex.), also expressed his opposition to Clinton's constitutional claims. See *Congressional Record* (April 12, 1999): H 1835.

42. U.S. House of Representatives, Committee on International Relations, "Situation in Kosovo," (April 21, 1999): 30.

43. Ibid., 30–31.

44. Gebe Martinez, "Campbell Maneuvers to Force an Ambivalent Congress to Choose," *Congressional Quarterly Weekly* (April 24, 1999): 970; Jim Vandehei, "GOP Leaders Plan to Derail Campbell Bill: Top Republicans Avoiding Debate on War Powers Act," *Roll Call* (April 19, 1999).

45. Quoted in Jon Sawyer, "Congress Faces the Unpleasant Task of Going

on Record about War in the Balkans," *St. Louis Post Dispatch* (April 25, 1999): A12.

46. *Congressional Record* (April 28, 1999): H 2376.

47. Thomas Campbell (R-Calif.), *Congressional Record* (April 28, 1999): 2382; Joe Moakely (D-Mass.), ibid., H 2380; Lloyd Doggett (D-Tex.), ibid., H 2341; and Michael McNulty (D-N.Y.), ibid., H 2381.

48. *Congressional Record* (April 29, 1999), H 2383–84.

49. Ibid., H 2393.

50. Ibid., H 2394.

51. Ibid., H 2401.

52. Ibid., H 2405.

53. Ibid., H 2402.

Chapter 7

1. Bruce W. Jentleson, *With Friends like These: Reagan, Bush, and Saddam, 1982–1990* (New York: Norton, 1994): 31. Much of the historical discussion of Iraqi-American relations comes from Jentleson.

2. Ibid., 32–33.

3. Ibid., 39. See also Andrew Cockburn and Patrick Cockburn, *Out of the Ashes: The Resurrection of Saddam Hussein* (New York: Harper Collins, 1999): 74–77.

4. Jentleson, *With Friends like These*, 42–47.

5. Ibid., 51.

6. Ibid., 95–96.

7. See Jean Edward Smith, *George Bush's War* (New York: Henry Holt and Co., 1992). For a military chronology see Kevin Don Hutchinson, *Operation Desert Shield/Desert Storm* (Westport, Conn.: Greenwood, 1995). For an excellent compilation of the many political debates centering on the use of force, see *The Gulf War Reader: History, Documents, Opinions*, ed. Micah L. Sifry and Christopher Cerf (New York: Random House, 1991).

8. Quoted in Thomas Friedman, "The 1992 Campaign," *New York Times* (October 2, 1992): A1; Michael Wines, "U.S. Allies Say Flight Ban Will Start Today," *New York Times* (August 27, 1992): A1.

9. For extended analysis of the Bush Administration's views on this point, see Smith, *George Bush's War*, chapter 6.

10. Public Law 102-1 (January 14, 1991).

11. George Bush, "Statement on Signing the Resolution Authorizing the Use of Military Force against Iraq," *Public Papers of the Presidents* (January 14, 1991): 40.

12. George Bush, "Letter to Congressional Leaders on the Situation in the Persian Gulf," *Public Papers of the Presidents* (May 17, 1991): 521–22.

13. Douglas Jehl, "Raid on Baghdad," *New York Times* (June 29, 1993): A1. James Vicini, "U.S. Officials Told That Iraq Plotted to Kill Bush," Reuters (May 20, 1993).

14. Bill Clinton, "Letter to Congressional Leaders on the Strike on Iraqi Intelligence Headquarters," *Public Papers of the Presidents* (June 28, 1993): 940–41.

15. Bill Clinton, "Address to the Nation on the Strike on Iraqi Intelligence Headquarters," *Public Papers of the Presidents* (June 26, 1993): 938.

16. *Dellums v. Bush*, 752 F. Supp. 1141, 1145 (D.D.C. 1990). See also Neil A. Lewis, "Standoff in the Gulf: Lawmakers Lose a Suit on War Powers," *New York Times* (December 14, 1990): A15.

17. John Aloysius Farrell and John W. Mashek, "Clinton Reaping Political Gain from Raid," *Boston Globe* (June 29, 1993): national/foreign section, p. 1.

18. Farrell and Mashek, "Clinton Reaping Political Gain."

19. Richard L. Berke, "Raid on Baghdad," *New York Times* (June 29, 1993): A7. See also transcripts from *Nightline*, June 29, 1993, LexisNexis, general news file. An ABC news poll indicated a 12-point increase in public approval. Farrell and Mashek also cite a CNN–*USA Today* poll showing that 66 percent of Americans approved of the strike on Baghdad.

20. *Congressional Record* (June 28, 1950): 9319–20.

21. George Stephanopoulous, *All Too Human* (Boston: Little Brown and Company, 1999): 156–62.

22. International Court of Justice, *Reports and Judgements, Advisory Opinions, and Orders 1984* (The Hague, 1984): 169–70.

23. Ann Devroy, "U.S. Warns Iraq to Pull Back," *Washington Post* (October 15, 1994): A1; John F. Harris, "U.S. Doubling Air Power in Persian Gulf," *Washington Post* (October 28, 1994): A1.

24. Steven Lee Myers, "Raid on Iraq, The Prelude; A Race against Time: U.S. Tried to Head Off Iraqis," *New York Times* (September 5, 1996): A1.

25. Bill Clinton, "Remarks Announcing a Missile Strike on Iraq and Exchange with Reporters," *Weekly Compilation of Presidential Documents* (September 3, 1996): 1469.

26. Bill Clinton, "Remarks to the National Guard Association of the United States," *Weekly Compilation of Presidential Documents* (September 3, 1996): 1471.

27. Bill Clinton, "Remarks on the Missile Strikes on Iraq and an Exchange with Reporters," *Weekly Compilation of Presidential Documents* (September 4, 1996): 1476.

28. *Congressional Record* (September 5, 1996): S 9935.

29. Carroll J. Doherty, "Senate Struggles over Response to Clinton's Attack on Iraq," *Congressional Quarterly Weekly* (September 7, 1996): 2535.

30. For additional analysis of this argument see Louis Fisher, "Military Action against Iraq," *Presidential Studies Quarterly* 28, no. 4 (Fall 1998): 796.

31. Craig R. Whitney, "Raid on Iraq: The Reaction from Allies, U.S. Hears Mild Applause or Silence," *New York Times* (September 4, 1996): A10.

32. *Congressional Record* (September 5, 1996): H 10095.

33. Ibid., S 9936.

34. Adrianne Flynne, "GOP Senators Displeased at Being in the Dark on Iraq," *Arizona Republic* (September 6, 1996): A13.

35. Public Opinion Online, *Los Angeles Times* (September 12, 1996), Lexis-Nexis. Other polls suggested even higher levels of support for the president. See Public Opinion Online, *USA Today* (September 9, 1996), LexisNexis.

36. Adam Nagourney, "Raid on Iraq: The GOP; Muting His Criticism of Clinton, Dole Backs Troops in Iraq Raid," *New York Times* (September 4, 1996): A1. See also Doherty, "Senate Struggles over Response," 2535.

37. "Iraq Again Bars UN Inspectors," *Facts on File* (January 15, 1998): 9–10.

38. Bill Clinton, "Remarks by the President on Iraq to Pentagon Personnel," *Public Papers of the Presidents* (February 17, 1998): 231–35. See also "Press Briefing by Mike McCurry," White House Press Release, Office of the Press Secretary (February 10, 1998).

39. Madeleine K. Albright, "Statement before the House International Relations Committee," Office of the Spokesman, U.S. Department of State (February 12, 1998). See also Albright, "Remarks at Tennessee State University," Office of the Spokesman, U.S. Department of State (February 19, 1998). For President Clinton's written views, see Bill Clinton, "Letter to Congressional Leaders Reporting on Iraq's Compliance with United Nations Security Council Resolutions" *Public Papers of the Presidents* (February 3, 1998): 163.

40. *Congressional Record* (January 28, 1998): S 180.

41. Donna Cassata, "'Big Stick' Approach to Iraq Masks Uncertainty on Hill" *Congressional Quarterly Weekly* (February 7, 1998): 327.

42. Cassata, "Big Stick."

43. *Congressional Record* (February 12, 1998): S 712.

44. Donna Cassata and Chuck McCutcheon, "Public's Worries about Iraq Policy Echo Concerns in Congress," *Congressional Quarterly Weekly* (February 21, 1998): 448.

45. *Congressional Record* (February 12, 1998): S 714.

46. Pat Towell, "Senate Urges Trial of Saddam," *Congressional Quarterly Weekly* (March 14, 1998): 682.

47. *Congressional Record* (February 11, 1998): H 433. See also *Congressional Record* (February 12, 1998): H 495.

48. *Congressional Record* (February 24, 1998): H 499.

49. *Congressional Record* (February 26, 1998): H 677.

50. Michael Barone and Grant Ujifusa with Richard E. Cohen, *The Almanac of American Politics* (Washington, D.C.: National Journal Inc., 1997): 288. See also *Congressional Record* (August 12, 1994): H 8044.

51. For more on Specter, see Richard F. Fenno Jr., *Learning to Legislate: The*

Senate Education of Arlen Specter (Washington, D.C.: Congressional Quarterly Press, 1991).

52. UN Security Council Resolution 1154 (March 2, 1998).

53. Barbara Crosette, "UN Rebuffs U.S. Threat to Iraq If It Breaks Pact," *New York Times* (March 3, 1998): A1.

54. Steven Lee Myers, "U.S. Insists It Retains Right to Punish Iraq," *New York Times* (March 4, 1998): 10.

55. Bill Clinton, "Address to the Nation Announcing Military Strikes on Iraq," *Weekly Compilation of Presidential Documents* (December 16, 1998): 2495.

56. Bill Clinton, "Letter to Congressional Leaders on the Military Strikes against Iraq," *Weekly Compilation of Presidential Documents* (December 18, 1998): 2513. Secretary Albright made similar references to UN authorization in her public remarks and exchanges with the press. See Madeleine K. Albright, "Remarks on Air Strikes against Iraq," Office of Spokesman, U.S. State Department (December 16, 1998).

57. Clinton, "Letter to Congressional Leaders on the Military Strikes against Iraq."

58. Stephen Fidler, "Planning for Strike Began as Earlier Mission Aborted," *Financial Times* (December 18, 1998): 2; Mimi Hall and Bill Nichols, "A Day of Drama, a Day of Big Decisions: President Forced to Deal with Iraq and Impeachment," *USA Today* (December 17, 1998): 7A.

59. Fidler, "Planning for Strike Began."

60. White House, Office of the Press Secretary. "Press Briefing by Joe Lockhart," (December 16, 1998); Associated Press, "The Congressional Response," *Minneapolis Star Tribune* (December 17, 1998): A17.

61. Quoted in Miles Pomper, Chuck McCutcheon, and Pat Towell, "GOP Leaders Refuse to Close Ranks with Clinton on Bombing of Iraq," *Congressional Quarterly Weekly* (December 22, 1998): 3359.

62. Quoted in Jim Drinkard, "Congress Presents Disunited Front in Attack," *USA Today* (December 17, 1998): 3A.

63. *Congressional Record* (December 17, 1998): H 11726, H 11727, H 11729. See also the remarks of Congressmen James Traficant (D-Ohio) and Ron Paul (R-Tex.).

64. William Drozdiak, "Disparate Reactions to Raid within UN Security Council," *Ottawa Citizen* (December 17, 1998): A4.

65. "Public Backs Attack on Iraq," Gallup poll (December 19, 1998).

66. Public Opinion Online, Roper Center (December 18, 1998, accession no. 0317448, question no. 007) at LexisNexis, polls and surveys.

67. On ONW see www.fas.org/man/dod-101/ops/northern_watch.htm. On OSW, see www.fas.org/man/dod-101/ops/southern_watch.htm.

68. For the no-fly zones over Bosnia, see UN Security Council Resolution 781 and UN Security Council Resolution 786.

69. U.S. Senate, Committee on Foreign Relations, "Facing Saddam's Iraq: Disarray in the International Community," (September 28, 1999); U.S. Senate, Committee on Foreign Relations and Committee on Energy and Natural Resources, "New Proposals to Expand Iraqi Oil for Food: The End of Sanctions" (March 17, 1999); U.S. Senate, Committee on Armed Services, "U.S. Policy toward Iraq," (January 28, 1999); U.S. Senate, Committee on Foreign Relations, "U.S. Policy toward Iraq: Mobilizing the Opposition" (June 23, 1999).

70. See John G. Stoessinger, *Why Nations Go To War* (Boston: St. Martin's, 2001) especially chapter 7 on this point.

71. Bill Clinton, "Letter to Congressional Leaders Reporting on Iraq's Compliance with United Nations Security Council Resolutions," *Weekly Compilation of Presidential Documents* (August 2, 1999): 1540. Even the title of Clinton's letter suggests the liberal and precarious application of international law, especially since ONW and OSW are addressed in the letter and considered part of the "compliance."

72. Quoted in Jacqueline Soteropulos, "Presidents of Today Strike Quick, Tell Congress Later," *Tampa Tribune* (December 18, 1998): 13.

Chapter 8

1. For a recent discussion of these issues, see Brien Hallet, *The Lost Art of Declaring War* (Urbana: University of Illinois Press, 1998).

2. For more on Clinton's inexperience and even lack of interest in foreign affairs, see David Halberstam, *War in a Time of Peace: Bush, Clinton, and the Generals* (New York: Scribner, 2001).

3. Langhorn A. Motley, "The Decision to Assist Grenada," Department of State Current Policy No. 541 (January 24, 1984). See also David P. Forsythe, *The Politics of International Law: U.S. Foreign Policy Reconsidered* (Boulder, Colo.: Lynne Rienner, 1990): 72–77.

4. George Bush, "Statement on Signing the Resolution Authorizing the Use of Military Force against Iraq," *Public Papers of the Presidents* (January 14, 1991).

5. U.S. House of Representatives, Committee on International Relations, "The U.S. Role in Kosovo," (February 10, 1999): 17.

6. For broad studies of Congress's role in foreign policy making after the cold war, see Ralph G. Carter, ed., *Contemporary Cases in U.S. Foreign Policy: From Terrorism to Trade* (Washington, D.C.: Congressional Quarterly Press, 2001); James M. Scott, *After the End: Making U.S. Foreign Policy in the Post–Cold War Era* (Durham, N.C.: Duke University Press, 1998); Eugene Wittkopf and James McCormick, "Congress, the President, and the End of the Cold War," *Journal of Conflict Resolution* 42, no. 4 (1998): 440–46; Eileen Burgin, "Assessing Congress's Role in the Making of Foreign Policy," in *Congress Reconsidered*, 6th ed.,

ed. Lawrence C. Oppenheimer and Bruce I. Oppenheimer (Washington, D.C.: Congressional Quarterly Press, 1997); James M. Lindsay, *Congress and the Politics of U.S. Foreign Policy* (Baltimore: Johns Hopkins University Press, 1994); Randall B. Ripley and James M. Lindsay, eds., *Congress Resurgent: Foreign and Defense Policy on Capitol Hill* (Ann Arbor: University of Michigan Press, 1993). For more issue-specific treatments see William P. Avery, "Domestic Interests in NAFTA Bargaining," *Political Science Quarterly* 113, no. 2 (1998): 281–306; Paul Stocktom, "Beyond Micromanagement: Congressional Budgeting for a Post–Cold War Military," *Political Science Quarterly* 110, no. 2 (1995): 233–59.

7. For example, see Donald M. Snow and Eugene Brown, *Beyond the Water's Edge* (New York: St. Martin's, 1997): 190–93.

8. Jimmy Carter, *Keeping Faith: Memoirs of a President* (New York: Bantam Books, 1982): 513–14.

9. *Congressional Record* (July 30, 1998): S 9444. The Congressional Leadership Group would consist of the Speaker of the House and president pro tempore of the Senate, the majority and minority leaders of the Senate and House, and the chair and ranking minority member of the Senate Committee on Foreign Relations, Committee on Armed Services, and Select Committee on Intelligence and the House Committee on International Relations, Committee on National Security, and Permanent Select Committee on Intelligence.

10. Louis Fisher and David Gray Adler, "The War Powers Resolution: Time to Say Goodbye," *Political Science Quarterly* 113, no. 1 (1998): 1–20.

11. See Hallet, *Lost Art of Declaring War.*

12. Todd S. Purdum and Alison Mitchell, "A Nation Challenged: Capitol Hill; Bush, Angered by Leaks, Duels with Congress," *New York Times* (October 10, 2001): A1.

13. Arthur M. Schlesinger Jr., *The Imperial Presidency* (Boston: Houghton Mifflin, 1973).

Index

2029